THEORIZING
SATIRE

THEORIZING SATIRE

Essays in Literary Criticism

EDITED BY
Brian A. Connery and Kirk Combe

ST. MARTIN'S PRESS
NEW YORK

"Portrait d'Une Femme" from Ezra Pound: *Personae.*
Copyright 1926 by Ezra Pound. Reprinted by
permission of New Directions Publishing Corp.

Scholarly and Reference Division,
St. Martin's Press, Inc., 175 Fifth Avenue,
New York, N.Y. 10010

First published in the United States of America in 1995

Printed in the United States of America

ISBN 0-312-12302-7

Library of Congress Cataloging-in-Publication Data

Theorizing satire : essays in literary criticism / edited by Brian
    A. Connery and Kirk Combe.
        p. cm.
    Includes bibliographical references and index.
    ISBN 0-312-12302-7
    1. Satire—History and criticism.   I. Connery, Brian A.
    II. Combe, Kirk.
    PN6149.S2T44 1995
    809.7—dc20   94-29335
                                                                CIP

Interior design by Digital Type & Design

.Contents.

*We are grateful for support from
Denison University, Oakland University,
and the National Endowment for the Humanities.*

For Marlene and Carina;
Brenda, Clayton, Olivia, and Hannah

.List of Contributors.

Fredric V. Bogel is Professor of English and currently Fellow for the Humanities at Cornell University. He has authored *'The Dream of My Brother': An Essay on Johnson's Authority* (Studies in English Literature Series, University of Victoria Monographs, 1990), *Literature and Insubstantiality in Later Eighteenth-Century England* (Princeton UP, 1984), and *Acts of Knowledge: Pope's Later Poems* (Bucknell UP, 1981). His articles on satire include "Dulness Unbound: Rhetoric and Pope's *Dunciad*," (*PMLA* 97: 844–55); "Irony, Inference, and Critical Uncertainty," (*Yale Review* 69: 503–19); and "Deconstructive Criticism: The Logic of Derrida's Differance," (*Centrum* 6:50–60). He is currently at work on a book tentatively titled *The Difference that Satire Makes*.

Christiane Bohnert is an independent scholar and translator. She has written two books: *Brechts Lyrik im Kontext: Zyklen und Exil* (Atheneum, 1982) and *Satire* (Metzler, forthcoming 1993). She is currently writing a reference work on satire, and has published articles on Kant's ethics in contemporary Western culture, Lessing's *Nathan the Wise*, E.T.A. Hoffmann, GDR literature, and Bertolt Brecht.

John R. Clark is Professor of English at the University of South Florida. He has written and published more than sixty satires himself, as well as publishing numerous articles on satire in journals including *Classical Philology, College English, Explicator, Journal of Popular Culture, Philological Quarterly, Seventeenth-Century News, Studies in Philology, Novel,* and *Renaissance Drama*. His books include *Form and Frenzy in Swift's 'Tale of a Tub'* and *The Modern Satiric Grotesque and Its Traditions*.

Kirk Combe is Assistant Professor of English at Denison University. He is the author of "Dryden's Allusion to Horace in *Mac Flecknoe*" (*Notes and Queries,* September 1987); "Clandestine Protest against William III in Dryden's Translations of Juvenal and Persius" (*Modern Philology,* August 1989); "'But loads of Sh— almost choked the way': Shadwell, Dryden, Rochester, and the Summer of 1676" (forthcoming in *Texas Studies in Literature and Language*); as well as numerous book reviews in the area of Restoration and eighteenth-century British literature. Currently, he is writing a book on Rochester's politics.

Brian A. Connery is Associate Professor of English at Oakland University and the author of essays on Jonathan Swift, twentieth-century narrative satire, and composition theory. He is grateful to the National Endowment for the Humanities and to Professor John Sitter for an NEH Summer Seminar during which some of the work on this book was completed. He is currently completing a book on satiric authority in the works of Jonathan Swift.

Christian Gutleben traveled throughout the world before settling down to study English literature at Grenoble and then Strasbourg University. He has spent two years at Oxford on a doctoral research grant and is now teaching at Strasbourg University while completing a dissertation on the British campus novel, a subject upon which he has published several articles.

Erin Mackie is an Assistant Professor of English at Washington University, St. Louis, where she teaches eighteenth-century literature, contemporary youth culture, and feminism. She is currently preparing for publication a study of fashion and taste in the early eighteenth-century periodicals, *The Tatler* and *The Spectator*, and working on an selected edition of those papers for Bedford's Cultural Editions series. She has written on Charlotte Charke, Swift, the hoop-petticoat, and on the relations among the imagination, shopping, and museumification. She plans to explore further issues of style and taste in eighteenth-century racial and ethnic sociocultural divisions.

Richard Nash is Associate Professor of English at Indiana University, Bloomington. He has published on Pope and Swift and the relations of literature and science in the eighteenth century, and is currently at work on a book on eighteenth-century constructions of "the wild man" in literature and science.

Jon Rowland teaches English Literature and Rhetoric at the University of Toronto. Some of his work has appeared in *Studies in Eighteenth-Century Culture*, and his book, *Faint Praise and Civil Leer: The "Decline" of Eighteenth-Century Panegyric* has been published by the University of Delaware Press. The latter is a fuller, historical treatment (roughly 1600 to 1760) of some of the arguments presented in Chapter 6, from the first panegyric in English by Samuel Daniel to the panegyrical satires of Charles Churchill. Versions of "From Cheated Sight to False Light" were presented at meetings of the East-Central/American Society for Eighteenth-Century Studies, whose members offered much collegiality and support during the long writing process.

Gay Sibley is an Associate Professor in the English Department at the University of Hawaii, Manoa. Her work has appeared in *American Literature, Studies in the Novel, Nineteenth-Century Prose, English Journal,* and *The Dictionary of Literary Biography,* and she is currently working on a book-length study of the "ethical alien" in the novels of George Eliot.

Linda V. Troost is Associate Professor of English at Washington and Jefferson College. Her publications on satire include "Poetry, Politics, and Puddings: The Imagery of Food in Butler's *Hudibras*" (*Restoration* 9) and "The Characterizing Power of Song in Sheridan's *Duenna*" (*Eighteenth-Century Studies* 1986–87). Her entry "Samuel 'Hudibras' Butler" appears in the *Dictionary of Literary Biography* (Seventeenth-Century Poets Series 2). She also has published articles on English opera as well as choreographed and sung choral and principal roles in numerous Gilbert and Sullivan operas.

Theorizing Satire:
A Retrospective and Introduction

Brian A. Connery and Kirk Combe

Reading, at its best, entails an open-mindedness that can be perilous. We bring to the text what we know of the world, of others, and of ourselves, and we place this knowledge at the disposal of an absent author's words, with the understanding that our mental furniture, as reinstalled by the text, may be radically rearranged and that some pieces may be junked altogether. We risk even wholesale cognitive remodeling—the elimination of walls, the adjustment of ceilings, the construction of curious add-ons. We hope the text's structural integrity will enhance the durability of our own ideas; that the art of the text will achieve an attractive interior decoration; that the design and discrimination of the text will open up pathways of consciousness while reducing clutter. Such a project is not to be entered into lightly, and the wary reader checks the text's references carefully.

Reading satire is doubly perilous, for satirists specialize in demolition projects. The one thing we know about satire is that it promises to tell us what we do not want to know—what we may, in fact, resist knowing. One is apt to find one's former consciousness uninhabitable when the work of the satirist is done. Like tragedy, as Northrop Frye suggests, satire is a form that desire rejects. Although a few utopian satirists are noted for construction rather than destruction, their materials are often criticized as insubstantial. Most often, the interior of satire is messy, cluttered, and smelly as well. The taste and discrimination of satirists are questionable, and their references stink. In spite of this, they appear proud of their work and thus compound their offense. Knowing that the market may be closed to their trade, they often participate in fraud—advertising themselves as something else, appearing in disguise. But even when such artifice wins contracts with readers and admission to the asylum of the canon, their disruptive behavior leads to segregation under the discipline of literary studies.

Reading satire publicly, as the critic proposes to do, is triply dangerous. Satire establishes oppositions between good and evil, text and reader, reader and society, even between the reader and herself. In aligning ourselves with the satirist, we find ourselves in unattractive company and subject to the fear and loathing of the society of dulness the satirist opposes. Conversely, in aligning ourselves in opposition to the satirist, we risk being derided as hypocrites. If we try to transcend the satiric fray by ascending to the Olympian regions of literary theory and criticism, we risk losing touch with the earthly and material origins of satire within particular time periods and societies. Thus, to write critically on satire amounts to an exercise in feigning scholarly immaculacy while strolling in a mire: Our efforts to remain unsullied may sink us more deeply into the ooze.

The peculiar nature of satire has always been its monstrosity, its doubleness and self-bifurcation. One easily understands how more than several centuries misunderstood the etymology of the word, believing that *satire* derived from *satyr,* and thus was a kind of literature that one would suppose the product of a rude and lustful sylvan brute. As satires in the form of beast fable make clear, satire tells of the descent of humanity below itself. Like Jonathan Swift's Houyhnhnms, satire is simultaneously humane and inhuman in its treatment of the world. This same duality is manifest in a peculiar form of doublethink in satirists' descriptions of their own work. Most satirists—indeed, virtually all English satirists from the late sixteenth to the late eighteenth century—*claim* one purpose for satire, that of high-minded and usually socially oriented moral and intellectual reform; however, they *engage* in something quite different, namely, mercilessly savage attack on some person or thing that, frequently for private reasons, displeases them. The veneer of civilized behavior serves to mask great primitive urges. Thus, satire is a literary Trojan horse for which polite (or politic) artfulness produces a dissembling form, serving first to contain and conceal, and then to unleash the primitive passions of the satirist.

Critical commentary on the genre of satire has a long though not always distinguished tradition in English and, by extension, American letters. It has become clear, via commentators such as William of Conches describing the satires of Juvenal (see Minnis and Scott), that classical satire made its mark on English letters well before the less-than-distinguished critical efforts of William Webbe (*A Discourse of English Poetrie,*1586) and George Puttenham (*The Arte of English Poesie,* 1589). In those treatises, Webbe and Puttenham, wrestling with the linguistic, stylistic, and cultural obscurities of Horace, Persius, and Juvenal, set the misguided theoretical tone for the rather bizarre Elizabethan outburst of classically based satire by poets as generally forgotten as Thomas Lodge, Joseph Hall, Everard Guilpin, and John Marston, or as currently eminent as John Donne. Despite the estimable satiric efforts of Sir Thomas Wyatt earlier in the sixteenth century—not to mention Geoffrey Chaucer in the fourteenth century—the satire of the 1590s customarily has served as the jumping-off point for twentieth-century studies of English satire.

State censorship, driven as much by fears of political and religious dissent as by an aversion to obscenity, subsequently drove satire underground during the first four decades of the seventeenth century, only to have the breakdown of official censorship accompanying the onset of the Civil War loose the flood-gates of a satiric tidal wave after 1641. By this time, the social and critical conditions in England were significantly different from those of the 1580s and 1590s. English society itself was in upheaval, which not only permitted but encouraged an overtly politicized use of satire as, in effect, a modern weapon of propaganda. Equally, the neoclassical influence of French critical theories on satire was being felt in England. Isaac Casaubon's pivotal study *De Satyrica Graecorum Poesi et Romanorum Satira* had been available, albeit only in Latin, since 1605. The work of French classical scholars, such as Heinsius (both the elder and the younger), Nicolas Rigault, André Dacier, and Louis Desprez, was being read as well. Simultaneously, the French neoclassical *practice* of satire was introduced to English poets of the seventeenth century via the works of Mathurin Régnier and, more notably, Nicolas Boileau. In fact, after roughly 1660, the satiric works and critical judgments of Boileau had a prominent hand in shaping English satiric conventions during the Restoration and early eighteenth century, exerting a tremendous influence, for instance, on early Restoration satirists such as the Earl of Rochester and John Oldham. All of the above-named French sources greatly influenced John Dryden both in his own satiric works and in the critical thinking in his *Discourse concerning Satire*. In turn, Dryden's satire and criticism were integral in the formation of English satire at arguably its high point in England during the first half of the eighteenth century. The much-studied satire of Swift and Alexander Pope represents not an isolated instance of satiric genius, but a culmination of numerous cultural and literary forces at work in English society, with the consequence, as Dustin Griffin suggests, that theorists of satire currently look at Swift's work as paradigmatic (*Satire* 2–3).

As Alvin Kernan has pointed out, very little serious criticism supported the practice of satire between Dryden's seventeenth-century *Discourse* and Northrop Frye's mid-twentieth-century *Anatomy,* although one should note that important work in philosophy and psychology was accomplished (that of Louis Bergson, Ferdinand Schiller, Søren Kierkegaard, and Sigmund Freud, for instance), which now informs much current analysis of satire. Stuart Tave's *The Amiable Humourist* and, more recently, Claude Rawson's *Satire and Sentiment 1660–1830* offer largely accurate accounts of the eighteenth-century English controversy about the propriety of satire and of the consequent eclipse of the satirist by the humorist and novelist. Satire's low view of human nature certainly accounts for its unattractiveness to the majority of Romantics (excepting, of course, Robert Burns and Lord Byron). Percy Bysshe Shelley's unpublished fragment of "A Satire against Satire" explicitly proscribes satire and prescribes instead a private form of admonishment for personal correction;

the nonpublication of the poem may itself be seen as an enactment of this proscription. While the poet may ultimately be the "unacknowledged legislator of mankind," Shelley implicitly rejects the more immediate judiciary possibilities of poetry and abandons satire's capacity for correction through punishment. Subsequently, it is easy to account for satire's rejection by the Victorians simply on the basis of its tastelessness. In the twentieth century, the development of the criticism of satire may still best be regarded as fitful. Distorted by biographical criticism and generally ignored by New Criticism, in the first half of the twentieth century, satire was explored most productively by analytic approaches peripheral to the New Critical mainstream: philology, anthropological criticism, and rhetoric.

The Johnsonian tradition of biographical criticism, fortified by modern psychology, may have created more misunderstanding than understanding of satire in the twentieth century. For biographical critics still under the influence of the Romantic sense of the poem as self-expression, satire's insistence upon both its historicity and its efficacy seems to have reinforced the credibility of the satirist's conventional professions of unaffected sincerity to such an extent that readers too frequently confounded satiric personae with satirists themselves. Biographical and psychoanalytic critics tend to account for satire, then, as a manifestation of personality disorders, thereby ignoring the art of the text and simultaneously defending the societies and individuals under attack by satire as the unfortunate victims of the anger of maladjusted scribblers.[1] Alternatively, these same critics sometimes make the mistake of taking the satirist at his or her word. Notably, in his satires, Dryden often has been trusted as a reliable arbiter of literary taste and political doctrine.

Five factors seem most important in understanding the malign neglect of satire by the New Critics in the middle of the twentieth century. First, satire's insistence upon its historical specificity, its torrential references to the peculiarities of the particular individuals in the society that it represents (peculiarities that, it has been assumed, "great art" transcends) worked to exclude it from the consideration of those who insisted on the self-containment of literary texts. The question continues to be raised today: can a satire, say Pope's *Dunciad*, legitimately be considered an enduring work of Literature when filled with references to now unfamiliar people, places, and events? As Edward Rosenheim has suggested, the study of satire necessarily blurs the boundary between historical scholarship and literary criticism (32–34), a boundary that New Criticism, in its struggle against the dominance of philology, attempted to establish in boldface. Thus, according to such critical principles, satire would seem extraliterary at best; most frequently, of course, as a consequence of residual Victorian taste, it was pronounced subliterary.

Second, satire more than other genres emphasizes—indeed, is defined by—its intention (attack), an intention that again refers the reader to matter outside the text. Contrary to W. H. Auden's proclamation that "Poetry makes nothing happen," satire insists on its efficacy, its ability to chasten, chastise, reform, and warn. Thus, late in the reign of the New Critics, Robert Elliott's *The Power of Satire: Magic, Ritual, Art* had to argue that satire becomes art (as distinct from magical ritual) and, thus, worthy of critical analysis, exactly at the moment when the belief in its efficacy is extinguished. That is, just as tragedy metamorphoses from ritual sacrifice to art as it is secularized and divorced from propitiatory intent, so satire transforms itself into art when the belief in its power to hurt has dissipated. While this declaration of satire's inefficacy makes it acceptable to New Critics, it also denies satire's self-proclaimed purpose, which is social rather than aesthetic: to lash vice and to make folly ridiculous.

Third, satire tends towards open-endedness, irresolution, and thus chaos. Closure, in most cases, would turn a narrative satire into either comedy or tragedy and thus contradict the satirist's representation of evil as a present and continuing danger. Dryden could not put a more gratifying ending onto *Absalom and Achitophel*—as Dr. Johnson complained—because at its time of writing the political crisis itself was unresolved. In his pose as an impartial historian of current events, neither could Dryden in the poem reconcile Monmouth to his father (though Dryden expresses the desire to do so in the prefatory "To the Reader"), nor could he portray Charles actually crushing Shaftesbury. The first event was never to come and the second was yet to come, so these more heroically satisfying conclusions simply were not available to the satirist. Similarly, for Pope, the Universal Darkness burying All at the close of *The Dunciad* was an ongoing, distressing state of affairs for British society. For a New Critic interested in demonstrating the integration and coherence of a text, the well-wroughtness of the satiric urn, open-ended or entropic conclusions are impasses, signs of aesthetic failure.

Fourth, satire's own frequent formlessness forces it to inhabit the forms of other genres (as in the mock-heroic), and makes satire resistant to simplistic versions of a formalist approach; the incongruity created by satire's parasitic appropriation of other forms can create friction between form and content that runs counter to the prescriptions of formalism. Often, satire's habitation of other forms is so successful that it is mistaken for those forms, and condemned, thus, on a false basis, as unsuccessful. To see the problems this creates, one need only to read the abundant criticism of a text like Nathanael West's *A Cool Million,* nearly all of which condemns the work as an unsuccessful novel.[2]

The problem of bifurcation between form and content points to the fifth problem that satire poses to New Critics: its militant disunity. Perhaps more than any other genre, satire is constructed or structured on the basis of oppositions or hierarchies; in satire, these oppositions are represented in their extremes in order to achieve maximum tension. The most common rhetorical figures of satire—irony, paradox, and oxymoron (all three based upon opposites)—are those that maximize the imaginative tension of the text and produce in the reader a consequent sense of discomfort. (Observing this, one understands how a satiric Rochester or Samuel Butler can be a contemporary of a metaphysical Andrew Marvell. One wonders if, in fact, the "metaphysical" poets were not a necessary precondition for the flourishing of satire in seventeenth-century England.) Where other writers might use simile or metaphor, the satirist uses hyperbole—stretching the limits of possible comparison. Where other writers might use hyperbole, the satirist uses understatement to intensify through irony the sense of incongruity. Thus, unlike metaphysical poetry, the yoking together of disparate matter in satire serves to reveal not wit but imminent incoherence.

As Mary Clare Randolph perceived in her analysis of formal verse satire, the formal structure of satire depends upon the juxtaposition of extreme vice and extreme virtue, and, rather than achieve a satisfying equilibrium between the two, the satirist most often dwells upon vice, creating an imbalance that the reader resists. The tension between the representations of vice and those of virtue is intensified by the satirist's tones toward each; as Thomas Drant writes, in 1566, the satirist is "Testie and wrothe with vice" but "courteous and frendly to the good."[3] Others have viewed satire as less discriminate; Joseph Addison, for example, in a description of a gathering of personifications of genres, says "Satire had Smiles in her Look, and a Dagger under her Garment." In this century, David Worcester observes that the satirist is "simultaneously amiable and hostile"; consequently, the reader is attracted by the satirist's amiability and the appeal of virtue while simultaneously repelled by the satirist's hostility and the gross representation of vice.

The tension created in these oppositions is frequently cited as that which constitutes the "art" of satire, as in Dryden's famous observation of the "vast difference betwixt the slovenly Butchering of a Man, and the fineness of a stroak that separates the Head from the Body, and leaves it standing in its place. A man may be capable, as *Jack Ketch's* Wife said of his Servant, of a plain piece of Work, a bare Hanging; but to make a Malefactor die sweetly, was only belonging to her Husband" (*Discourse* 71).[4] Defenders and/or apologists have insisted that satire be distinguished from some of its less sociable and more unruly relatives, like invective, by the presence of a controlling intelligence that denatures and refines the production of satire. In his essay on satire as behavior, Alvin Kernan suggests that satire is distinguished by the presence of the irrational emotion of hostility, normally repressed, with a simultaneous "brilliant play of rationality" ("Aggression and Satire" 124). However, it might just as easily be argued that if all art is the product of a sublimation and masking of primal emotion, then satire is the work that exposes and thereby desublimates art. Satire creates masks that are designed to be transparent.

It is no wonder, then, that satire criticism did not flourish in the early years of New Criticism; indeed, it *is* a wonder that satire criticism achieved a renascence in the forties through the sixties, beginning with the work of Maynard Mack and Northrop Frye, followed by a seemingly serendipitous confluence of interest on the parts of Alvin Kernan, Robert Elliott, Ellen Leyburn, and Ronald Paulson. Leyburn's *Satiric Allegory: Mirror for Man* and Frye's *Anatomy of Criticism,* particularly his attention to the Menippea, made it possible once again to consider narrative satire as well as the formal verse satire. Frye begat Elliott, Paulson, and more recently Michael Seidel—who, taking a hint from René Girard's sense that art is civilization's way of covering up the violence of history, proclaims that satire is culture's way of exposing the violence that civilization conceals.

The history of satire criticism for the past fifty years can easily be defined in terms of attention to one or the other of the poles implied in the oxymoronic definitions of satire. Attention to the "agitation" or "feeling" of the satirist has produced psychological studies of the satirist and anthropological studies of satire as a form of social and cultural behavior with ritual roots and a continuing function in culture. Attention to the "intelligence" has produced what might be called a rhetoric of satire. While both directions are embodied in Frye's *Anatomy,* the distinctively anthropological approach was begun with Robert Elliott's *The Power of Satire,* which harked back to F. N. Robinson's philological work on Irish satirists. The rhetorical work is clearly present both in Worcester's 1940 *The Art of Satire* and in Mary Clare Randolph's analysis of the medical metaphor in Renaissance satire, but, as Worcester acerbically explains, rhetoric itself had fallen into disrepute, and their leads lay dormant for two decades before Worcester's book was republished along with a flurry of works bearing such titles as *The Satirist's Art, The Art of the Satirist, Jonathan Swift and the Satirist's Art,* and *Satire's Persuasive Voice.* Most recently, George Test's *Satire: Spirit and Art* has extended our view of satire by relating satire to a number of cross-cultural phenomena and reinvestigating satire as a form of social behavior thereby, as his title suggests, attempting to reunite the rhetorical with the social, cultural, and behavioral.

The continuation of the rhetorical work of Worcester and Randolph was made possible by an important essay by Maynard Mack, "The Muse of Satire," part of his project to rehabilitate Alexander Pope, which confuted biographical and psychoanalytic deflection of satire by insisting upon the separation of the historical author from the satirical persona. Building upon Ricardo Quintana's analysis of Swift as a just man masking himself as an unjust man, Mack demonstrated the ways in which Pope's *Epistle to Arbuthnot* actively constructs a speaker characterized by the necessary ethos of a just man, not necessarily bearing a resemblance to Pope himself, who opposes the dulness that the satire attacks. While such a distinction seems commonplace today (indeed, it has now been attacked as overly commonplace—see Irvin Ehrenpreis's "Personae"), Mack's essay seems to have been the necessary demonstration that an art, susceptible to analysis and criticism, was in fact at work in satire, in spite of satire's own frequent disingenuous claims of artlessness. Indeed, in a subsequent work, Robert C. Elliott returns repeatedly, in his attempt to distinguish satire as art from satire as ritual, to the distance of the writer from the spokesperson as a crucial characteristic of the art of satire. Most recently, Dustin Griffin's essay, "Venting Spleen," has continued the separation between satirist's life and art by claiming that not only should the satirist's claims about him- or herself be regarded as fictitious, but satire's claims about its historical context and its efficacy and power within that context should be regarded as a rhetorical convention rather than a statement of belief or fact.

A bustle of important work, thus, continued through the fifties and sixties. Yet fundamental issues remain unresolved: the definition of satire, for instance. Again, Frye is responsible for the groundwork of future criticism in his suggestion that "Two things . . . are essential to satire; one is wit or humor founded on fantasy or a sense of the grotesque or absurd, the other is an object of attack. Attack without humor . . . forms one of the boundaries of satire [i.e., invective or denunciation]. The humor of pure fantasy [forms] the other boundary of satire" (*Anatomy* 224-25). Frye demands a *fiction* as drapery over the moral standard that acts as the framework for the satire. *Fantasy, humor,* and *attack* appear to be the primary factors in subsequent definitions. Insisting that satire cannot be quite so general as Frye's description indicates, Edward Rosenheim suggests that satire is an "attack by means of a manifest fiction upon discernible historical particulars" (31). This definition enhances Frye's a bit: the fiction must be apparent to the reader, i.e., the reader must *not* mistake persona for author or content for reportage. And Rosenheim, as noted earlier, insists upon satire's rootedness in the historical moment of its production. Leon Guilhamet, focusing upon the form of satire in *Satire and the Transformation of Genre,* extends the discussion of the "manifest fiction" in his claim that satire, itself formless, is mimetic of other forms of discourse. In a short 1988 piece, Don Nilsen adds a few more "necessary conditions" that distinguish satire: irony, negativity, distortion, and humor. Perhaps most important, Nilsen adds an anthropological reader-response touch, suggesting that satire unifies its audience, bonding them against the enemy under attack. In a recent review of satire criticism, Stephanie Barbé Hammer concludes with the following composite tripartite definition: "1.) Satire is a literary kind which borrows its form from other sorts of writing, 2.) satire is characterized by an attack or censure of vice and evil in society which fuses the aesthetic and ethical, and 3.) satire is characterized by its use of rhetorical and dramatic irony to effect its critique" (12). Hammer's definition adds, it should be noted, like Rosenheim's, the restriction that the attack of the satire must be directed at a *social* evil.

Thus, the definition of satire has become increasingly restrictive. However, in general usage, "satire" remains less an identifiable genre than a mode, and an astonishingly wide range of vastly varied works have been placed under its rubric. This seems particularly true in the area of late modern and postmodern works, particularly narrative, in which irony and, increasingly, parody are crucial characteristics. In this area, a restrictive definition has proven even more problematic. Taking a hint from Frye's description of "satire of the high norm," John Tilton, in his discussion of Anthony Burgess, John Barth, and Kurt Vonnegut, has attempted to define "cosmic satire" as a form of narrative satire that transcends topical social satire, creating "a profound and ultimately tragic satiric vision by probing the psychic cosmos where behavior originates" (5). While Tilton's observations have an air of truth and echo Kernan's definition of satire as the literary creation of "symbolic worlds constructed to reveal the nature and workings of dulness" (*The Plot of Satire* 5), such definitions, in their generality, become difficult to apply. As Thomas Lockwood has observed, regarding the history of the attempt to define satire, the "more general and therefore satisfying definitions are least useful when most needed" (5). That is, Tilton's definition cannot help us determine ways in which we would read *Slaughterhouse-Five* as a "cosmic satire" that are fundamentally different from the ways in which we would read it as a novel or as a more particularized satire tied to its social and historical locality.

In closing his latest essay on satire, Alvin Kernan frets that the entire project of the study of satire "stands at risk, of course, as various new kinds of criticism deconstruct not only single works of literature but critical formulations of individual genres like satire, and even literature itself" ("Robert C. Elliott" 4–5). Were it not for his subsequent work (*The Death of Literature*), we would suspect that Kernan here is simply overcome by an elegiac mood. Believing that the best of satire criticism, including Kernan's, is well-founded in some or another form of "theory," we are much more sanguine about the future of the criticism and theorizing of satire.

Indeed, it seems to us that the last thirty years of debate on critical theory have served generally to tease out and elaborate many issues that were central to the study of satire prior to the emergence of post-structuralist analyses, and current movements within critical theory and practice seem to us quite capable of producing increased insight into satire—without voiding the pioneering work of readers like Kernan. Because satire has always claimed to have an effect upon the reader, the rhetorical work of the 1950s and 1960s has served as a firm foundation for current reader-response analyses of satire. Recent theory has, in fact, incorporated many of the ideas of earlier satire criticism, and has exploded some of the New Critical barriers against which earlier critics and theorists had to struggle. Stanley Fish's groundbreaking reader-response analysis of *Paradise Lost* in *Surprised by Sin* (1967) is, for instance, in one of its major aspects, an application of Henry W. Sams's 1959 rhetorical insight into reading satire, articulated in "Swift's Satire of the Second Person."[5] Reception theory, a near relation to reader-response, seems also to be a promising means of exploring issues originally raised through rhetorical analyses of satire.

Similarly, satire criticism and theory have always tended toward interdisciplinarity. The examination of satire as cultural behavior, from Robinson to Frye to Elliott to Test, can only be extended by the current interest in the works of Victor Turner, Mikhail Bakhtin, René Girard, and Clifford Geertz. New currents in psychology, especially the continuing critique of Freud's work, may be fruitful as well. Satirists, long the subject of Freudian analysis, have recently been examined from the perspective of Jacques Lacan and Julia Kristeva in ways that echo the investigations of satiric reflexivity inherent in the now long-recognized convention of the satirist satirized. At the same time, such conventions are now readily recognizable as having both psychological and rhetorical bases. Contemporary "humorology," as is argued in Paul Lewis's *Comic Effects,* has produced a host of multidisciplinary approaches to humor, few of which have yet to be applied specifically to the critical study of satire. In particular, satire studies, with its emphasis on audience and social impact, may be well informed by sociology, psychology, and even fields like market research.

Certainly, structuralist poetics, arising out of linguistics and anthropology, was ideally suited to investigate the oppositions inherent in satire discussed earlier. In structuralist genre theory, genre is constituted by conventions or normative structures (langue), and the individual work is distinguished by its variations upon and transgressions of these conventions and structures (parole). Thus, structuralist poetics calls attention to satire's peculiarity as itself a transgressive form, a genre constituted by transgression against genre. In a seeming paradox, it purports to reinforce social norms in the very act of transgressing literary norms. Satire itself, then, is in fact deconstructive. Moreover, satire has always focused upon the aporia created by ironic difference, for its rhetoric of exposure is based upon the demonstration of its victims' differences from themselves. Post-structuralist poetics, like deconstruction, continuing to work with the destabilizing of oppositions and hierarchies, seem well-designed to reconsider the problems of irony and indeterminability that readers of satire have sensed all along. As other genres and modes are increasingly revealed to be subject to indeterminacy, satire's relevance to critical theory increases. Indeed, readers of Douglas Atkins's *Reading Deconstruction/ Deconstructive Reading*'s analyses of *Tale of a Tub* and *The Dunciad* must have recognized that the readings produced by a deconstructive poetics were not in any substantial way really new but were newly clear. Moreover, post-structuralism's problematization of what, if anything, lies outside of the text reduces the previously supposed problem of literary integrity against which critical and theoretical apologists for satire have struggled for so long.

Having suffered at the hands of critics who wished to exclude history from literature, satire can only gain by the resurgence of historicism. The reconsideration of the power of literature and the literature of power, basic in the new historicism, raises in a new way issues that have been fundamental to satire study. Although both Pope and Swift explicitly claimed that satire was a supplement to the law, readers seem to have forgotten this relationship; but as the recent work of Ian Bell and Jerome Christensen seems to indicate, Michel Foucault has reminded us of writing's implication in the grids of power and may enable us to analyze in new ways satire's relation to law and its capacity to discipline and punish. Similarly, since satire has always called attention to both its materiality and its moment of production, neo-Marxian considerations can be expected to be fruitful. Satire's habitual construction based on thesis and antithesis, the same oppositional principle that produces structural readings, is susceptible to dialectical analysis as well. Moreover, recent reinvestigations and refinement of our concept of ideology should be pertinent to studies of the potential for satire as a site of resistance to cultural and political hegemony—as well as for satire's implication within hegemonic discourse. Although as yet only a few identity theorists and critics have begun to investigate ways in which satire can unify marginalized or colonized people, one suspects that satire theory will be instrumental in the continuing investigation of colonial and post-colonial literatures. While readers of the lyric may protest against the politicization of poetry, readers of satire have long recognized that as a form it is always already political. Satire, as a literature of power and attack, has been seen as radically masculinist, and in fact a form of power exerted frequently against women. Felicity Nussbaum's and Ellen Pollak's pioneering works have traced the ways in which satirists have been openly and covertly misogynistic (*The Brink of All We Hate; The Poetics of Sexual Myth*). On the other hand, however, little work has appeared to recuperate eighteenth-century English women of letters, such as Hetty Wright and Lady Mary Wortley Montagu, who responded to such attacks and wrote their own satire. Interestingly, feminist critics have most often referred to the power of women's "humor"—rather than satire—implying that satire is indeed gendered; the work of examining this distinction and of the many issues that underlie this difference has only just begun.

Certainly, all of this work cannot be done in a single volume. The present collection of essays aspires to be only a continuation and an expansion of the horizon surveyed by the many critics mentioned earlier. The essays contained here continue to reflect satire criticism's historically narrow focus upon male writers in Britain, principally during the seventeenth and eighteenth centuries, even as they attempt to enlarge the scope of both our vision and our understanding. Each author here offers a theory of or regarding satire, but each theory is worked out with reference to historically rooted texts. We believe that much of what has been said (and is being said) about writers in the seventeenth and eighteenth centuries has special interest to those who would study satire in other periods and in other countries, and we hope that this volume will make available to a feminist, modern Americanist, for instance, many of the tools she needs in order to analyze the role of satire in the first American wave of feminism. At the same time, we hope, by including writers from other periods and from other national literatures, to expand the horizon of those readers whose attention has been fixed primarily upon the British satiric scene in the eighteenth century.

Part I of this book, "Reading Satire," offers examples of two synchronic approaches to satiric texts: one utilizing an analysis of the recurring tropes and images of satire, and one based on a combination of psychoanalysis and reader-response theory. John R. Clark investigates the parodic nature of satire, as it seeks to reflect the vulgarity of the culture that it embodies and thus criticizes. Fredric V. Bogel offers a Lacanian-based reader-response theory of satire, articulated through the example of a reading of Swift's poems.

Part II, "Geneses and Genealogies," offers a chronologically organized overview of the punctuated evolution of satire. Beginning with Gay Sibley's re-investigation of the classical etymology of satire in *satura* and her exploration of the contemporary American case of Joe Bob Briggs, this section moves through Kirk Combe's analysis of how and why satire superseded the medieval complaint in the seventeenth century; Richard Nash's examination of the relations between the satirist and the archetypal figure of the wild man; Jon Rowland's theory of the relation between satire and panegyric as it is manifest in the writings of Swift. Finally, Christian Gutleben, after tracing its generic roots back to Renaissance college "saltings," uses the example of the history of a modern "satirical" form—the academic satire—to distinguish satire from modern and postmodern comic playfulness. Throughout Part II, satiric form and content are related to historically specific social norms in order to historicize the literary conventions of satire.

Part III, "Satire and Society," investigates relations between culture and the production of satire, beginning with Christiane Bohnert's chapter summarizing and revising the history of post-Enlightenment satire criticism. Erin Mackie offers an analysis of the impact of the marketplace upon literature, and specifically upon women as signs in satire through the example of Swift. And Linda V. Troost examines economic and social satire in the comic operas of W. S. Gilbert.

As this introduction has emphasized, one elusive, and probably illusory, goal of the critic of satire, always has been to define the genre—to tell precisely what its elements or qualities are, or what its ultimate purpose must be. The Elizabethans conceived satire in terms of a crabbed style and a shrill narrative voice; conversely, the Augustans favored polished meter and urbane intonation. Happily (and, we think, wisely), as editors of this volume, we assume no obligation to set such limitations on the concept of satire. Our intention is not to engage in the folly (and, on occasion, the knavery) of solving the dilemma of what satire is or ought to be. Rather, we feel it is appropriate and timely to attempt to represent the critical diversity of the late twentieth century as it is applied to the subject of satire. In this way, we hope to accomplish two things. First, this collection should enact the often dizzying array of current critical approaches and concerns as practiced on satire of widely different times and cultural bases. Undergraduate, graduate, and specialist alike should find challenge and increased understanding in the chapters that follow. Second, in adding these voices of the 1990s—three hundred years after Dryden's great retrospection on satire—to the continuing debate over this perplexing literary form, we want to extend yet one more step, and we trust with distinction, the abiding tradition in English letters of critical commentary on satire.

NOTES

1. A particularly arresting (if not dumbfounding) manifestation of this critical approach to
    satire comes early in this century with Johannes Prinz writing on the life and works of
    Rochester (*John Wilmot Earl of Rochester: His Life and Writings*, Leipzig, 1927).
    Commenting both on Rochester individually and on satirists generally, Prinz decrees
    that, "In order to have the impetus and the convincing power of the true satirist, it is
    essential that a considerable admixture of sadistic propensities should be included in
    the constitution of the writer. Only a person to whom it is a source of never ceasing
    voluptuous pleasure to inflict pain and discomfort upon his fellow-beings will continue
    to compose satirical works" (155). As Fredric Bogel argues in his chapter in this book,
    satire creates an unease in its readers. Accounting for the unease by reference to the
    satirist's disease is one way of simultaneously disowning and discounting the discom-
    fort. An encyclopedic compilation of such explanations for satire may be found in
    Leonard Feinberg's *The Satirist.*
2. It is notable and representative that the two major works of criticism of satire during
    the 1940s were Mary Clare Randolph's essays on verse satire, the only form of satire
    with a detectable regularity of form (although, as Randolph explains, the binary form
    is grossly asymmetrical).
3. British Library microfilm No. T. 733(2). Quoted by Mary Clare Randolph in "Thomas
    Drant's Definition."
4. Note as well the inherent contradiction in Dryden's statement. The goal of satire is cul-
    tivated brutality, artful destruction; a victim is to be dispatched—but sweetly.
5. After Fish's work had refined that of Sams, satire criticism reappropriated such rhetor-
    ical analysis as is evidenced in essays in the special issue on "Reader Entrapment" in
    satire published by *Papers on Language and Literature,* 18.3.

WORKS CITED

Addison, Joseph. *The Spectator* 63 (May 12, 1711).
Atkins, G. Douglas. *Reading Deconstruction/Deconstructive Reading.* Lexington: UP of Kentucky,
    1983.
Bell, Ian. "Satire's Rough Music." *Literature and Crime in Augustan England.* London and New
    York: Routledge, 1991. 147–82.
Bloom, Edward A., and Lillian D. Bloom. *Satire's Persuasive Voice.* Ithaca: Cornell UP, 1979.
Casaubon, Isaac. *De Satyrica Graecorum Poesi et Romanorum Satira.* (1605). Delmar, NY:
    Scholars' Facsimiles and Reprints, 1973.
Christenson, Jerome. "*Marino Faliero* and the Fault of Byron's Satire." *Studies in Romanticism*
    24 (1985): 313–33.
Dryden, John. *A Discourse concerning the Original and Progress of Satire.* Vol. 4. *The Works of
    John Dryden.* Eds. E. N. Hooker and H. T. Swedenberg, Jr. 20 vols. to date. Berkeley:
    U of California P, 1956—.
Ehrenpreis, Irvin. "Personae." *Literary Meaning and Augustan Values.* Charlottesville: U of
    Virginia P, 1974. 49–60.
Elliott, Robert C. *The Power of Satire: Magic, Ritual, Art.* Princeton: Princeton UP, 1960.
Feinberg, Leonard. *The Satirist: His Temperament, Motivation, and Influence.* Ames: Iowa State
    UP, 1963.
Frye, Northrop. *Anatomy of Criticism: Four Essays.* Princeton: Princeton UP, 1957.
Kropf, Carl, ed. *Reader Entrapment in Eighteenth-Century Literature.* Special Issue. *Studies in the
    Literary Imagination* 17 (1984).

Griffin, Dustin. *Satire: A Critical Reintroduction.* Lexington: U of Kentucky P, 1993.
———. "Venting Spleen." *Essays in Criticism* 40 (1990): 124–35.
Guilhamet, Leon. *Satire and the Transformation of Genre.* Philadelphia: U of Pennsylvania P, 1987.
Hammer, Stephanie Barbé. *Satirizing the Satirist: Critical Dynamics in Swift, Diderot, and Jean Paul.* New York and London: Garland, 1990.
Kernan, Alvin. "Aggression and Satire: Art Considered as a Form of Biological Adaptation." *Literary Theory and Structure: Essays in Honor of William K. Wimsatt.* Eds. Frank Brady and John Palmer. New Haven: Yale UP, 1973. 115–29.
———. *The Plot of Satire.* New Haven: Yale UP, 1965.
———. "Robert C. Elliott 1914–81." In *English Satire and the Satiric Tradition.* Ed. Claude Rawson. New York and London: Basil Blackwell, 1984. 1-5.
Lewis, Paul. *Comic Effects: Interdisciplinary Approaches to Humor in Literature.* Albany: State U of New York P, 1989.
Leyburn, Ellen Douglas. *Satiric Allegory: Mirror for Man.* New Haven: Yale UP, 1956.
Lockwood, Thomas. *Post-Augustan Satire: Charles Churchill and Satirical Poetry 1750–1800.* Seattle: U of Washington P, 1979.
Mack, Maynard. "The Muse of Satire." *Yale Review* 41 (1951): 80–92.
Minnis, A. J., and A. B. Scott, ed. *Medieval Literary Theory and Criticism c. 1100–c.1375.* Oxford: Clarendon P, 1988.
Nilsen, Don L. F. "Satire—The Necessary and Sufficient Conditions—Some Preliminary Observations." *Studies in Contemporary Satire* 15 (1988): 1–10.
Nussbaum, Felicity. *The Brink of All We Hate: English Satires on Women 1660–1750.* Lexington: UP of Kentucky, 1984.
Pollak, Ellen. *The Poetics of Sexual Myth: Gender and Ideology in the Verse of Swift and Pope.* Introd. Catharine C. Stimpson. Women in Culture and Society Series. Chicago: U of Chicago P, 1985.
Prinz, Johannes. *John Wilmot Earl of Rochester: His Life and Writings.* Leipzig: 1927.
Quintana, Ricardo. "Situational Satire: A Commentary on the Method of Swift." *University of Toronto Quarterly* 17 (1948): 130–136.
Randolph, Mary Clare. "The Structural Design of Formal Verse Satire." *Philological Quarterly* 21 (1942): 368–84.
———. "The Medical Concept in English Renaissance Satire." *Studies in Philology* 38 (1941): 125–57.
———. "Thomas Drant's Definition of Satire, 1566." *Notes and Queries* 180 (1941): 416–18.
Rawson, Claude. *Satire and Sentiment 1660-1830.* Cambridge: Cambridge UP, 1993.
Robinson, Fred Norris. "Satirists and Enchanters in Early Irish Literature." *Studies in the History of Religions Presented to Crawford H. Tory.* Eds. D. G. Moore and G. F. Lyons. New York: Macmillan, 1912. 95–130.
Rosenheim, Edward, Jr. *Jonathan Swift and the Satirist's Art.* Chicago: U of Chicago P, 1963.
Sams, Henry W. "Swift's Satire of the Second Person." *ELH* 26 (1959): 36–44.
Seidel, Michael. *Satiric Inheritance: Rabelais to Sterne.* Princeton: Princeton UP, 1979.
Tave, Stuart. *The Amiable Humorist: A Study in the Comic Theory and Criticism of the Eighteenth and Early Nineteenth Centuries.* Chicago: U of Chicago P, 1960.
Test, George. *Satire: Spirit and Art.* Tampa: U of South Florida P, 1991.
Tilton, John W. *Cosmic Satire in the Contemporary Novel.* Lewisburg: Bucknell UP, 1977.
Worcester, David. *The Art of Satire.* New York: Russell & Russell, 1940.

Part One

Reading Satire

•1•

Vapid Voices and Sleazy Styles

John R. Clark

*There cannot be one color of the mind: an other of the wit. . . . Doe wee
not see, if the mind languish, the members are dull? Look upon an effem-
inate person: his very gait confesseth him. If a man be fiery, his motion is
so: if angry, 'tis troubled, and violent. So that wee may conclude:
Wheresoever, manners, and fashions are corrupted, Language is. It imitates the publicke riot. The excesse of Feasts, and apparell, are the notes
of a sick State; and wantonesse of language, of a sick mind.*

(Jonson 8.592–93)

The idea cited here, from Ben Jonson's *Discoveries*, is hardly new:[1] we think of Buffon's *Le style est l'homme même*; you *can* judge a book by its cover, or at least by its superficies and supernumeraries—style, layout, introductory and concluding matter, publisher, grants, fellowships, patrons, accolades, and friends. When the individual or his society is atilt or collapsed, the evidence will be patently obvious by the literary productions of the body politic and the collective cultural brain. Jonson himself certainly produced and paraded in the plays his own bathetic bevy of "humorous" professional Elizabethan sickies; his priests, doctors, lawyers, dissenters, lovers, poets, nimblewits, philosophers, hawkers, cutpurses, and conycatchers continuously mass-produce and spew out—orally and in writing—a language of jargon and pseudo-learning, vapor, and puffery. This language Jonson designates *cant*.[2] His characters are made to stand (or lean) as exemplars of civic obfuscation, quagmire, and distemper. They are avatars, as Robert Burton or Jonathan Swift would aver, of Aeolism and the Edifices of Air.

Voltaire once put it epigrammatically another way. He was sickened by the so-called aristocratic French refinement that found the beauties of the biblical "Song of Songs" too crude and simplistic. He countered wittily à propos of his contemporaries: "Whence comes our delicacy? it is because the more manners are depraved, the more language becomes circumspect; it is believed that one can replenish in language what has been lost in virtue" ("Lettre de M. Eratous à M. Clocpitre. . .," 9.499).[3]

At first, it might appear that Voltaire's barb actually contradicts Jonson, suggesting as it does that a decadent society struggles hypocritically to polish its language and conceal (or even compensate for) its loss of decency in manners and mores. But a little thought should convince us that Voltairean irony actually *confirms* Johnson, for it indicates (as Henry Fielding was fond of affirming) that a depraved society exposes itself precisely *because of* its inflated language, its exaggerated affectation of sophistication and delicacy. The stunted *and* the bloated scrub are self-exposing. "By their fruits ye shall know them" (Matt. 7:20). George Orwell puts it this way: "The inflated style is itself a kind of euphemism. . . . The great enemy of clear language is insincerity. When there is a gap between one's real and one's declared aims, one turns as it were instinctively to long words and exhausted idioms, like a cuttlefish squirting out ink" ("Politics and the English Language" 167). The atmosphere in the vicinity of knaves and fools is, as the satirist repeatedly demonstrates, replete with feathers and fatuousness, smokescreens and folderol.[4]

As a matter of fact, the great satirists—Aristophanes, Petronius, the *Reynard* authors, Geoffrey Chaucer, François Rabelais, the creator of *Lazarillo*, Jonson, Molière, Jonathan Swift, Gustave Flaubert, Robert Browning, Mark Twain, Robert Musil, Günter Grass, Gabriel Márquez—have always displayed a remarkable ear for the public's utterance, its abstruseness and humbug. And this talent is compounded by the satirist's mimic skill: the greatest satirists are perfectly capable of parodying and replicating such chaff and clatter. It is to their pages we turn to recover any age's prevalent language of blather and cliché, babble and decay. For satirists are master recording technicians bringing us high-fidelity—nay, stereophonic and DAT—reproductions of each era's outstanding yammer and scam. Satirists' incredible ability to isolate the fleet and the fake and the ephemeral in vast mausoleums of the satire's careful contriving is tantamount to enshrining drivel in temples of gold or of brass, so we are forced to inspect our linguistic shortcomings in an eternal (and public) resting place. As Alexander Pope has remarked, we are coerced into beholding a hair or grub interred in amber; we gape at the insect and admire its fabulous urn, but wonder how the devil it got there ("Epistle to Dr. Arbuthnot" lines 169–72 in Pope 603).

In such a sense, then, our satirists are linguists of a very special order, for they are perennially sensitized to auditioning and preserving the languages of Babel. They will never forgive the vocabulary of fools, the punctuation of profligates, the syntax of disorder or disgrace. For the satirist's permanent *mythos* postulates and dramatizes the sad tale that his culture is in discombobulation and decay. In his pages doomsday is quotidian, transpiring in every place.

Therefore it should not surprise us that a number of our satirists are specifically known outside satire as the scholars and antiquaries of language, rhetoric, usage, and style; one need merely think of such authors as Varro, Lucian, Rabelais, Erasmus, Samuel Johnson, A. E. Housman, H. L. Mencken, George Orwell, or E. B. White. In their satires, therefore, satirists may be rightly regarded as the vigilantes of crapulous usage and abusage.

Hence, in this chapter, I would like to range extensively, exploring the satirists' principal investigations, imitations, manipulations, and, as it were, sensible recordings of coarse and cretinous language in action. In these pages, my central focus will be upon satire's broad, overriding concern with voice and diction, with language and style. What the satirist does very well indeed is to present and mimic foolish and impudent voices and styles: he blankets us with a host of imitations of decadent verbosity.

It should be noted that the satirist, as a result, is often faulted as a defective artist because of some of his own deficient organization, skewered styles, and other unpleasant writing practices. But in fact he is merely giving us a near-replica and precise overdosage of our own customs and abuses—our own disease: If our jargon be heavy, if our sense of form deficient, our language and thought atrocious—why, then, the satirist hath done no more than to confront us with our own widely prevalent sins. If satire be considered allopathic, we might accordingly assert that satire's injection of limited apportionments of prescribed medicine are intended to cure us of the larger intellectual diseases that infect our society.

As a matter of fact, the satirist is able to make these presentations best by direct dramatic confrontations. He dons a mask, adopts an alien voice or antic pose.[5] As one scholar has noted, revengers and malcontents in Jacobean theater tap into a new vein of power by "role-playing. Disguise serves as more than a convenient trick. It involves a definite loss of the habits, values, and restraints of one's normal identity. It frees the disguiser to do things which would be otherwise inconceivable, as he in a sense becomes what he poses as" (Wharton 24). Indeed, all men sense this kind of "release" when wearing a disguise. Young Jack in *Lord of the Flies* gains an almost maleficent power. Aspiring to become a hunter, he paints his visage red and white, forging "a new face." Thus disguised, he commences to frighten the other boys, and actually begins to assume a new personality—capering, dancing, laughing, snarling: "the mask was a thing on its own, behind which Jack hid, liberated from shame and self-consciousness" (Golding 80).[6]

Doubtless there is some weight of grim irony in the fact that satirists utilize exactly the same device that has proved so suitable to savages, robbers, masqueraders, and con men. To be sure, of course, this practice on the part of a satirist is generally resented. It virtually goes without saying that people suspect the character and the motives of someone who wears a mask (especially if he be a wit). Apparently, the thin and threadbare lines between the *eiron*, the pretender, the fakir, and the bandit tend to disappear. The Greek word for hypocrite (*hupokrites*) was originally benign; it designated one who answers, and was applied to professional actors, those who played a role. We well remember Prince Hamlet's shock and chagrin when he discovered that a mere indifferent player could so movingly feign a genuine grief, even to the point of displaying "Tears in his eyes, distraction in's aspect" (*Hamlet* II.ii.581).

But, then again, *everyone* is guilty of this selfsame usage; it is "the way of the world," society's usual modus operandi. Indeed, we had better concede at once that all men fashion dozens of personae and selves in the course of any typical day. As La Rochefoucauld has wittily and satirically noted, "In all the professions, each man affects a mien and outward appearance so as to seem to be what he wants us to believe he is. Thus, one can say that the world is composed entirely of false-faces" (No. 256, 93). Perhaps that is precisely why the satirist so dearly loves this ploy: he dons his masks, exactly as *toute le monde* does from day to day; but he does so with the deliberate dash and excess of the parodist, taunter, ventriloquist, and clown. He draws upon the same power source that supplies Everyman, but he does so to wreak havoc, to electrify the enlightened citizenry, and to short circuit the system.

Jonathan Swift, palpably our greatest satirist, is virtually notorious for this usage; in his study of personae, Robert C. Elliott notes that "Swift's feats of impersonation operate according to rules which every reader senses but which no critic I know of has been able to specify very precisely. The game is this: Swift must express himself through a zany alter ego, say truth by means of a lie, speak sense through a madman's lips. He must manipulate a persona whose utterances simultaneously expresses [sic] and unwittingly condemns [sic] the folly Swift is pursuing" (*Literary Persona* 125). In fact, satire over the ages has regularly tended to turn fictional and to create "voices" that are, among other things, self-exposing. Consider some of the great satiric characters in the tradition: Petronius' Encolpius and Eumolpus; Horace's "Horace," Davus, and Cook; Chaucer's Pardoner and Wife of Bath; de Rojas' La Celestina; Shakespeare's Falstaff; Cervantes' Historian Cid Hamet Benengeli; Rabelais's

Chronicler Alcofribus Nasier; More's Hythloday; Pope's Martinus Scriblerus; Swift's Lemuel Gulliver; Sterne's Tristram; Browning's "Men and Women"; Nabokov's Humbert Humbert; and Roth's Portnoy. Created voices are absolutely necessary for fictional satire. As for Swift's case, one critic flatly proclaims: "The fact is that we should not have Swift at all, his terrible truths . . . if his imagination did not work through the psychologies of the outrageous figures he officially hates. Their indecorums, their far-fetched metaphors, their absolute egotism fill his imagination . . ." (Traugott 99). It is unquestionably true that Swift is deservedly famous for the brilliance with which he adopted the personae of his enemies and buffoons, somehow ennobled thereby to speak enchantingly like an oracle through their distorted masks.

In any event, we cannot stress enough the fact that the satirist is a first-rate mimic, a creator of tones and styles and voices. In fact, Scott Elledge claims that Jaques (in *As You Like It*), like many a satirist, displays a "preference for mitigating the boredom of life by the exercise of a gift for satire. He enjoys the creative act of composing satirical speeches." In short, just as the satirist pleases himself by his creativity, so, as concerns his audiences, he is seeking "more often to please than to reform," Elledge maintains; hence, entertainment and play are his central priority, transcending the conveyance of mere "message" (33, 23). Such a viewpoint is almost diametrically opposed to conventional definitions of satire, which stress its earnest rhetoric, its message, its zeal, and its quest to induce reformation. Yet, if we give it some thought, major satire usually appeals to us by its wit, its indirection, its spurts of artistic creativity, its fantastic settings and outrageous vocabularies, by its almost scandalous renunciation of boundaries and constraints. The present chapter, therefore, stresses, not his reformation or his message, but the satirist's plethora of masks and voices, his creative posturings, and his carpetbag of styles.

What the satirist does frequently and does well is to adopt the tone and character of his victims. And, in fact, sometimes the satirist can, with a single brush-stroke, effect a full-scale portrait. Pope does just this in capturing the essence of the vacuous Sir Plume. Plume is, you will recall, the Lord who tries in vain to get the Baron after the rape to restore Belinda's lock.

> 'My Lord, why, what the Devil?
> Z—ds!! damn the lock! 'fore Gad, you must be civil!
> Plague on't! 'tis past a Jest—nay pritchee, Pox!
> Give her the Hair'—he spoke and rapp'd the Box [of Snuff].
>   ("The Rape of the Lock" 4.127–30, *Poems* 236)

As a swearing Lord, Sir Plume excels Fielding's Squire Western; he cannot utter half a line without an execration or an expletive. He is in the same case with the modern Hippy; eliminate his jargon and his cant phrases, and there is literally nothing left. Hence, Sir Plume is a speechless advocate, an illiterate Lord, a comically sputtering noble ruin. Paradoxically, by exaggerating furiously, Pope captures his very essence. What is more, this single portrait manages to call into question almost the entirety of the aristocracy: they seem to be idle, opulent, and inchoate fops. Even the best of the Restoration's satiric comedies never manages so handsomely or so swiftly to do them in.

Voltaire achieves the same absurd oxymoronic effect repeatedly in *Candide*. The tale is narrated with the speed and gallop of a race horse, but there is no goal or finish line; and indeed, in his whiplash celerity, the narrator often transports himself into the realm of splendid nonsense. Here is a wonderful mishandling of a recognition scene between Candide and the brother of his beloved Cunegonde: "Both of them fell over backwards, embraced, and shed streams of tears" (56). It would require a contortionist to be able to fall down backward while simultaneously pressing forward into an embrace—but no matter; in this absurdist landscape and marathon, that's precisely what happens. There is no time to pause or rectify this splendid flow of arrant ineptitude.

At times, to be sure, mere nonsense can be made to turn acerbic and nasty. During World War II, e.e. cummings caustically imitates an ardent American patriot:

> ygUDuh
>
>> ydoan
>> yunnuhstan
>
>> ydoan o
>> yunnuhstan dem
>> yguduh ged
>
>> Yunnuhstan dem doidee
>> yguduh ged riduh
>> ydoan o nudn
>> LISN bud LISN
>
>> dem
>> gud
>> am
>
>> lidl yelluh bas
>> tuds weer goin
>> duhSIVILEYEzum
>
>>> ("ygUDuh" *Poems* 343)

Ruthlessly these lines dramatize the dire effects of propaganda upon the provincial mentality. The Brooklyn bum portrayed here is barely articulate; notice how close he is to the rhetoric and clarity of Sir Plume. For this nominal American, the Japanese are "gooks"—scarcely human little animals. In contrast, he, the speaker, is a prime exemplar of The American Way; he will bring Understanding and Civilization to the Far East.[7] Of course, this is a grand instance of the pot calling the kettle black. Cummings outdoes himself in capturing the empty clichés and gutteral gasps of an American Neanderthal.

William Blake nicely portrays the ironic potential—always a real possibility—for satirist and victim to intersect, and even to change places. He encapsulates this possibility in a single brilliant two-line epigram:

> A petty sneaking knave I knew—
> 'O Mr. Cromek, how do ye do?'
> (*The Poems* 595)

Here, the single-minded satirist is just commencing (and comfortably warming) to the denunciation of his enemy. But Mr. Cromek's sudden appearance upon the scene throws all into *bouleversement*. All at once, in the second line, the satirist must himself turn to obsequious fawning, and become the petty, sneaking knave—assuming the selfsame hypocrisy in conduct that he had at the outset condemned in another![8] What a reversal is here: in a trice, the satiric archer becomes his own target. For it is certainly true (or at least we like to think it is so) that all too many a satirist is guilty of the very spite and malice that he lashes and impugns in others. Blake has fashioned well in his epigram an instantaneous piece of poetic justice, that encompasses *two voices*—that of the challenger, and that of the victim.

A similar metamorphosis besets the voice in Ezra Pound's "*Portrait d'une femme*"; the speaker is apparently extolling a *ficelle*, a London matron who has spent her life merely in sitting still, receiving visits and retailing gossip. She is hailed as "our Sargasso Sea":

> Great minds have sought you—lacking someone else.
> You have been second always. Tragical?
> No. You preferred it to the usual thing:
> One dull man, dulling and uxorious,
> One average mind—with one thought less, each year.
> Oh, you are patient, I have seen you sit
> Hours, where something might have floated up.
> (*Personae* 73)

We are primarily struck by the verse's dull, prosaic tone throughout. All events and ideas are diminished here, or calmly negated. All is adrift and aimless, as if soggy, waterlogged, and helplessly afloat. Here there is a metamorphosis before our very eyes. Describing a woman who is like the Dead Sea, the speaker himself, as if mesmerized, drifts into gossip and passive inanity. It is almost as if he has been captured among the Lotus Eaters; he himself becomes a convert to comme ci, comme ça entropy and inaction. And in doing so, Ezra Pound in 1912 very handsomely formulates and mimics what was to become a major "voice" of the twentieth century: the dispassionate analyst, the prosaic journalist, the inventory-taking statistician and C.P.A., the burnt-out case—all of them toneless and scientific, yet also on the verge of infinite boredom—hopeless, soporific, all worn out. The powerful woman he describes (emblematic of Victoria herself or of Victorian London) is virtually the essence of the age; she is a witch of sorts, like Circe, who converts everyone—including the poet himself—into figures of listlessness, ennui, and exhaustion.

Much the same had transpired in Pope's *Dunciad,* when the Goddess Dulness, the princess of her era, had afflicted the entire populace—including the tedious modern Poet reciting his ineffectual modern epic—with stupor, and the whole world was consumed by the rising floodtide of invincible bad taste. Here is one of Satire's great and recurring impersonations—of the afflicted, tired, and defeated little man, worn down by his age's unheroic ineptitudes and plenteous bad taste. Jonathan Swift's poet/lover is in as bad a case, as he wracks his brain to employ all the standard terms of love poetry, with all of the usual classical allusions. The first stanza of his "Love Song" proffered a feeble paean to Cupid. A second stanza of some sort will obviously have to follow.

II.
Mild *Arcadians*, ever blooming,
   Nightly nodding o'er your flocks,
See my weary Days consuming,
   All beneath yon flow'ry Rocks.
                  ("A LOVE SONG. In the *Modern* Taste,"
                  Poems 2.660.5–8)

In this verse, the Arcadians, blossoming like tulips and pansies, are asked, though asleep at night, to watch a clutch of tired days that are apparently consuming themselves—and where are these days wasting themselves away? O simple: underneath a clutter of blooming boulders. Indeed, the entire performance here might properly be termed flowery poetry, since everything—whether animal, vegetable, or mineral—is budding and flourishing mightily.

Except the poet's verse. If, for some reason unknown to common sense, a person should feel a pressing need to contemplate hilariously bad poetry, why, then, here is God's plenty!

Romance fares no better in satiric prose. Anton Chekhov almost perfectly simulates the thought processes of the smug, self-confident lover. The great Russian writer imitates the voice of Gurov speaking to the young Anna Sergeyevna, his latest amatory conquest. They are seated outdoors in a romantic setting, facing the ocean. In a manner anticipating stream-of-consciousness and free association, Chekhov traces Gurov's rather jumbled flood of ideas as he watches the sea:

> In Oreanda they sat on a bench not far from the church, looked down on the sea, and were silent. Yalta could scarcely be seen through the morning mist. White clouds lay motionless on the mountain tops. Not a leaf stirred on the trees, the cicadas chirped, and the monotonous, hollow roar of the sea, coming up from below, spoke of rest, of eternal sleep awaiting us all. The sea had roared like that down below when there was no Yalta or Oreanda, it was roaring now, and it would go on roaring as indifferently and hollowly when we were here no more. And in this constancy, in this complete indifference to the life and death of each one of us, there is perhaps hidden the guarantee of our eternal salvation, the never-ceasing movement of life on earth, the never-ceasing movement towards perfection. Sitting beside a young woman who looked so beautiful at the break of day, soothed and enchanted by the sight of all that fairy-land scenery—the sea, the mountains, the clouds, the wide sky—Gurov reflected that, when you came to think of it, everything in the world was really beautiful, everything but our own thoughts and actions when we lose sight of the higher aims of existence and our dignity as human beings. ("Lady With Lapdog" 270)

The poor, becalmed Thinker commences with ideas of "rest" and "eternal sleep." This train of thought turns to a recognition of two rather contradictory qualities of the ocean: "constancy" and "indifference." Somehow, both are rather a non sequitur as concerns man's eternal restfulness. Yet, in spite of logic, the ocean's almost callous disinterestedness suddenly sparks in Gurov a discovery of the "guarantee of our eternal salvation." No reader could be expected to anticipate that auspicious and mind-boggling leap in subject and in faith. Nor could contemplation of the ceaseless flow of winds and tides prepare us for Gurov's discovery that such changelessness and repetition teach him about "the never-ceasing movement towards perfection." Thus, Gurov's mood swings to one of self-satisfied well-being, and he considers that every thing is a "fairy-land." He handsomely concludes with a grand notion: *all things* are beautiful—except for people who don't have grand thoughts about "higher aims," and meaningfulness, and human "dignity." In short, it is all infallibly beautiful if you think it so.

The reader ought to be breathless from the panoramic sweep and swoop of Gurov's volatile reflections. What has the ocean's Indifference to do with Salvation? With Perfection? What has either to do with fairy-land? But, then, if "everything" is beautiful, there's not much to be said, by way of discrimination. But still, one wonders what Gurov's sordid little tryst with a recent high-school graduate has to do with man's supernal dignity, his "higher aims," and his "salvation." The answer, of course, is: nothing whatsoever. Gurov's hilarious rumination takes him pretty much where he wanted to be in the first place: His immediate physical needs and recently sated appetites are now in abeyance, and he exudes a soft miasma of self-gratulation and happy imaginings—these can by no means be termed "thoughts"—as he dreamily and complacently flounders about on his extensive ego trip. The satirist could hardly have exposed a man more baldly or better presented the idle fancies of the nearly mindless egotist.

Another masterful narrator of desiccated romance is Petronius' ex-slave Encolpius. Returning from a dinner party, the drunken homosexual lovers— as usual—lose their way. Fortunately, Giton has marked every column with chalk, and the lovers find their route back to the inn. But they are locked out. After much chagrin and wringing of hands, they manage to induce a passerby to smash down the inn door for them. Now, the fond lovers are safe at home— alone together, and in bed at last!

> O gods in heaven, what a night we kept, how soft the bed! together warmed, we slept so twined in love, so crossed upon a kiss, it seemed his soul was mine and mine was his. Goodbye, I thought, to every grief to man. Farewell, all care!—That night my doom began.
>
> Alas, I boasted of my happiness too soon. For the instant my drunken hands relaxed their grip on Giton, Ascyltus, that wizard of my destruction, ravished the boy away in the darkness to his own bed and took his pleasure of another man's love. Whether Giton felt nothing at all, or merely pretended not to notice, I do not know; but all night long, oblivious of every moral law, every human right, he lay with Ascyltus in adulterous embrace. Waking, I went groping with my hand for the boy's body in the bed and found, O gods, my treasure stolen! For one instant—if the word of a lover can be believed—I was tempted to run myself through with my sword and join, as the poets say,
>
>> that sleep I slept to the endless sleep of death.
>
> But in the end prudence prevailed. (*Satyricon* 85)

The reader can only smile at the vapid changes, quick reversals, the rocketing speed of every turn and tergiversation. The lovers are free. The lovers are lost. The lovers find their way. The inn door is barred and they are helpless. Someone smashes it down for them. Now, there is time for sexual bliss (a bliss never fully obtained heretofore in the long course of this truncated satiric romance). But, alas, a "wizard of destruction" steals Encolpius' beloved away, and now Giton is "oblivious of every moral law"—as these characters habitually are.

Here is a whirligig of change. We commence with the epic "return"—the chalked markings remind us of Theseus in the Labyrinth (or of Hansel and Gretel). This theme gives way to an inn-side brawl of low comedy and farce, where doors are broken down. Then follows a lover's scene with a hymn to sensual pleasure, that at once turns melodramatic with the theft of the "insensate" paramour. Thence follows tragedy: the heady posturing and threats of suicide—an elevated strain that is quickly abandoned. The whole transaction is magnificently undercut and put down by the wonderful insertion: "if the word of a lover can be believed." For, of course, these picaresque lovers and posturers can in no way be believed for more than a single instant: every mood, every scene, every vow, and every action is tortured upon a rack and overthrown, and a new spate of literary posturing takes its place. Single-handedly, the *Satyricon* intensively parodies almost every single type of literature, bringing literally dozens of genres onto the chopping block. And through it all, the lover's voice, overfull of pious platitudes and shallow ineptitudes, presides over this glorious send-up.

Let us next turn to the most diffuse and most prosaic of genres. Voices loudly proliferate in the world of nonfiction. For this is the great medium of the modern ages, ages devoted to essays, lectures, histories, analyses, advertisements, commentaries, editorials, "articles," and "criticism." In this realm, Bustos Domecq, the creation of Jorge Luis Borges and Adolfo Bioy-Casares, is something of an amphibian: part literary critic, part popular essayist, at once an aspirant sociologist and chronicler of popular culture and events. Needless to say, he tends to be pompous, overly serious, and something of a vaporous windbag. He opens one conventional essay thus:

> The nuclear age, the curtain-drop on colonialism, the rise of the military-industrial complex, the challenge of the left, the zoom in the cost of living and concomitant shrinking of the pay envelope, the Papal call

to peace, the threat of the devaluation of the dollar, the spread of sit-down strikes, the proliferation of supermarkets, the conquest of space, the population shift from rural life to city slums, the passing of rubber checks—all these spell quite an alarming panorama and, when you come right down to it, give the man of the Sixties food for thought. ("The Idlers," *Chronicles* 129)

This catchall listing proves to be something of a fisherman's net: a tawdry miscellany of items manages to get itself dredged up. Some problems are distinctly weighty and even of ominous import: nuclear matters number among them, as would the spread of strikes, and any loss of pay or shrinkage of monetary value (these last two are suspiciously repetitive); but we cannot equally weigh and consider a number of the lesser items that in wholesale fashion invade his list: the Pope's commendation of peace, the bouncing of a few checks, and the increase in the number of supermarkets. The categories—and their valuation—are senselessly inclusive and random. Umberto Eco refers to the "fungibility" of *kitsch*, of tasteless prose, its tendency, like fungus, to spread and flow and flourish (*Open Work* 182). That is precisely the case with Bustos Domecq's prose. Almost anything and everything is of importance to this essayist—*if and when* he thinks of it. His enormous sentence finally collapses in a monstrous (and trifling) anticlimax: contemporary man is given pause; he ought even—to do some *thinking*. The descent is further abetted by the choice of a ringing cliché at the close: all this distasteful clutter should provide "food for thought." Yech. One more sweeping conglomerative editorial assessment of all our most pressing contemporary "problems" is well under way.

This critical tone of inflated arrogance and self-importance, accompanied by tedious and toneless generalization and bombast, is one that we have all too frequently to reckon with: for it is the manner of our teachers, our textbook writers, our ministers, and our highbrow (and pseudo-highbrow) magazines. Here again, in the same vein, is the voice of another "scholar," Diedrich Knickerbocker, pressing ineluctably forward in unfolding his *History of New York*:

CHAPTER II

Having thus briefly introduced my reader to the world, and given him some idea of its form and situation, he will naturally be curious to know from whence it came, and how it was created. And, indeed, the clearing up of these points is absolutely essential to my history, inasmuch as if this world had not been formed, it is more than probable that this renowned island, on which is situated the city of New York, would never have had an existence. The regular course of my history, therefore, requires that I should proceed to notice the cosmogony or formation of this our globe.(Irving 38)

Just like a fool to value his own topic as worthy of defining the apex and terminus of all history! And just like a pompous scholar to undertake a "brief" survey of the entire history of the universe—down to the present—before he can permit himself to begin to approach his rightful topic, New York City. Ah, there's nothing more authoritative than a capsule history or a thumbnail sketch of—Everything. Like Laurence Sterne's Tristram Shandy, Knickerbocker wants to begin his subject ab ovo: from the real, honest-to-God beginning. And he has to belabor us with slow, nagging trains of pseudo-reasoning about the patently obvious: perhaps the City of New York would not now be in existence if God had not created the World beforehand. Hmmmmm. As our esteemed Bustos Domeq would say, that whole question just happens to be empty enough to give us food for thought. (If you are given to "thinking" about food.)[9]

From this selfsame mold comes a whole crib and choir of modern "scholars"—the literary "critics," so finely mocked by Erasmus, Rabelais, and in the persons of pseudo-scholars: the authors of the Epistolae Obscurorum Virorum, Jonathan Swift's Modern, Alexander Pope's Martinus Scriblerus, Thomas Carlyle's Teufelsdröckh, and Vladimir Nabokov's Charles Kinbote. By some kind of incredible accident, book reviews and notices have become virtually the undergirding of a whole literary wharf of pious and pretentious "criticism" and "scholarship." But, in the long perspective, such critics and newspaper journalists count for very little. To employ an aphorism after Schopenhauer, Every literary masterpiece begets a load of criticism, but loads of criticism never beget a single masterpiece. Unless we should wish to claim (as I certainly do), that the field of criticism has directly inspired humanist parodists and satirizers since the Middle Ages. Here, of course, is the exception that proves my aphoristic rule.

Moreover, there are far too many times when the disease of critical confusion is catching, and artists themselves help to spread the infection. Indeed, some writers even appear unable to compose a sensible "Forward" to their book. Wearing the distorted mask of such authors, the satirist cheerfully plays the role of the inept and braggadocio author—trying to tout his own composition and generate a little P.R. That is exactly the case with the supposed author of La Vida de Lazarillo de Tormes.

Prologue

I certainly consider it fitting that Matters so remarkable, and perhaps never heard of or seen before, should come to the notice of many and not be buried in the tomb of oblivion; for it could be possible that someone reading them may find something pleasing to him and those who do not delve too deeply may be delighted.

> And in this regard, Pliny says that there is no book, however bad it may be, that does not contain something good. Especially since tastes are not all one; but what one does not eat, another dies for. And thus we see that things regarded of small account by some are not so regarded by others. And for this reason, nothing should be destroyed or repudiated, unless it be very detestable; but it should be communicated to everybody, especially if it is harmless and if some benefit could be derived from it.(3)

The speaker in this Prologue is an author wonderfully inept. He commences at once with egocentric self-assurance, but then becomes hopelessly mired in a long drawn-out chain of reasoning that comes to upset reason itself. Yet, despite all of his wordiness, he never does get around to stating openly what it is that he so patently wants: all men, women, and children to buy his book. Indeed, he never even directly mentions his book at all, speaking only circumspectly. Thus, he exemplifies the con man too ineffectual to bring off his own small-scale scam.

Overall, the logical mess he makes of his argument is hilarious. Remarkable "things," he tells us (meaning his own writings), should be brought to everyone's attention (especially when they are unique). Why? Because *maybe* someone *might* find something pleasing in such a work, especially if the reader be superficial. Already, this speaker has helplessly commenced to undercut his own work, implying that it is remarkable (though unheard of), and opining that somebody just conceivably *might* find something pleasing about it. Every book, after all, must have something of value in it.

At this point, the hapless author trundles Pliny onstage to introduce a series of monumental commonplaces: Nothing can be all bad. Tastes are different. *De qustibus non est disputandum.* One man's meat is another man's potatoes. Conclusion therefrom: most writings should be preserved, and *all* such writings should be required reading—*for everybody!* Thus, without mentioning his own work, this inconsequential writer has managed, by a dislocating and knotty string of reasoning, to conclude that all men should be forced to read his book.

Nevertheless, his ineptitude suggests, between the lines, precisely the opposite: for throughout this passage there are recurring images of worthlessness and injury conveyed by such words as "unheard of," "tomb," "oblivion," "bad," "die," "detestable," and "harm." Subliminally, this author firmly implants in the reader's mind the distinct warning that there is something positively dangerous about this work that he is so anxious to foist upon the palate of the entirety of humankind.

Furthermore, if we put aside the mountain of infelicities and ineptitudes that our author has so laboriously assembled, we can enjoy the parody of an infinite number of Prefaces, Forewords, To the Readers, and the like, that have inundated the modern printing-press world. For, isn't it, after all, the tricky business of *every* author in his introduction (1) to pose as being humble, typical, and full of decorous humility, while nonetheless managing (2) to tout his own rare and ravishing productions, toot his own authorial horn, and induce every reader he possibly can to purchase his volume? Behind the mask, behind the voice, the satirist here manages very brilliantly to impugn his own would-be writer while mocking innumerable authors of any (nay, of every) age.

➼⊹╫⊹⊱   ⊰⊹╫⊹⊱

But the satirist is by no means confined to imitating a single staid or steady voice. On the contrary, some of his more ingenious creations involve him in devising unusual speakers—madmen, group voices (utilizing "we"), and even group narrators.

The group voice is a challenging endeavor, but provocative and necessary. At times, the satirist may want to exaggerate to the extreme, pushing his creations as far as they will go. In *Le Dictionnaire des Idées Reçues* Gustave Flaubert does just that, reducing the common opinions of his detested bourgeoisie, the middle class, to that of a single voice; accordingly, he sees to it that their fixed opinions, notions, and hunches are duly codified and catalogued, in alphabetical order.

> APRICOTS. None to be had again this year.
> ACTRESSES. The ruin of respectable young men. —Are fearfully lewd, give themselves over to orgies, squander millions, and end up in the poorhouse. —Ooops, sorry! Some of them are excellent mothers! In well-to-do families!
> AFFAIRS. (Business). Come first. —A woman must not mention hers. —The most important thing in life. —That's all there is.
> ALABASTER. Used to describe the most beautiful portions of a woman's body.
> ALCOHOLISM. The cause of every modern ailment.
> ANTIQUITY. And everything connected with it: old-hat, boring.
> ARTS. Perfectly useless, because they've been replaced by machines which make the same things faster.
> ATHEISTS. A nation of atheists could not survive.
>   (*Oeuvres* 2.955–56)[10]

Needless to say, clichés abound, and settled opinions are devoid of any scrap of intelligence or learning. The trick for this group is to *appear* informed on every subject. Members of this class are blissfully unaware that their ideas are abysmally provincial, not to mention, of course, handsomely contradictory. They condemn the cash nexus that they themselves have enshrined; they everywhere elicit a sexual primness and prudery that is undermined by their protesting overmuch; and they everywhere display complacent self-satisfaction with middle-class values while simultaneously revealing respect (and longing) for the status of "established" and "well-to-do" upper-class families. And, to be sure, Flaubert's most damning irony consists in his maintaining that an entire nation of shopkeepers can be reduced to the complacent murmur and bombination of a single voice, and in pretending that their empty and ephemeral platitudes and pieties for a single minute deserve to be preserved in anything like an "encyclopedia."

At the opposite pole from mass men confined in a state of uniformity stands the lonely modern individual. He, too, has become the victim of schizoid tendencies. He is an ironist, but, by detecting irony virtually everywhere, he ultimately paralyzes himself. Perhaps it is only appropriate (ironically speaking) that some of our best poets have been able to describe, portray, and explore this dreadful condition.

Certainly, one of the most complex lyric achievements in the twentieth century is attained by John Berryman. At one extreme, T. S. Eliot's verse had insisted too much upon the artist's "extinction of personality," fostering a great distance between "the man who suffers and the mind which creates" (Eliot, *Essays* 7,8). Such a platform promotes a species of acute dissociation of the artist's work from the suffering self. At the other extreme, Robert Lowell has been attempting to revitalize "confessional" poetry, where the "I" virtually speaks with the poet's own voice. Berryman followed both courses at once; he wrote confessionally—almost exclusively—about his own mind, his own emotions and fears, his own actions and reactions. But he did so by establishing a literal echo chamber of various voices. "Henry" is the primary persona of the poet, who often speaks of himself in the third person. In addition, Henry will imitate others, and don the mask of minstrelsy—a black face disguise behind which he can further hide, tease himself and others, and cavort.[11] In addition to all of these, we have to allow for Berryman's quick-change artistry of temperament; he can flash from one mood to another faster than a snake can bite.

> *Nullius addictus iurare in verba magistri,*
> *Quo me cumque rapit tempestas, deferor. . . .*
> (Horace, *Epist.* 1.1.14-15)[12]

> (Not bound by law to any master,
> Wherever the tempest tosses me, I'm carried. . . .)

Thereby, Berryman displays what others have termed his "mixed mind" (Haffenden 314) and a "rabid self-irony" (Galway Kinnell in Haffenden 398) that is frequently satiric in the extreme. Hence, his poetry crackles with various electric charges of energy along numerous temperamental wires, displaying the tense stichomythia of debate continuously ongoing among a rampant crowd of tones and speakers.

All of this internal agony is dramatically apparent in a late poem, "Henry by Night" (1969, 1971).

> HENRY'S nocturnal habits were the terror of his women.
> First it appears he snored, lying on his back.
> Then he thrashed & tossed,
> changing position like a task fleet. Then, inhuman,
> he woke every hour or so—they couldn't keep track
> of mobile Henry, lost
>
> at 3 a.m., off for more drugs or a cigarette,
> reading old mail, writing new letters, scribbling
> excessive Songs;
> back then to bed, to the old tune or get set
> for a stercoraceous cough, without quibbling
> death-like. His women's wrongs
>
> they hoarded & forgave, mysterious, sweet;
> but you'll admit it was no way to live
> or even keep alive.
> I won't mention the dreams I won't repeat
> sweating & shaking: something's gotta give:
> up for good at five.
>
> ("Delusions, Etc. of John Berryman," *Recovery* 52)

Aloofly, Henry commences by describing his own "nocturnal habits." Then, increasingly, he assumes the voice of his "women" (doubtless Berryman's wife Kate, and daughter Martha): they commence a catalogue of complaints—although this report is simultaneously called into question by the word "appears": how accurate is their inventory of alleged "wrongs"? And how legitimate? The very fact of their "hoarding" up such an assemblage of "wrongs" against themselves makes them appear overly scrupulous and self-righteous. And the comments about farts and snores leads one to suspect that they are prissy. Indeed, the very fact that they find such an itemized listing "mysterious and sweet" and even the alacrity with which they are "forgiving" of the "wrongs" they have so patiently assembled and endured renders them suspect, perhaps paranoid and clearly intolerant and holier-than-thou. Moreover, they immediately punctuate their forgiveness with a trite conviction that cancels out their supposed forbearance: appealing to any- and everyone, they concede that "it is no way to live."

Yet, from another perspective, there is irony and exaggeration in this entire presentation. And we soon recognize that this is really *Henry's* projection, *his* dramatic (and slanted) portrayal of his long-suffering antagonists. He is in fact indicting them for being at the least impatient, mean-spirited, and picayune. Insofar as they *enjoy* their exasperation and pain, they are masochistic and somehow self-serving. However, because *it is his* projection, we must recognize that it is Henry who overrides any and all criticism by anticipating it, and even dramatically staging it in trite and melodramatic form. Henry, in short, is nicely defending his regularly indefensible behavior.

Up to this point, we would have to say that the whole subject has been exacerbatingly overplayed, anticlimactic. Henry's mere tossing in bed and experiencing insomnia is hardly the criminal offense that his intimates, like Job's Comforters, appear to be wishing to make out. Many a man, we recollect, can suffer from sleeplessness, and many a poet, in the throes and agonies of poetic inspiration, wakes while others sleep. Doubtless it is once again the cruel outside world that fails to appreciate the poet and respect his prodigious suffering.

Nevertheless, the women here have *some* point: it is not entirely the "pure poet" who stays up all night "reading old mail," or indulging in "cigarettes" and "drugs." There is some justification for their recriminations.

Yet, as we have seen, the women's chorus is—let us not forget—the poet's own doing; he has engineered this scene and colored it with his own dramatic ironies, caustic exaggerations—and even justifications. After all, they *are* a prudish chorus, and appear to relish their tormentor's sins and their own precious martyrdom.

But just at this very moment, when the two points of view seem farthest apart, they suddenly coalesce: Henry comes full-circle, even *endorsing* their histrionic cliché about him:

> . . . it was no way to live
> or even keep alive.
> Suddenly Henry speaks for the first time in his own first-person voice:
> I won't mention the dreams I won't repeat
> sweating & shaking

He can—poignantly—add still more data to support their complaint: he is not merely the insomniac, but one ridden by nightmares, and on the brink of something like an epileptic seizure. Worse, he appears close to an all-out crackup. Almost defiantly he uses the 1955 Johnny Mercer slangy song title to memorialize his terrible case: "something's gotta give." Even more ominously to the point: Marilyn Monroe had been working upon Cukor's projected film, "Something's Got To Give" before she committed suicide in 1962.

Then, at that moment, Henry's intimate first-person voice as suddenly subsides. The next voice is newly aloof and controlled, as if matter-of-factly signing off in a C.P.A.'s diary: "up for good at five."

Possibly more than any other recent poet, Berryman has here captured the anguish and the drama of the modern period's "divided self." His hosts of voices and dictions, his quick-change alteration in pronouns, posturings, and moods, and the pervasive sense of conflict, guilt, and malaise all help to devise an exhausting but convincing picture of the disturbed sensibility caught in the fast track of kafkaesque modern life.[13] This route is presented as a terrible dead end: lots of drive and activity/nowhere to go. Acute sensitivity/loss of feeling, atrophy. Painful awareness of others/solitude and isolation.

> combers out to see
> Know they're goin somewhere but not me
> . . . .
> I'm scared a lonely
>
> I'm scared a only one thing, which is me. . . .
> ("Dream Song" No. 40, lines 3–4, 6–7)

Both telescope and microscope in our scientific era are conscripted to focus upon the shattered self. With acerb facility, John Berryman studies all of a man's interior shades in tumult. And indeed, it is all of this ruthless self-scrutiny that seems to imprison us with the self:

> . . . this' where we
> cry oursel's awake.
> ("Dream Song" No. 40, 11–12)

That is the very heartland of Berryman's "Dream Songs": where the suffering self is besotted with dreams, shivers into insomnia, contemplates self-murther, and from thence composes beautiful lyrics about his infernal torments. With John Berryman, we stand at the outer limits of manifold voicing and satiric masking. In these precincts, the cynical ironist turns his biting speeches into a deft and searing elegiac music—discordant and beautiful music—about himself.

At this point it might well be asked whether the satirist, by simultaneously donning the mask and stripping it off, by going so far as even to make fun of himself, has left the realm of satire behind and entered the kingdom of universal cynicism. We might consider the story by Kilgore Trout in which, upon an alien planet, because of extreme rigor in the administration of the law, eventually *everybody* was thrown behind bars! (Trout, Ch. 19) Here we have a reductio reply to Juvenal's poignant query about militant justicers (satirists included): "Who will guard the guardians?" (*Satire* 6.347–48). In the terms of Trout's story: no one will; all are equally incarcerated and impugned.

Yet who can doubt that Trout's story is itself satiric? Why not indict oneself—and many another? Consider the alternative: the obnoxious satirist who affirms that most men are foolish and vicious—except himself and a few select friends. Only the very knavish or foolish satirist would venture to credit that claim. For, on the contrary, what the satirist comes to appreciate (if he is to be major and profound) is that there is some quanta of vice and folly in us all.[14] Instead of despairing at such a consideration, the savvy satirist busily sets to work weighing and considering, assessing percentages and shares.

According to Socrates, the Oracle had doubtless designated Socrates the wisest of men because he alone knew that he did not know ("Apology" 5E–6E). The satirist aspires to attain to that same category, for he knows only too well that he partakes of folly and vice. On the other hand, the archetype of the failed satirist is nicely represented in Nathaniel Hawthorne's short story, "The Minister's Black Veil" ([1836] 285–99). There, the minister, sensing that men disguise their motives and intentions, hiding a species of blackness in their souls, ardently wanted to teach his congregation this lesson, and accordingly opted to wear a black veil as emblem of man's dissembling. He adamantly persisted in wearing that black veil *for the rest of his life.* No one could dissuade him from his singular resolve, and, indeed, since he made such a dark and morose appearance, men increasingly shunned his presence. Thereupon, the minister himself grew more and more grim and somber, negative and despairing of mankind, dying a lonely and hopeless outcast. Patently the irony is that the minister, in intending to "teach" his fellow men, actually drove them out of the classroom! The mask of blackness that he wore eventually muddied his own perception, and, like a pair of dark-colored glasses, they afflicted his vision and impaired his sight. Finally, the minister *became* the selfsame blackness that he had sought to inveigh against, by singling out the ebony in man's heart and giving it sole place in his interpretation of nature, he himself became the bête noir he wanted men to avoid. He became the ultimate scapegoat—bearing the entire burden of vice that he had originally sought to isolate and expunge.

Seneca the philosopher once remarked that what some men perceive as faults in the outside world are in fact projections, owing to defects in the eye—and the mind—of the beholder. That is certainly the case with Hawthorne's priest. Seneca goes on to reflect that this eventuality is similar to that of a straight stick that appears bent and larger-than-life to the viewer when it is immersed in water (*Epistle* 71.24). Yet the two cases are not exactly alike, since the stick in water is not tilted because of some defect in the observer. But the bent twig phenomenon is appropriate as an emblem of the way that parody functions. The actual piece of wood might appear flawless and upright to the casual eye (however many little defects it might possess), but when it is submerged in the solution of parody, its blotches and blemishes are magically magnified, and its crookedness—however minuscule—rendered more apparent, even to the average man's careless quotidian gaze. In short, the traits and tendencies of many a character and many a custom or fad are little regarded or understood, until they are subjected to scrutiny through the lens of parody, whereupon their actual qualities are, by means of distortion, more readily detected. Such mimickry is an inspired and visionary way of seeing, and quintessential in the art of satire.

Nor should we fear that the adroit satirist will be apt to falter and, because of his own skill as masker and parodist, ensnare himself. Indeed, the satirist's facility as quick-change artist permits him to maintain aesthetic distance, to mimic hundreds of characters and stances; he has no time to be overwhelmed by a single idée fixe. Au contraire, if he mimics enough types and acquires a masterful brilliance at his work, then he does, by a species of conjury and legerdemain, finally transform negatives into positives; he comes to depict the vast assortment of people that make up humankind. He becomes a Chaucer or Shakespeare, a Dickens or Dostoevsky—wonderfully representing the broad spectrum of men. In fact, his welter of faces augments his portrayal of and participation in the enormous variety of human experience. He becomes like any other great artist—giving us vital glimpses and insights into the human condition itself. Edmund Burke once said of an inferior imitation of Samuel Johnson's style that "it has all the contortions of the Sibyl without the inspiration" (Boswell 1110); but the great parody has them both. It speaks at secondhand, but is first-rate; it talks to us through a mask, but tells the truth. Umberto Eco proposes that the best parody precedes and even dictates to nature. "If its aim is true, it simply heralds what others will later produce, unblushing, with impassive and assertive gravity" (*Misreadings* 5). That is just like great satire, to mimic all our yesterdays, all of our today—and all our tomorrows too.

NOTES

1. Cicero (in *Tusc disput.* 5.47) attributes the saying, "Man's speech is like his life" to Socrates, and Seneca devotes the entirety of no. 114 of his *Epistulae Morales ad Lucilium* to expounding this topic.
2. See examples of professional *canters* (the politician, doctor, lawyer, poet) and their *cant* in Act IV, scene iv of Jonson's *A Staple of News* (1625).
3. Unless otherwise noted, all translations are my own.
4. Under the term *Ilinx,* George Test discusses satiric strategies aimed at dizzying or disorienting readers; he includes under this umbrella a host of practices, such as dislocation of language by means of nonsense, macaronics, doggerel, base diction, clichés, and wordplay (133 ff.).
5. I am, of course, fully aware that some critics have for several decades frowned upon one's using the term *persona* or *mask.* See, especially, Ehrenpreis ("Personae" 25–37). The idea was debated (SNL 89–153) and more recently the term has been resuscitated (Elliott, *Persona*).
6. Bakhtin (39–40) holds the "mask" to be seminal in the folk culture's celebration of "carnival." The mask represents joyful change, metamorphosis, playfulness, and mockery; it favors relativity and variety, negating uniformity and conformity.
7. In fact, this statement is made in wartime. What Americans will actually "bring" to Nippon are bullets, shells, and atomic bombs.
8. It should be added, however, that this seeming discomfiture for the satirist is nonetheless slyly offset by a clear gain: his opponent, Mr. Cromek, is thereby exposed as "sneaking knave" *by name.*
9. Perhaps Professor Knickerbocker should have given some thought to his grammar. The opening sentence commences very forthrightly with a dangling modifier; the Introducer should be the author, not the reader.
10. Similar satires include Swift's *A Complete Collection of Polite and Ingenious Conversation* (1738), Ambrose Bierce's *The Devil's Dictionary* (1906), and Victor L. Cahn's *The Disrespectful Dictionary* (1974).
11. "The poem then, whatever its wide cast of characters, is essentially about an imaginary character (not the poet, not me) named Henry, a white American in early middle age sometimes in blackface, who has suffered an irreversible loss and talks about himself sometimes in the first person, sometimes in the third, sometimes even in the second; he has a friend, never named, who addresses him as Mr. Bones and variants thereof. Requiescant in pace" (Berryman, "NOTE," *Dream Songs* vi).
12. Horace's own lines are themselves contradictory and heavily ironic: "I'm a free man ravished by every storm."
13. On Kafka, consult "Dream Songs" Nos. 310 and 247.
14. On the topic of "The Satirist Satirized," see Elliott (*Power* 130–222), and Hammer.

WORKS CITED

Anon. *La Vida de Lazarillo de Tormes y de sus fortunas y adversidades.* Eds. Everett W. Hesse and Harry F. Williams. Madison: U of Wisconsin P, 1961.

Bakhtin, Mikhail. *Rabelais and His World.* Tr. Helen Iswolsky. Cambridge, Mass.: M.I.T. P, 1968.

Berryman, John. *The Dream Songs.* New York: Farrar, Straus and Giroux, 1974.

———. *Recovery. Delusions, Etc.* New York: Dell Delta, 1973.

Bierce, Ambrose. *The Devil's Dictionary.* Garden City: Doubleday Dolphin, n.d.

Blake, William. *The Poems of William Blake.* Ed. W. H. Stevenson. London: Longman, 1971.

Borges, Jorge Luis and Adolfo Bioy-Casares. *Chronicles of Bustos Domecq.* Tr. Norman Thomas di Giovanni. New York: E. P. Dutton, 1976.

Boswell, James. *Life of Johnson.* Ed. R. W. Chapman. Oxford and New York: Oxford UP, 1983.

Cahn, Victor L. *The Disrespectful Dictionary.* Los Angeles: Price/Stern/Sloan, 1974.

Chekhov, Anton. *Lady with Lapdog and Other Stories.* Tr. David Magarshack. Harmonsworth: Penguin, 1964.

"Concept of the Persona in Satire, The: A Symposium." *Satire Newsletter* 3 (1966), 89–153.

cummings, e. e. *Poems 1923–1954.* New York: Harcourt, Brace, 1954.

Delacroix, Eugène. *The Journal of Eugène Delacroix.* Tr. Walter Pach. New York: Crown, 1948.

Eco, Umberto. *Misreadings.* Tr. William Weaver. New York: Harcourt Brace, 1993.

———. *The Open Work.* Tr. Anna Cancogni. Cambridge, Mass.: Harvard UP, 1989.

Ehrenpreis, Irvin. "Personae," in *Restoration and Eighteenth Century Literature: Studies in Honor of H.D. McKillop.* Ed. Carroll Camden. Chicago: U of Chicago P, 1963. 25–37.

Eliot, T. S. *Selected Essays.* New York: Harcourt, Brace, 1950.

Elledge, Scott. "The Fool in the Satirist," in *The Range of English.* Champaigne: National Council of Teachers of English, 1968. 21–43.

Elliott, Robert C. *The Literary Persona.* Chicago: U of Chicago P, 1982.

———. *The Power of Satire: Magic, Ritual, Art.* Princeton: Princeton UP, 1960.

Ellmann, Richard. *Yeats, The Man and The Masks.* New York: Dutton, 1948.

Flaubert, Gustave. *Ouevres.* Eds. A. Thibaudet and R. Dumesnil. 2 vols. Paris: Galimard, 1946–48.

Golding, William. *Lord of the Flies.* New York: G. P. Putnam's Capricorn, 1959.

Greene, Robert. *The Honourable History of Frier Bacon and Frier Bungay [sic].* London: Jean Bell, 1655.

Haffenden, John. *The Life of John Berryman.* Boston: Routledge and Kegan Paul, 1982.

Hammer, Stephanie Barbé. *Satirizing the Satirist: Critical Dynamics in Swift, Diderot, and Jean Paul.* New York and London: Garland, 1990.

Hawthorne, Nathaniel. *Great Short Works of Nathaniel Hawthorne.* Ed. Frederick C. Crews. New York: Harper & Row, 1967.

Herzog, Arthur. *The B.S. Factor. The Theory and Technique of Faking It in America.* New York: Penguin, 1974.

Irving, Washington. *A History of New York from The Beginning of the World to the End of the Dutch Dynasty. . . .* New York: G. P. Putnam's Capricorn, 1965.

Jonson, Ben. *Ben Jonson.* Eds. C. H. Herford, Percy and Evelyn Simpson. 11 vols. Oxford: Clarendon P, 1925–63.

Juvenalis, Decimus Junius. *Juvenal and Persius with an English Translation.* Ed. G. G. Ramsay. Rev. ed. Cambridge, Mass.: Harvard UP, 1979.

La Rochefoucauld, François, Duc de. *Maximes* Ed. F. C. Green. Cambridge: Cambridge UP, 1946.

Orwell, George. *A Collection of Essays.* New York: Doubleday, 1954.

Petronius. *The Satyricon.* Tr. William Arrowsmith. New York: New American Library, 1964.

Plato. *Plato in Twelve Volumes with an English Translation.* Ed. Harold North Fowler. London: William Heinnemann, 1971.

Pope, Alexander. *The Poems of Alexander Pope.* Ed. John Butt. New Haven: Yale UP, 1963.

Potter, Stephen. *Lifemanship, or The Art of Getting Away With It Without Being an Absolute Plonk.* New York: Henry Holt, 1950.

———. *The Theory and Practice of Gamemanship, or The Art of Winning Games Without Actually Cheating.* New York: Henry Holt, 1948.

Pound, Ezra. *Personae. Collected Shorter Poems of Ezra Pound.* London: Faber and Faber, 1952.

Seneca, Lucius Annaeus. *Ad Lucilium Epistolae Morales with an English Translation.* Ed. R. M. Gummere. 3 vols. Cambridge, Mass.: Harvard UP, 1969–71.

Seymour-Smith, Martin. *The Bluffer's Guide to Literature.* Intro. David Frost. New York: Crown, 1971.

Swift, Jonathan. *The Poems of Jonathan Swift.* Ed. Harold Williams. 2nd. ed. 3 vols. Oxford: Clarendon P, 1958.

———. *The Prose Works of Jonathan Swift.* Ed. Herbert Davis. 14 vols. Oxford: Blackwell, 1939–68.

Test, George A. *Satire. Spirit and Art.* Tampa: U of South Florida P., 1991.

Traugott, John. "'A Tale of a Tub,' in *The Character of Swift's Satire: A Revised Focus.* Ed. Claude Rawson. Newark: U of Delaware P, 1983. 83–126.

Trout, Kilgore [Philip José Farmer]. *Venus on the Half-Shell.* New York: Dell, 1975.

Voltaire (François Marie Arouet). *Candide ou l'optimisme.* Ed. Lester G. Crocker. London: U of London P, 1958.

———. *Oeuvres complètes de Voltaire.* Ed. Louis Moland. 52 vols. Paris: Garnier Frères, 1877–85.

Wharton, T. F. *Moral Experiment in Jacobean Drama.* New York: St. Martin's P, 1988.

·2·

The Difference Satire Makes: Reading Swift's Poems

Fredric V. Bogel

While my interest in satire predates my entry into the teaching profession, there is a sense in which the project I've been working on for the past few years grows directly out of the undergraduate classroom. More particularly, it is a response to the evident discomfort students feel when reading satire, especially satire of the Restoration and eighteenth century. There are many ways to account for this discomfort, as any specialist in the field knows. For one thing, the language of Augustan literature is both dense and rhetorically intricate, yet different from the dense and intricate language of Spenser or Blake, Browning or Berryman. For another, Augustan satiric literature is dauntingly allusive, filled with historical names like Charles and Charter[i]s, Walpole and Walter, or type-names like Rufa, Orgilio, Bays, and Booby—type-names, moreover, that may or may not refer obliquely to historical personages. And then there are the elliptical names consisting of an initial letter followed by a number—sometimes significant, sometimes not—of asterisks, or dashes, or perhaps by one long dash covering a multitude of effaced or nonexistent signifiers. The need for frequent annotation, moreover, is not simply an annoyance. Glancing anxiously and repeatedly from text to footnote, the student may come to feel that he or she has been led into a ritual display of ignorance, and that the text has maneuvered its readers into a position uncomfortably like that occupied by the figures it satirizes: a position of duncical incompetence. Difficulties like these, one would think, are more than sufficient to account for the discomfort felt by readers of Augustan satire.

Nevertheless, students themselves, when encouraged to meditate on their encounters with satire, acknowledge the difficulties I've outlined but don't feel that these are the heart of the matter. Moreover, if my experience is representative, student response has changed significantly over the years, for when formalist criticism was dominant in America, and just after, satire generated considerably less discomfort. Of course, insofar as formalist approaches to satire stressed the fictionality and universality of the mode, and not its embeddedness in social reality, they tended to ease somewhat the imperative to historical knowledge. But that fact has little to do with the readerly discomfort that I am mainly concerned with—which is a discomfort with the act of satiric judgment itself. Or rather, with a particular conception of this judgment that was just one part of the formalist critics' revision—and recovery—of the satiric mode. For a long time, the formalist account of satiric judgment, providing as it did both a rationale for satire and secure definitions of the roles of satirist, satiric object, and reader, actually served to win for the mode a less compromised literary status and a more accepting readership. But when the critical climate began to change in the seventies, the formalist picture of satire—as of the act of satiric judgment and the authority that supports it—began to prove less pleasing, and readers began to resist those texts that they had previously been taught to revere.

What is curious in the case of satire, though, is that in one sense readers *always were* resisting. Swift's and Pope's contemporaries found them petty or overly ambitious malcontents; nineteenth-century readers found them unpoetic or pathological, or both; twentieth-century critics—even sympathetic critics—displaced the charges of personal unpleasantness and moralistic superiority into an account of rhetorical convention, but neglected to tell us why a smug or vindictive persona should arouse less resistance than a smug or vindictive poet. And our students tell us in numerous ways that they are made uneasy by the spectacle of the satirist sitting in judgment on a wide range of real and imagined poetic or moral failures. More than the difficulties of line and couplet rhetoric, or literary and political allusion, it is this act of judgment that chills the sympathetic current of the undergraduate soul.

At the present moment in critical history then, traditional resistance to satire is seconded, and given interpretive and theoretical legitimacy, by the skeptical or resistant modes of critical reading that are currently in the ascendancy. Finding ourselves uneasy with the satirist's claims to authority, *and* empowered by a generalized critique of literary authority as such, we may not look closely enough at the assumptions underlying either position. For these very different modes of skepticism assume that satire expects us to endorse the satirist's authority, tacitly asks us to align our reading selves with the satirist and therefore to set ourselves against the object of satire. Each sort of reader—the Augustan contemporary or the undergraduate or the modern negative hermeneuticist—has a different reason for resisting such claims for endorsement and alignment, but all agree implicitly that the "reader position" projected by the satiric mode is one in which there is a fairly simple assent to the satirist's ethos and values, that we are to endorse both judgment and judge, playing a role like that of the listener—the second person—in Freud's account of the telling of a tendentious joke (98–102). This assent, moreover, is not an isolated phenomenon, since the rhetoric of satirist-reader relations is bound up with the rhetoric of the relations between satirist and satiric object. The clarity of our alignment with the satirist and of our opposition to the satiric object reproduces and is compact with the clarity of the opposition between satirist and satiric object.

I think that this assumption is fundamentally mistaken, and that most satire does not ask of us a clear alignment with the satirist and a clear opposition to the satiric object, but something more complicated and more likely to generate that "unease" that Patricia Spacks finds to be the characteristic emotion generated by the reading of satire. But this assumption is connected with several others, also in need of revision. First, the idea that satire is a response to a perceived threat in the world external to the text, and to a preexisting difference between satirist and satiric object, seems to me not quite true. It makes at least as much sense to treat references to figures "out there" as part of a convention of referentiality establishing the satirist as a person in touch with the external world rather than someone simply generating fantasy-figures to attack. More important, it is at least as likely that we attack a figure, distance ourselves from him, because we sense his threatening proximity to us as that we attack him because he is already so different from us.

I am contending, then, that satire is not a response to a prior difference but an effort to *make* a difference, to create distance, between figures whom the satirist—who is one of those figures—perceives to be insufficiently distinguished. Why, though, should readers have persisted for so long—and in the face of their own considerable uneasiness—in assuming that satire does affirm clear norms, does establish clean distinctions between satirist and object, does invite our unambiguous alignment with the satirist and against the object, and that in the mechanism of satire perception of difference precedes attack? In part, because that assumption allows us to mask our own ambiguities of identity, our own troubled connectedness with satirist and satiric object alike, and thus to affirm an internally consistent subjectivity. By casting out the satirist's intricate and complex involvement with the objects of his satire, we cast out our own as well. In this connection, as Michael Seidel has already made clear in his study of *Satiric Inheritance,* the work of René Girard on doubling, mimetic rivalry, and the violence these engender is extraordinarily useful, as is Mary Douglas's account, in *Purity and Danger,* of the extent to which "pollution behavior"—the effort to cast out or classify or terminologically corral dangerous forces and agents—is rooted in the threat those forces and agents offer to cultural differences and distinctions. What Girard and Douglas tell us, in their different ways, and what Roland Barthes also tells us in *S/Z,* is that it is not difference but the erosion or annihilation of difference that requires acts of ritual boundary-policing, acts among which I would include a sizable number of satiric texts.

The more powerful form of this argument would contend not that satire sometimes begins in a relation of threatening proximity and then works to establish difference but that it *always* does. The writer who has done most to think through the groundwork for such a contention is Kenneth Burke, in his explorations of identification and division in rhetoric. If we were to adapt Burke's argument about rhetoric to satire, and employ the strongest version of it—structural rather than psychological—we would say that satire must begin in partial identification, since if it did not there would be no reason to establish or insist on the otherness of the satiric object. If the separation were absolute to begin with, says Burke, "there would be no strife . . . since opponents can join battle [and note the wonderful play of identification and division in that idiom] only through a mediatory ground that makes their communication possible, thus providing the first condition necessary for their interchange of blows" (85). Satire, then, would be that literary form that works to convert an ambiguous relation of identification and division into one of pure division. If we take that initially ambiguous state to reflect an internal division in the satirist, or anxiety about such a division, then we would take the satiric act as an effort to move, in Barbara Johnson's phrase, from differences within to differences between (x–xi, 3–4). And we would conceive the task of literary criticism to be, in part, the recovery and exploration of that initially ambiguous state, and of its modes of persistence in the satiric text, on the theoretical grounds that, as Burke says citing Coleridge, "*inter res heterogeneas non datur oppositio*"—(between heterogeneous things there can be no opposition)—"a notion that . . . [Coleridge] also expresses by observing that *rivales* are opposite banks of the *same* stream" (414).

This is, as I said, the strong form of the argument, and I'll attempt to demonstrate its usefulness and the intricacies of reading that it generates by turning to Jonathan Swift's "Cassinus and Peter," a poem that illustrates some of the work satire can perform, some of the differences it can make, and some of the challenges it poses to readers.

To interpret this poem in terms of the history of satire criticism since the Victorian period may also be to read it in terms of the natural history of reader response. The first stage in this fancied progression is shock, distaste, and some sort of condemnation of Swift: He hates women, he hates humankind generally, he's repulsed by the body, and he is to be rejected. The second stage, roughly identifiable with American formalism's insistence on the artistic status and aim of satire and on the separation of both poetic characters and poetic speakers from the author, finds Swift holding Cassinus' attitude toward women up to ridicule: an attitude that so powerfully and so ludicrously idealizes the female sex that the swain is entirely undone by his discovery that the heavenly Celia "shits." Having made this discovery, he converts his positive fantasy into a negative fantasy that is equally distant from reality. There is a great deal in the poem to support this reading. Cassinus' naiveté is suggested by his sophomoric status; by the "rapture sweet" in which he and Peter discourse on "love and books" (perhaps best understood as a single, as-yet-undifferentiated topic); by the pastoral setting with which he is identified, a setting of nymphs and swains, of "kind Arcadians," and of a conventional harmony between the human and natural that leads Cassinus (usually) to salute Aurora with his flute as "The finch, the linnet, and the thrush,/Their matins chant in every bush." And, of course, the tenacity of Cassinus' hold on the fantasy world that Arcadia represents, especially its conception of women, is clearest in his response to the incontrovertible evidence of Celia's bowels: unable to deny her bodily reality, he nevertheless refuses her representativeness. Like the Brobdingnagians who "classify" Gulliver by labeling him a *lusus naturae*, Cassinus confers on Celia a singular, criminal, status that quarantines her from the rest of humanity, especially female humanity: hers is "a foul disgrace," "a crime that shocks all humankind;/A deed unknown to female race," and Peter is not to reveal it to his own "nymph" lest her virgin soul bemoan "A crime to all her sex unknown!"

Such an interpretation is clearly an advance on simple disgust at Swift's imagination. It can account for much of the poem's detail; it grants the poem more than symptomatic status; and it provides precisely that clarity of function and role with which formalist critics sought to replace an inchoate and scandalized biographical impressionism. With this reading, we know where we are: aligned with the satirist Swift and against the satiric object, Cassinus. As one critic says, "Cassinus' extreme affectation of sensibility is Swift's means of allowing his reader the healing grace of detachment and humorous condemnation" (Rodino 273). Or in another critic's terse formulation: "Poet and reader can unite in regarding Cassinus's view as a joke" (Barnett 178).

If we follow Douglas's account of pollution behavior, however, we might say that Cassinus is a figure of considerable and threatening ambiguity since he is at once a typical college lad (one of an initially matched pair of "college sophs of Cambridge growth") *and* a monstrously distracted fantasist. In consequence, the satiric or critical decision to regard his views as a joke, to consign him to the category of the pathological (or the sheerly ridiculous), *produces* rather than registers his difference from us, ensconcing him safely in the category of the aberrant and placing both reader and satirist safely on the side of the normative. Satire, and this way of reading satire, *makes* a difference. It does not simply take note of a difference that is already comfortably in place. Thus when another critic writes that "Cassinus' fastidious horror convicts him of the same absurd pride as Gulliver, who sought to renounce his human form" (Nokes 372), we must recall that at the end of the fourth Voyage, this pride is uneasily reproduced by the reader who feels securely superior to the absurd Gulliver. More on this in a moment.

A third approach to the poem, more alert than formalist analysis usually was to the politics of gender and the ideological work performed by literary gestures, would ask what is at stake in Cassinus' horror. What distinctions is he attempting to secure or impose by his rejection of Celia and her "horrid fact"? Perhaps sexual difference itself is what is threatened by Cassinus' discovery. Ellen Pollak has noted the insistent bodily dirtiness of Cassinus—his legs "well embrowned [frequently a "fecal" word in this period] with dirt and hair"; his proximity to the chamber pot; and so on—and has argued that Cassinus suffers from the threat of castration consequent on loss of those mediating idealizations that protected him from "visual knowledge of 'the Fact' of woman's body" (166–67). This reading can be broadened by taking sexual difference, and not merely secure phallic self-possession, as the value threatened by Cassinus' discovery. Cassinus is horrified not by an experience of the female body that figures in its genital femaleness his own potential castration but by a female appropriation of what he had taken to be strictly male attributes—defecation and gross physicality as such—and thus by an undoing of sexual difference that threatens his very singleness of identity: threatens not to take something away from him but to add something, the female, just as Celia's "crime" has added maleness to her identity. Celia's *chief* crime—whatever Cassinus thinks—is not defecation but a subversion of sexual difference.

There is a real appropriateness, then, in the appearance of all those figures (especially female figures) of superabundant bodily parts (especially phallic bodily parts): Cerberus of the three heads and the snaky mane or tail; Alecto, with snakes in her hair and a whip of scorpions in her hand; and of course, the snaky-locked Medusa. And the link between these mythological figures and Shakespeare's *Macbeth,* which Cassinus quotes in his ravings, is twofold: first, it is a play in which crime and guilt are insistently associated with transgression of the boundaries of gender; second, the earlier of the two passages Cassinus quotes when he bursts out, "ye cannot say 'twas I" is, in Shakespeare's text: "Thou canst not say, I did it: *never shake/Thy gory locks at me*" (3.4.49–50, my emphasis). Cassinus is, in effect, haunted by the specter of the breakdown of sexual difference and the threat that that breakdown poses to a certain idea of womanhood and a certain idea of his own identity.

And where are the satirist and the reader in this account of the poem? If, as before, we take Cassinus to be a purely pathological or purely ludicrous figure, then we find ourselves securely aligned with the satirist, Swift, in secure opposition to the satiric object, Cassinus. But, again, we should recall that Cassinus is initially twinned with Peter as one of a pair of figures remarkable only for their typicality (typicality, recall, is what Cassinus anxiously wishes to refuse to Celia). Moreover, that second figure, Peter, functions powerfully as a reader-surrogate in the poem; it is he who enacts our suspense and curiosity, and who performs our normalcy in registering Cassinus' distractedness and asking the most commonsensical questions ("Is Celia dead?"); and it is he whom we are encouraged to identify ourselves with at the end of the poem, when Cassinus prepares to die and Peter is about to be left behind, like the reader at the conclusion of a text. Now, if we simply distinguish between Cassinus and Peter, we can align ourselves with the latter and against the former. But if we resist suppressing the connection between these "Two college sophs, of Cambridge growth,/*Both* special wits, and lovers *both*" (my emphasis), then we preserve a measure of continuity between them and, therefore, between Cassinus and ourselves. If this seems like an overly tenderhearted approach to take, we should recall that the likeliest alternative—writing Cassinus off as sheerly aberrant, a pure "satiric object"—is roughly what we have been laughing at Cassinus for doing to Celia.

Moreover, when we take Celia's alleged transgression as the subversion of difference, and Cassinus' response as an effort to restore that difference—to isolate Celia from the "female race" and from "all humankind"—we may well grow suspicious of *all* attempts to establish unambiguous alignments and oppositions marked by identity alone or difference alone. For the poem allows us to experience the compensatory or invested or narcissistic character of the wish for such alignments and oppositions.

It also allows us to experience, however obliquely, an alternative: alignments that difference gradually invades, or that exhibit either a contamination of their categoricality or signs of the artifice required to sustain it. If Cassinus and Peter, despite our sense that their names are not only different but drawn from separate linguistic registers, begin as two peas in a pod, they nevertheless grow very different in the course of the poem, much as Cassinus' initially paired stockings do. And if the octosyllabic couplets do not exactly separate into unmatched lines, they do, as so often in Swift's verse, make plain the labor—even the violence—that has produced their uniformity.

A sharper and more self-conscious challenge to the notion of crisply opposed and internally homogeneous categories appears in the poet's parenthetical appeal to the muse in the opening lines:

> Two college sophs of Cambridge growth,
> Both special wits, and lovers both,
> Conferring as they used to meet,
> On love and books in rapture sweet;
> (*Muse, find me names to fix my metre,*
> *Cassinus this, and t'other Peter*)
>   (my emphasis)

Swift's aside, taken alone, playfully acknowledges poetic artifice, but in the context of these opening lines, it also generates a contradiction between two conceptions of poetry: as the account of a reality that preexists the poem (Cambridge, two sophomores, etc.), and as the construction of a fictional scene. Whether we call this an opposition between the mimetic and the conventional, or between the referential and the rhetorical, or even the constative and the performative, is not too important. What is important is that these two categories are treated as though they might coexist with perfect ease when in fact each is the denial of the other; their co-presence, therefore, is a powerful instance of contamination, of internal heterogeneity. Just the sort of thing that, in the sexual realm, threatens to destroy Cassinus and that he seeks to deny by every means available to him.

Having shown that pollution rituals clarify cultural rules by mastering the anomalies and ambiguities that threaten those rules, Mary Douglas nevertheless goes on to affirm the *need* for such threats. They are necessary because cultural norms and unambiguous categories, taken alone, forestall the possibility of transformation, of change, of self-criticism. Such threatening figures are dangerous, but they are also locations of power, and if a cultural system is to be vital as well as coherent and perspicuous it must incorporate some of that power. This is why the Lele people hunt, cook, and eat the scaly anteater called the pangolin, an animal that is in many ways a kind of cultural nightmare since it threatens so many of the classificatory systems on which that society is founded. To participate in this ritual is to acknowledge, and seek to draw upon, the power of the anomalous, the ambiguous, the self-contradictory. It is dangerous to do so, and safer always to master or quash such locations of power, but the vitality of cultural life—as opposed to its orderliness or intelligibility or unity—depends on these partly calculated efforts to incorporate otherness.

One could read the first six lines of Swift's poem as just such a moment, in which the poet's exemplary embrace of heterogeneity is set against the maniacal conceptual tidiness of Cassinus (in matters of sexual difference, at least). Such a reading is very tempting. It is analogous to those readings that presume that all of the misogyny in Swift's poems is *exemplary*—the dramatizing of a position in order to satirize it, not the taking of that position by the author. Interpretations like these permit us to accommodate troubling details of a text, and to do so while still reading "with the grain." Moreover, in allowing us an author whom we endorse, they also provide us with a self we can admire. They permit us to look into the mirror of the text, as Swift says elsewhere, and see everybody's face but our own. Much as, in reading his poems about bodily disintegration or fragmentation, such as "A Beautiful Young Nymph Going to Bed," we are provided with not only the contrasting sense of bodily coherence that the poem presumes in its dramatic audience but also the analogous coherence of the reader-position itself, which functions as a kind of rhetorical analog to the ego.

But this stage is itself a trap, one that reproduces the tidiness for which Cassinus is willing to sacrifice his very life. What it ignores, what it *needs* to ignore, is the possibility that what we take to be exemplary incoherence is simply incoherence, that, say, the misogyny we understand as quoted or ventriloquized is actually being uttered and endorsed. This sort of ultimately recuperative reading certainly produces a readerly ego of considerable coherence, but it is a Lacanian ego: built on denial, self-aggrandizing, artificially coherent, and the product and emblem of a fundamental—but hidden—alienation from ourselves. The ego, says Lacan, "is the human symptom par excellence. The ego is human being's mental illness" (qtd. in Felman 12). I think there is more than a casual or fanciful connection between Lacan's mirror and Swift's. When Swift says we look into satire's mirror and see everybody's face but our own, he is certainly pointing to a defensive strategy. But in a sense Swift suppresses a term. The reason we don't see our face in the satiric mirror is not that it doesn't exist (though that is another implication of the image—that the admirable ego or the face that symbolizes it is a fantasy). Rather, its invisibility attests precisely to its normativeness. We are invisible as ideology is invisible: because we have learned to call it—to call our own identity—Nature, or Normalcy. In upholding the satirist's apparent failings or incoherences as intended, as exemplary, as normative, we are also defending a readerly ego that is coherent, flattering, and disastrously alienated.

The task of reading satire must be to move beyond this stage and dismantle that ego, in part by resisting those alignments with the satirist's voice that make us uneasy in any case, and in part by exploring the identities of both the readerly ego and the satirist with the satiric object, as well as their differences. This will plunge us into a state of considerable unease, but I think that is where we must be if we are to read satire in meaningful ways. It is a mistake to read most satire as though it simply asked readers to identify themselves with the satirist and set themselves against the satiric object. That would only be possible if the satirists themselves enacted such unambiguous rituals of identification and rejection, and I do not think they do. They ask us, instead, to meditate on the problematic intricacies of identification and difference by which we define our own identities and our relations to others of whom we cannot fully approve or disapprove. Reading satire is not so much about finding a position we can plug ourselves into as about exploring the complexity of what it means to take a position.

But to say that the satirist "asks us" to meditate on the problematic relations of identity and difference, or that he plunges us into uncertainty about whether a particular position is being endorsed or quoted dismissively, is still to assume an authorial intention that is both single and operative, and a readerly self that is unproblematically aligned with it. To engineer indeterminacy is—*as an intention*—no different from engineering determinacy. When Pollak, for example, explores the question whether certain of Swift's poems express or satirize misogyny, she concludes—correctly, in my view—that "There is virtually no textual certainty." But she then adds what I take to be a damaging qualification: "Indeed, it seems to be precisely one of Swift's tactics of authorship to have left this very question unresolved" (169). Such a position does nothing to disturb the comforting fixity of the satiric triangle—satirist, reader, satiric object—and nothing to disturb the mystified coherence of the readerly ego. You can't lose. In this case, though, if you can't lose you can't win either, because the power to which one opens oneself in embracing ambiguity and anomaly cannot be had without the risk of danger; things must always *be able* to go wrong if they are to have a chance at going right.

It is from precisely such danger that we are saved by the postulate of an ulti-mately intending satirist and its corollary, a coherent readerly ego aligned with that satirist and against a satiric object that is securely "other." If we are to find our way here, we must be able to lose it, and that means allowing the satirist to fail and ourselves to be uncertain whether the satirist has failed or not. *Really* uncertain. Satire can't empower us as readers unless it also threatens us. Consequently, the discomfort that I began by speaking about—a discomfort with the satirist's acts of judgment and with the expectation that we as readers will endorse them—must be replaced by a more profound discomfort, the discomfort produced by the most important difference satire can make: a difference between readers and themselves.

NOTES

1. Jonathan Swift, *The Complete Poems,* ed. Pat Rogers (Hew Haven and London: Yale UP, 1983), 463–66. All citations will be from this edition.
2. See Douglas 168–69 and also 94–95.

WORKS CITED

Barnett, Louise K. *Swift's Poetic Worlds.* Newark: U of Delaware P, 1981.
Barthes, Roland. *S/Z.* Tr. Richard Miller. New York: Hill and Wang, 1974.
Burke, Kenneth. *A Grammar of Motives and a Rhetoric of Motives.* Cleveland and New York: Meridian Books, 1962.
Douglas, Mary. *Purity and Danger: An Analysis of the Concepts of Pollution and Taboo.* London and New York: Routledge, 1991.
Felman, Shoshana. *Jacques Lacan and the Adventure of Insight: Psychoanalysis in Contemporary Culture.* Cambridge, Mass. and London: Harvard UP, 1987.
Freud, Sigmund. *Jokes and their Relation to the Unconscious.* Tr. James Strachey. New York: Norton, 1963.
Girard, René. *Violence and the Sacred.* Tr. Patrick Gregory. Baltimore and London: Johns Hopkins UP, 1977.
Johnson, Barbara. *The Critical Difference: Essays in the Contemporary Rhetoric of Reading.* Baltimore and London: Johns Hopkins UP, 1980.
Lacan, Jacques. *Le Séminaire, livre I: Les Ecrits techniques de Freud.* Paris: Seuil, 1975.
Nokes, David. *Jonathan Swift, A Hypocrite Reversed: A Critical Biography.* Oxford and New York: Oxford UP, 1985.
Pollak, Ellen. *The Poetics of Sexual Myth: Gender and Ideology in the Verse of Swift and Pope.* Chicago: U of Chicago P, 1985.
Rodino, Richard. "Swift's 'Scatological' Poems." Rpt. in David Vieth, ed., *Essential Articles for the Study of Jonathan Swift's Poetry.* Hamden: Archon, 1984.
Seidel, Michael. *Satiric Inheritance: Rabelais to Sterne.* Princeton: Princeton UP, 1979.
Spacks, Patricia Meyer. "Some Reflections on Satire." *Genre* 1 (1968): 13–20.
Swift, Jonathan. *The Complete Poems.* Ed. Pat Rogers. New Haven and London: Yale UP, 1983.

Part Two

Geneses and Genealogies

·3·

Satura from Quintilian to Joe Bob Briggs: A New Look at an Old Word

Gay Sibley

The Latin word *satura* has been interpreted variously by several to mean a number of things. Further, every indication exists that what ingredients of *satura* have survived in garden-variety "satire" are not among the most telling and significant. My purpose is to look at *satura* anew, and to suggest that when this early literary vehicle does appear in its purest form—as it did in Petronius, for example, and as it does in the work of a contemporary author, John Bloom, writing under the pseudonym of "Joe Bob Briggs"—tremendous pressure arises to ensure that such writing is relegated to beyond-the-pale, acanonical territory. Quintilian, by claiming that *satura* belonged exclusively to the Romans, has confused generations of scholars who had assumed its origins were Greek. Given what we now accept as "satiric" in the Greek writings from Homer to Julian, G. L. Hendrickson, in his explication of Quintilian's assertion, notes that it "must seem therefore somewhat of a paradox to read in the comparative survey of Greek and Roman literature which Quintilian presents in his tenth book the much quoted dictum: *satura quidem tota nostra est*" (47). Hendrickson's article then goes on to demonstrate that what was "wholly Roman" about satire is a definition of the word that was more specific than what we now recognize as satire, and asserts that "when [Quintilian] says *satura tota nostra est* he means that the special type of literature created by Lucilius, dominated by a certain spirit, clothed in a certain

metrical form fixed by the usage of a series of canonical writers, and finally designated by a name specifically Latin, is Roman and not Greek" (58).

What is needed here to understand (and defend) Quintilian's claim, it
seems, is a common denominator underlying that specificity of spirit, form,
and usage; without such a linchpin, identifying Lucilius or any other Roman
writer as either the originator or the best example of "the type" is moving too
soon. While I agree with Professor Hendrickson that the confusion comes from
different interpretations of *satura,* I think it possible that the key to the essential difference is inherent in the word itself as metaphor, rather than in the techniques or modes of any particular writer. Further, the function of this
metaphor can be seen as universal over both time and space. Although the definition provided by Diomedes, a grammarian and a "late writer" appearing after
Quintilian, has been at least in part refuted, his pointing to the literary use of
satura as metaphor is significant, and worth quoting in full:

> Now *satura* or satire received its name either from the satyrs, because
> in this kind of poetry humorous or off-color things are discussed
> which are just like the things brought up or acted out by satyrs in
> plays, or else it took its name from the plate which was filled with
> many different first offerings and presented to the gods at a religious
> festival by the early Romans. The plate received the name *satura* from
> its abundant and overflowing contents. . . . Or else *satura* comes from
> a certain kind of stuffing which Varro says had this name applied to
> it because it was filled with many ingredients. There is also this
> observation in the second book of his *Plautine Inquiries:* 'Satura is
> raisins, barley, and pine-nuts sprinkled with winehoney.' Others add
> pomegranate seeds to these ingredients. Still others say that satire
> received its name from a law called *satura,* which includes many pro-
> posals brought together in one enactment, apparently because many
> poems are brought together in the poetic version of *satura.*[1]

As Hendrickson points out, the connection to "satyr" has been refuted,
"finally exploded by Casaubon, in his famous study of Roman satire and the
Greek satyr-drama in the year 1605" (60). And according to Ulrich Knoche, "we
can prune away the fourth exclamation of the grammarian—the connection
with the *lex satura*—for there never was a *lex satura* but only a *lex per saturam*
or a *lex in saturam*" (14). And Knoche concludes that "it is most likely that
Diomedes' third explanation is the correct one and that *satura* is taken from the
language of the kitchen" (15). In short, what has persisted into modern times
from Diomedes' definition has been the literal and mundane translation of
satura as a particular kind of food; and critics have seen the tenor of the
metaphor almost exclusively in terms of literary abundance and variety.

The argument for this particular metaphorical interpretation has never seemed quite sound to me. Whereas heretofore the explanation has centered on the advantage of "the mix" as appealing to a variety of tastes, my claim is that the possibility exists that, for Quintilian, the specifically Roman *satura* consisted of a mixture of ingredients that were blended in such a way that only those with "discriminating palates" could come close to knowing what it was they were tasting. In the event of such a possibility, the focus of my analysis of Roman *satura* is on the indiscernibility of the tastes provided, rather than on their variety.

➤┥┼┝┥ ┥┼┝┝◄

One example of Quintilian's *satura,* and one that he treated at some length, is the work of Varro. Among the notable characteristics of Varro's work is his designation of his own form of satire as "Menippean," referring back to the form started by the Greek Cynic, Menippus, therefore predating Lucilius. Mikhail Bakhtin, in his identification of what he calls "menippea" in Dostoyevsky's works, F. Anne Payne in her work on Chaucer, and Theodore Kharpertian in his study of Thomas Pynchon, have all listed characteristics attributed to Menippean satire: scandalous activity and words, the mixing of genres, and topicality (Bakhtin 93–97; Payne 7–11; Kharpertian 20–37).[2] And Kharpertian notes that, "in order to symbolize its critical attitude toward human folly and knavery, satire concentrates on the body. . . . on alimentation, elimination, and fornication as deflationary antitheses to lofty and hubristic delusions" (34). But none of these critics notes the use of food as a metaphor for taste and, by implication, for class. I see this omission as critical, for the moment the focus is on taste as metaphor, in that the palate's response to food is de facto linked with the aesthetics of everything else, we are awash in biological determinism. Whereas what we have left of Menippean satire appears to have attacked the alterable "what people think"—Northrop Frye refers to Menippus as having concentrated on "mental attitudes" (Frye 309)—the work of both Lucilius and Varro seems to go after the unalterable "what people are." Yet while Menippean satire appears to have trivialized loftier subjects—philosophical universalism, for example—in doing so it also attacks, by implication, the "bad taste" of those who would presume to educate others on such lofty subjects, particularly at a banquet. There is also good reason to believe that this idea of "taste-as-metaphor" existed in the early fertility rites that Robert C. Elliott and Ronald Paulson document as the origins of the Greek "satiric spirit," since its implications are universal (Elliot 4–6; Paulson 5–8). All people, comments Northrop Frye in his *Anatomy of Criticism,* "may be confidently excluded from the human race if they cannot understand the conception of food, and so any symbolism founded on food is universal in the sense of having an indefinitely extensive scope. That is, there are no limits to its intelligibility" (118). Indeed, it seems reasonable to assume that the amalgamation of the taste of the palate and all other tastes within a joint concept occurs at the point that any given society leaves off cannibalism, simultaneously deciding not only that consuming the flesh of one's own kind is in the worst possible taste, but that such flesh does not taste very good, either.

One of the universally documented characteristics of both Menippean satire and the ancient ceremonies is abuse. The "curse," or method of abuse in these early fertility rites, according to Professor Elliott, "was creative through denigration of the sterile"(5). Once the question is no longer general fertility, it then evolves into specific fertility, i.e. who *should* reproduce, and "the sterile" in *satura* are whoever is deemed insufficiently desirable. I would like to argue that both the Roman *satura* and the earlier satire as engendered by the Cynic Menippus had as their targets people who attempt to be what the satirist believes they can never be, and that the reasons for the satirist's targets' inevitable failure are implicitly, through the metaphor of taste, biological. If this is so, Menippus' apparent focus on ideas rather than on classes of people could be due to one of two things: Menippus went after the presumptuous educator (as Horace was correctly to do centuries later), inherently ridiculing any optimistic view of education; or, the "down and dirty" parts of Menippean satire, overtly using biological determinism as a basis, were trashed, to be reinstated in the works of Lucilius and Varro and to be critically identified by Quintilian as *satura*. In other words, when Quintilian says "*satura tota nostra est*," I believe he is staking a Roman claim for the synechdochical identification of a built-in metaphor, not for the creation of a genre. And the *satura,* or "mixed plate," in providing no discernible tastes, simply admits to obfuscation as a necessary ingredient of that genre.

The difference starts with the audience, and the need to obfuscate comes from the goal of the poet to preserve what he sees as standards threatened by that audience. If the satiric writer addresses a "safe" audience, he is in effect addressing a circle that is both his own and wide, a circle that includes those with political power, and he can accordingly poke fun at nearly everything he chooses with impunity. If, on the other hand, he represents a small circle of intellectuals completely at odds with most of his audience, or is in need of currying favor with an audience philosophically not his own, he must hide his intent in order that what he wishes to put forward will not be discredited or burned. He must preserve it, in other words, until the audience, probably a new audience, is eventually able and/or willing to choose from the "mixed plate" that he wants them to. All this seems fairly obvious, yet in the long debate over what Quintilian really meant, the technique of using "taste" leading to deliberate obfuscation as a possibly significant referent of Quintilian's claim has not been given due attention.

In any case, the position of the purveyor of Roman *satura* is the most conservative possible, in that the satire implies that classes of individuals, as revealed by their tastes, are and should be set in stone. Whereas the surface satire—the inherent "lecture" to a merely uninformed audience, for example— may often appear motivated by a belief in the benefits of education, the metaphor itself always and already undercuts such superficial optimism.

The problem with any discussion of "taste" in modern times, of course, is that it is very much a private matter—meaning that a denunciation of someone else's taste is allowable as gossip or opinion, but not as a universal representation of any standard, i.e. something that is very real but that somehow cannot be taught. For this reason, perpetuating the way that the early Roman satirists perceived "taste" is no more palatable now than it appears to have been then. Yet some basic factors regarding the use of "taste" in Roman satire have to be delineated.

First of all, in the *saturae* of most of the Romans, beginning with Lucilius, and including Varro, taste at the table is inextricably linked with morality: if one eats grossly, one also associates with prostitutes, brags about one's wealth, one's sex life, one's friends.[3] The numerous banquet scenes illustrating this point in satire occur among the Greeks as well; even Plato's *Symposium* qualifies within this limitation. But there is evidence that the pre-*satura* "satiric spirit" at least superficially acknowledged the power of education as a solution to the problem. What is notable about the Roman variety beginning with Lucilius is that "taste" is not only intertwined with morality, but is just as inextricably linked with "breeding," meaning that the underlying assumption behind much of the satire is that those who eat grossly not only lack restraint in everything else, but are also fat and ugly.[4]

If the original meaning of the Roman *satura* carried this unpleasantly deterministic component as part of its definition, and if this component is partly what made Quintilian insist that *satura* was the exclusive property of the Romans, we have some new answers, as well as some new questions, about the nature of satire then and now.

Another factor in the early *satura* is its peculiar use of language. If we take Quintilian at his word and begin with Lucilius, we see that what was new in

Lucilius's *saturae,* as compared to those of Ennius, at whose "primitive early satire" Quintilian "hints obliquely" (Coffee 4), was that Lucilius made "forceful attacks on named individuals" and "chose for all his later poems the dactylic hexameter, which became the medium accepted by subsequent writers of verse *satura*" (35). In short, we see in Lucilius the use of a written language that seems original. Not only did he write in the apparent speaking language of everyday people, but he appears to have invented words of his own, which is one of the reasons why his work was saved by the grammarians.[5]

As it happens, what the critics have most documented as being peculiar to *satura* is its "mixture" of language and structure. As Professor Knoche documents, "the characteristics that in the eyes of the ancients provided the most obvious link between Varro's satire and the diatribe of Menippus, at least as far as externals were concerned, was the prosimetric form" (58). Although this link is indeed the "most obvious," I believe that its function for *satura* has not been adequately understood. What the prosimetric form does do, as it turns out, is enable the writer to confuse an audience. The bounding back and forth from prose to poetry produces an uncertain ground in the mind of a reader. In other words, even if Menippus did not employ "taste" as a deliberate component to his form of satire, the need to obfuscate may be answered by Menippean form.

In Varro, there is the association of language with both taste and class. As Knoche points out, in Varro the "prose parts for the most part reproduce the colloquial idiom of the educated just as it appeared before its impoverishment through the classicistic movement" (66). When Horace came along to criticize Lucilius for this particular use of language, the later poet had often to defend himself against "blind admirers of Lucilius," who saw both him and Varro as "the proper counterweights to [an] advancing Hellenism" (80). It appears that what the speakers in Lucilian and Varronian *satura* were doing was incorporating into their Latin some Greek words, creating a kind of a linguistic pidgin. Says F. W. Walbank in *The Hellenistic World,* "For about three centuries, from the time of Flamininus onwards, most educated Romans were bilingual and open to the full impact of hellenistic culture. . . . Soldiers returning from eastern campaigns and Greeks coming to Rome as hostages, envoys, detainees, traders, professional men or slaves familiarized the Romans with the Greek language and Greek ways. . . . Romans of the old school like Cato resisted both, but half-heartedly and ineffectively" (247–48). The satire is therefore at least in part responding to a prevailing anti-Hellenism that had existed in bilingual Rome since Cato, the "Censor," had glorified Roman *gravitas* at the expense of Greek *levitas* more than a century before the writing of Lucilius and Varro. But the linguistic influence recorded by these examples of *satura* can also be seen as a reflection of class— the class of slaves, in particular. On the same page that T. J. Haarhoff comments that Lucilius "makes full use of Greek words and even mixes them with Latin in a curious way," he also says that "it is clear that the part played by slavery in promoting Hellenism in Italy was very great indeed" (230).

Unfortunately, there's no way of knowing for sure just what is represented in either Lucilius' or Varro's hybrid languages, since colloquial idioms become extinct almost at the moment they are uttered. This doomed language works well for *satura,* however, because it contributes to the necessary obfuscation; it also ties in with the ingredient attributed to Menippus: topicality. In the use of a soon-to-be-extinct "colloquial idiom," both Lucilius' and Varro's narrative stances become resistant to interpretation.[6]

Because of the mash of structure, language, and tone, everything remains speculative. Yet Varro's political position, as was the case with Lucilius before him, leads us to believe his audience was not the wider, safe one. In other words, Varro was from a wealthy family that owned a good deal of land; he was also a dilettante, who looked upon poetry as a hobby rather than a calling. And in his work, he was speaking "to people of his own class, to distinguished Roman citizens whom he wanted to make aware of certain shortcomings privately which could not be denied and which he could observe at close range in his circle of friends" (Knoche 57). But whether or not "the colloquial idiom of the educated" was held up to ridicule is moot, finally. The end result is its preservation, even if only in fragmentary form. In using taste as an implicit metaphor, however, Varro provides us with an important clue as to the true meaning of *satura.* And his pulling forward into Roman times some of the earlier Menippean techniques provided that *satura* with additional devices, enabling the poet, should he choose, to mask his intent. As it happens, there is every indication that the only group who might have perceived both Varro's and Lucilius' language as its own were likely to have been those who saw the use of "their" language flattering. In other words, Lucilius' "new" words may have been appearing in literature for the first time, but may also have been recognizable as street language before then. In Lucilius' case, from what we can glean from Horace, the earlier poet simply went too far. His "new words" and awkward constructions pointed to those without "taste," but also must sooner or later have given away the objects of the satire to the objects themselves. Although in his *Satires,* Horace frequently gives the nod to Lucilius' influence upon his own ventures into the genre, he indicts him "for his negligent use of language," which he sees as being "conditioned by a false pride. . . exhibit[ing] a lack of artistic conscience" (Knoche 80). Yet Horace also defends Lucilius, and interestingly, the defense hinges on audience: "Is no fault to be found in Homer? . . . It is a fair question, in reading Lucilius, to ask ourselves whether he or his subject was to blame for his want of polish and melody. If only he had belonged to our Augustan age, he would prune with care."[7]

It is not so much that Lucilius was on the wrong track, but that he simply was not sufficiently subtle. And there is no evidence to indicate that, in a pre-Augustan age, he was required to try for anything more. As an aristocrat and as a member of Scipio's entourage, *Sapiens* ("the Wise"), Lucilius was the mouthpiece of that circle, and many of his diatribes are geared to specific political opponents (Duff 47–49). Further, in matters of "taste," both of palate and of behavior, he was in accord with the widespread stance of his time, in that immoral and unrestrained actions were heavily censured by the state and "laws were introduced to control the extent of feasting" (50). The major difference, then, between the Horatian and the Lucilian satiric stances seems to be that "Horace's satire took on an educational function, as the poet represented it, through observation and precise description with the ultimate purpose of understanding and perfecting oneself" (Knoche 83). So although Horace does not leave "taste" behind—*Satires* 2.2, 2.4, and 2.8 all heavily rely on the "banquet" motif—the emphasis changes considerably. The concept of taste as inborn, unchangeable, is softened considerably with Horace's treatment, and with his distance as narrator/listener. But the concept still exists, allowing Horace entrance into what I see as Quintilian's limitation of *satura*. In Epistle xvii, as John Wight Duff brings to our attention, "Horace tells the story of Diogenes the Cynic, in the act of cleaning vegetables for a meal, calling out to Aristippus the Cyrenaic as he passed by, 'If Aristippus could put up with dining on greens, he would not want to associate with princes,' to which came the retort, 'If my critic knew how to associate with princes, he would turn up his nose at greens'"(76).

That Horace should have taken the stance he did accords with his position as a lowly born benefactor of the patronage of Maecenas and Augustus. They had befriended him, and he was there to learn what they knew. "In defending his patron and the circle of friends to which the humbly born author has been admitted, he touches [in Satire vi] on a subject which recurs in the *Epistles,* how to live with the great" (Duff 70). The switch from Lucilius' invective occurs through a switch in perspective: though speaking as a persona, instead of assaulting a specific person who dines without taste, Horace goes after a specific person who has the presumption to teach it. The implications of the "inborn" and "unalterable" view of taste are still there; but the persona comes off finally as the more tasteful because of his recognition that the thought of anyone's instructing anyone else in matters of taste is ridiculous. The idea of a universal standard has moved from the explicit to the implicit, becoming the more palatable to any and all audiences. In short, with Horace the ingredients within the *satura* are more skillfully blended, and the standards are therefore more likely to survive. And because he argues for humility in himself as regards taste along with everything else, we do not find it offensive that he argues for humility in his reader. And if making an unalterable taste implicit is a form of deception in narration, in that doing so reinforces an elitist position, we find the implication not as significant, finally, as having been instructed in how tastefully to respond to a presumptuous arbiter.

Charles Witke, in his *Latin Satire: The Structure of Persuasion,* devotes a chapter to the "Greek Satirical Spirit," then moves right to Horace, with only brief mention of Lucilius, whose influence Professor Hendrickson had earlier judged as paramount. The move would not be striking except that Witke devotes the last third of his work to individual chapters on "Theodulf of Orleans," "Hugh Primas of Orleans," and "Walter of Chatillon," while burying Petronius in "Petronius and Three Others." Justifying the burial, Witke defends himself in what I see as a loaded statement: "Satirists are not permissive and do not make moral allusions which can be interpreted in a variety of inconsistent and irreconcilable ways. Petronius may be making remarks about Roman economics, social mobility, sexual freedom and oriental religions. But his audience reacts according to whether or not it is respectively rich or poor, low or high born, wanton or not, an enthusiast for exotic cult or more conservative in religious habit" (155).

It is therefore at least possible that what Quintilian meant by *satura* was precisely what Lucilius started and what Petronius took to the limit—that element of cloudiness, in content and structure (Petronius' work is, like Varro's, a mixture of prose and poetry) that preserves a kernel the poet sees society in danger of losing—that kernel being most closely associated with what the poet perceives as an inherited taste. What Witke objects to, it seems to me, is Petronius' (and "three others'") taking *satura* to its indigestible extreme; and there is evidence to indicate that Witke is not the first to have made this moral judgment, and to have muted or censored entirely those pieces of literature providing no discernible "taste" for anyone.

In "Fortunata," the second chapter of Erich Auerbach's *Mimesis,* the author provides us with a passage from "Petronius' romance, of which only one episode—the banquet at the house of the wealthy freedman Trimalchio—is extant in full" (24–25). Here Petronius rises above the indulgence geared for a safe audience, and in doing so makes it easy for us to see why he was known as Nero's *elegantiae arbiter* (Ramage, et al. 99). The passage describes Trimalchio's wife Fortunata, and the description is given by one of the guests at the banquet, whose speech reveals him to be, in Auerbach's words, "a small or middling man." Through the candid rambling about the monetary ups and downs of his fellow diners, the speaker inadvertently describes himself. "In their linguistic form," says Auerbach, "[Trimalchio's stories] reveal themselves unmistakably as what they are, namely, vulgar chatter. . . . Inasmuch as the guest describes a company to which he himself belongs both by inner convictions and outward circumstances, the viewpoint is transferred to a point within the picture, the picture thus gains in depth, and the light which illuminates it seems to come from within it . . ." (26–27).

Because a reader is left on his or her own to judge the taste of the speaker, narrative responsibility darts out of reach. The Trimalchios of Petronius' time, should they have read this transcript, would have seen themselves as objects of positive attention rather than ridicule, as there is no narrative judgment to guide them anywhere else. And in addition to this subtle use of language, providing what Auerbach describes as "the ultimate limit of the advance of realism in antiquity" (27), Petronius also buries his own narrative stance even further by having Trimalchio's entire conversation retold by a pederast. In other words, were a reader to judge the diner's taste in conversation as "bad," that reader finds his own taste in accord with that of a pervert. Accordingly, no reader, not even one with the most refined of palates, is exempt from the satire.

The fact is, most of us would rather think that what Quintilian had in mind was a more ennobling genre than one either defined by a focus on an elitist, biological/aesthetic/moral "taste" or characterized by deception; would prefer to know our taste is in some accord with the poet's, to know when we are being manipulated; would prefer to see the sustaining characteristics of *satura* in someone like Horace, as the prime example of one who knew "how to live with the great." And our modern acknowledgment of satire-as-genre leans heavily upon the Horatian stance within its definition. With humility in matters of taste as a democratic goal, the work of Petronius is embarrassing, in that within these works, "reciprocal human figures [do not] figure as attractive or even achievable ends for human thought and conduct" (Witke 155). Such a judgment reflects a morality of criticism that probably has a great deal to do with the fact that, among those writers Quintilian lists as examples of the creators of *satura*, in that genre only Horace is represented in anything more substantial than fragments, and those fragments (of Lucilius, Varro, Petronius, and others) come down only through the efforts of grammarians, who were probably using them as illustrations of a sort of "pig Latin." In this sense, these earlier satirists were decanonized, and their contributions preserved only to discredit them.[8] To write any literature that argues for "attractive or even achievable ends for human thought and conduct" presupposes an audience generally agreed on what in human conduct is "attractive," as Horace apparently did in aligning himself with "the great"; and presupposes also the power of education to meliorate unattractive conduct. With Petronius, however, as the prime example, both his form and his function determine that no reader can "taste" anything for sure; and education does not exist as a meliorating factor. For the butt of *satura*, the message is, "You are unalterably what you are, and what you are is bad indeed." Under such circumstances, the satiric mash becomes liquid, and every reader could be swallowing the moral equivalent of arsenic. Although the ambiguity seems more acceptable in other genres (Witke notes William Golding's *Lord of the Flies* as a moral-free example paralleling Petronius' contribution [155]), history would indicate that when *satura* reaches this crucial point—a point I think was inherent in the particularly Roman variety to begin with—civilization tends to marginalize it, if not get rid of it altogether.

Fortunately for those interested in the evolution of satire, within the last decade a writer has appeared who makes my theory a good deal easier to document and demonstrate. In January of 1982, the Dallas *Times Herald* ran a movie review written by a young reporter named John Bloom, writing under the pseudonym of Joe Bob Briggs.[9] Bloom's idea was to review "bad" movies, but to review them from the vantage point of a viewer who could discriminate between what was good and what was bad in a "bad" film. As a satirist, Bloom has just enough of a fancy education to be suspiciously on the mark, and his use of Joe Bob Briggs as a Petronian narrator (lacking any concern whatever for the feelings of his audience) is so reminiscent of what I see as Quintilian's particular *satura*, that I have no doubt of its authenticity in the genre.

Joe Bob is a "redneck," a working-man/boy, who at nineteen has been married three times (giving him a credibility roughly equivalent to Petronius's Encolpius), and is "a drive-in authority of enormous experience," having seen "sixty-eight hundred movies" (Trillin 73). And Joe Bob remains, for many people, the "for real" author of what came to be a notoriously popular review column, "Joe Bob Goes to the Drive-In." The important thing about Joe Bob was that he talked in his own language; while author Bloom, a "soft-spoken, reserved, almost withdrawn young man who had graduated with honors from Vanderbilt" stayed completely in the background writing other essays in another English on the *nouvelle vague*. That "taste" is the focus of the satire in Bloom's creation seems indisputable; Bloom even claimed that he "had been thinking about doing a column from someone with a personality that is completely opposite of what we think is tasteful" (73). Inevitably, however, the question was to arise, "Who is 'we'?" And, indeed, the question arose. As Trillin points out, "What a country storyteller named Gamble Rogers once said of the ornery and fearlessly outspoken cracker was a central feature of Joe Bob's character: 'He don't care. He flat do not care'" (76). And in not caring, Joe Bob did precisely what we can imagine Lucilius, Varro, and Petronius to have done: through the narrator's speaking in his own language, and speaking to an audience to some of whom the language was their own, there came to be a "problem of whether the column [was] making fun of Joe Bob or of the people Joe Bob makes fun of" (76). Joe Bob's taste ran to films most of us, but not all of us, would perceive as tasteless. He rated movies, says Trillin, "according to the amount of innards displayed"(74):

> So this flick starts off with a bimbo getting chained up and killed by a bunch of Meskins dressed up like Roman soldiers in their bathrobes . . . Sixty-four dead bodies. Bimbos in cages. Bimbos in chains. Arms roll. Thirty-nine breasts. Two beasts (giant lizard, octopus). Leprosy. Kung fu. Bimbo fu. Sword fu. Lizard fu. Knife fu. Seven battles. Three quarts blood. A 39 on the vomit meter . . . Joe Bob says check it out. (74)

Predictably, some saw Joe Bob as a Southern cracker being satirized for their amusement; and just as predictably, the Southern crackers "were grateful that there was finally someone in the paper who wrote normal" (74). Finally, however, Joe Bob's passion for violence and sex offended the Baptists; then he said that the girls he knew were "dumb as a bunch of rocks" one too many times, applauded chainsaw vio/porn once too often, and some feminists began to get angry. Then some other feminists got angry at the angry feminists for not recognizing that the column was simply "making fun of the kind of people who go to watch those movies" (82). Generally, however, the column remained outrageously popular. When the editors of the *Plain Dealer* in Cleveland "decided to drop his column for tastelessness an avalanche of reader mail persuaded them to put it back" (83).

Soon, though, Joe Bob went too far. He set up a recording by "drive-in stars," as he said, "for the benefit of minority groups in Africa and the United Negro College Fund in the United States, cause I think we should be sending as many Negroes to college as we can, specially the stupid Negroes" (83). And the song lyrics evoke the *satura* banquet:

> We are the weird.
> We are the starvin,
> We are the scum of the filthy earth,
> So let's start scarfin . . .

There's a goat-head bakin
We're calling it their food,
If the Meskins can eat it,
They can eat it, too. (83)

In their response to Joe Bob's rantings, Afro-American leaders were predictably offended; but we could just as easily have anticipated the response in telephone calls to the *Times Herald* from fans: "The trouble is these colored people don't know good saytire when they see it" (Trillin 85).

Given what we have seen of the nature of *satura,* if Lucilius and Varro were seen as "proper counterweights to [an] advancing Hellenism," the implication is that the "advancing Hellenism" was a force that couldn't be reckoned with in any other way, a force inclined to mute any opposition and to eschew any compromise, however well-reasoned. In this sense, Joe Bob Briggs, taking on (and apparently in some cases befuddling) the contemporary bastions of feminism and multiculturalism, could easily be viewed as a modern-day "counterweight." In such a light, *satura* appears as a desperate genre, providing a voice that, were it not thus encoded, would otherwise be permanently silenced.

The disturbing factors in the writing of "Joe Bob Briggs" are tightly linked to the disturbing factors Charles Witke sees in Petronius: they provide "no attractive or achievable ends for human conduct." By creating characters whose language makes them objects of ridicule, but whose language is also used to ridicule others in such a way that there's neither a steady narrator nor a reliable audience, the writer of *satura* apparently dooms himself to canonical extinction. It also seems likely that what we naturally find unpalatable in Joe Bob Briggs is similar, in kind and in language, to what Horace found offensive in Lucilius and Varro. But it also seems possible that the "advancing Hellenism" to which Lucilius and Varro responded so evasively, so darkly, was advancing with a fascistic rigidity, conveying its own deterministic message: "You cannot change what you are, and what you are is bad indeed"; the kind of force that would provide the only justification for such an offensive retaliation.

Finally, though, one had to hope that John Bloom belonged to an elitist group of *sapiens* writing for nobody but themselves, and the newspaper's editors not only cut the column, but tried to retain the rights to "Joe Bob Briggs," in order to kill forever their association with him and everything he wrote. John Bloom continued to defend his creation and retain his copyright; however, one of Bloom's friends echoed the sentiments of many a disgruntled reader: "If John thinks no one else can kill Joe Bob, fine. Then at some point he should kill Joe Bob himself" (86). Bloom claims he will continue on with Joe Bob until he discovers "the heart of Joe Bob, find[s] out what about him disturbs people" (87). Although, according to Calvin Trillin, Joe Bob is "no longer a presence in Dallas," he does retain a position at the fringe, preserving his column in *The American Harpoon*, the *San Francisco Chronicle* (among other "liberal" newspapers), appearing in his cowboy hat on talk shows, providing a parodic piece during the television coverage of the 1992 Republican convention, and coming out with a 1993 book, *Iron Joe Bob*, which advises his male readers to "admit you're a weenie!" This latest book is interesting in that it veers away from multiculturalism altogether, focusing exclusively on gender. And despite Bloom's retention of the redneck Joe Bob narrative voice, the "narrative unreliability" of that voice is forgotten amid hundreds of pages of misogynistic invective. Unlike his earlier Dallas columns, this book would be unlikely to confuse the feminists. But Bloom's status at this point is marginal as a purveyor of the murky *satura*. For one thing, he seems to be going after wider, safer audiences. *Iron Joe Bob,* as a book, can say whatever it likes, and is probably admired at least in principle by most men weary of a feminist onslaught. And the news columns seem comparatively benign. A recent one in the entertainment section of the *San Francisco Chronicle* (July 25, 1993), for example, contains a satire on job application forms and a movie review of *Jurassic Park,* which review notably avoids issues of both multiculturalism and gender. In other words, these are columns that are not likely to be preserved, even in an acanonical sense, through the ages.

To conclude, the "liquid evil" critics over time have seen in the *satura* of Petronius, as well as in the likes of the early "Joe Bob Briggs," just as easily could have existed in the works of the earlier Roman satirists mentioned by Quintilian, and may very well have been the fundamental ingredient in Quintilian's concept of *satura* itself, which in its purest form seems to provide a shocking, though appropriately transient, counterweight to whatever "ism" is deemed "politically correct" at any given time.

NOTES

1. An excerpt from "the rhetorical treatise of the grammarian Diomedes," translated and quoted in Ramage, et al., and further explicated in Knoche (7–16), Witke (15–20), Coffee (12–13), and others.

2. See, in addition to these critics, Northrop Frye's *Anatomy of Criticism,* in which the author uses Burton's *Anatomy of Melancholy* as a paradigm of the Menippean legacy, and argues that "anatomical" elements, originating with Menippus, make up a part of the development of the novel. Although Varro and his satiric ancestor share the prose/poetry mixture, along with a treatment of the matter and manner of excessiveness and presumption, Burton's work appears to go after the thinker, while Varro's object is clearly the glutton.

3. The variations within early satire are well-documented by many scholars. For summary purposes, I have used Coffee, Hendrickson, Knoche, Ramage, and Witke.

4. So much of Western literature contains these implicit associations, in fact, that readers can be counted on to anticipate them. As an example, when Northrop Frye argues that "Thwackum and Square," the presumptuous and abusive schoolmasters in Henry Fielding's *Tom Jones*, "have Menippean blood in them" (309), he refers to their pedantry, their bigotry, their vanity, their presumption—all documentable Menippean characteristics. But to what degree are the reader's expectations thwarted when Square is described as "a comely man," and to what degree are those expectations gratified when Thwackum does "in countenance very nearly [resemble] that gentleman, who, in the Harlot's Progress, is seen correcting the ladies in Bridewell" (Fielding 139)? The reader does not need to know Hogarth's work in order to validate the already existing assumption that Thwackum is physically unattractive. Thinking as they do, appearing as they do, behaving as they do, such literary characters are expected to be "sterile," not only because they are presumptuous and abusive, but because presumption and abuse can be expected to occur "naturally" in people who think and appear and behave as they almost invariably do.
5. See Professor Heurgon's Sorbonne lectures for a discussion of Lucilius' use of slang.
6. In his work on Petronius, Gilbert Bagnani comments on the inevitable obscurity of anything written in a colloquial language: "We are beginning to see as through a fog the dim outlines of colloquial Latin; we are still very far from being able to detect its nuances and farther still from the possibility of dating its usages" (73–75).
7. *Satire IX*, translated and paraphrased (Duff 63).
8. In a recent article on "Canonicity," Wendell V. Harris argues that Alastair Fowler's "discrimination of six kinds of canons" (potential, accessible, selective, official, personal, critical) is not sufficient, and that there should be more: biblical, pedagogical, diachronic, nonce (112). In neither Fowler's nor Harris's categories do the *saturae* of Lucilius, Varro, or Petronius fit, inasmuch as they were never preserved with canonical intent, but quite the reverse.
9. For the summary of the career of "Joe Bob Briggs," I am indebted to Calvin Trillin's article in *The New Yorker* (December 22, 1986), 73–88.

Works Cited

Anderson, William S. *Essays on Roman Satire*. Princeton: Princeton UP, 1982.
Auerbach, Erich. *Mimesis: The Representation of Reality in Western Literature,* tr. Willard R. Trask. Princeton: Princeton UP, 1953.
Bagnani, Gilbert. *Arbiter of Elegance: A Study of the Life and Works of C. Petronius.* Toronto: U of Toronto P, 1954.
Bakhtin, Mikhail. *The Problems of Dostoevski's Poetics,* tr. R. W. Rotsel. Ann Arbor: U of Michigan P, 1973.
Briggs, Joe Bob. *Iron Joe Bob.* New York: Atlantic Monthly Press, 1992.
———. *Joe Bob Goes to the Drive-In.* New York: Delacorte Press, 1987.
Coffee, Michael. *Roman Satire.* London: Methuen and Co., 1976.
D'Alton, John Francis. *Horace and His Age.* New York: Russell and Russell, 1962.
Duff, John Dwight. *Roman Satire: Its Outlook on Social Life.* Berkeley: U of California P, 1936.
Elliott, Robert C. *The Power of Satire: Magic, Ritual, Art.* Princeton: Princeton UP, 1960.
Fielding, Henry. *The History of Tom Jones.* New York: Penguin, 1984.
Frye, Northrop. *Anatomy of Criticism.* New Haven: Princeton UP, 1957.
Haarhoff, T. J. *The Stranger at the Gate.* London and New York: Longmans, Green, 1938.
Harris, Wendell V. "Canonicity." *PMLA* (January 1991): 110–21.
Hendrickson, G. L. "*Satura Tota Nostra Est.*" *Classical Philology* XXII (January 1927): 46–60.
Heurgon, Jacques. *Lucilius.* Paris: Centre de Documentation Universitaire, 1959.

Kharpertian, Theodore D. *A Hand to Turn the Time: The Menippean Satires of Thomas Pynchon.* Cranbury and London: Associated UP, 1990.

Knoche, Ulrich. *Roman Satire,* tr. Edwin C. Ramage. Bloomington and London: Indiana UP, 1975.

Paulson, Ronald. *The Fictions of Satire.* Baltimore: Johns Hopkins UP, 1967.

Payne, Anne F. *Chaucer and Menippean Satire.* Madison: U of Wisconsin P, 1981.

Ramage, Edwin S., David Sigsbee, and Sigmund C. Fredericks. *Roman Satirists and Their Satire: The Fine Art of Criticism in Ancient Rome.* Park Ridge: Noyes Press, 1974.

Rankin, H. D. *Petronius the Artist: Essays on the Satyricon and its Author.* The Hague: Martinus Nijhoff, 1971.

Sullivan, J. P., ed. *Critical Essays on Roman Literature: Satire.* London: Routledge & Kegan Paul, 1963.

Trillin, Calvin. "The Life and Times of Joe Bob Briggs, So Far." *The New Yorker* (Dec. 22, 1986): 73–88.

Walbank, F. W. *The Hellenistic World.* Sussex: The Harvester Press, 1981.

Witke, Charles. *Latin Satire: The Structure of Persuasion.* Leiden: E. J. Brill, 1970.

·4·

The New Voice of Political Dissent: The Transition from Complaint to Satire

Kirk Combe

THEORY

As someone who for years has tried bravely and vainly to define satire—what it is, what it does, how it operates—I am quite aware of the frustrations inherent to critical discussions of the genre. Rule, or in the case of satire even description, implies exception. Unfortunately and inevitably, exceptions seem to heap upon even my broadest attempts to supply satire with "operational principles," "controlling baselines," or whatever other desperate and evasive term I give my regulations. I, and others, have found that even though rules for satire are not necessarily wrong, neither are they necessarily right.[1] Besides, whenever we define our inclination is to simplify in order to create neat categories. After all, what else is definition for? The Latin *definire* means not only to explain, but to limit in the sense of to put an end to. Definition, by definition, is a restrictive and exclusive business. However, one of the key dangers I see in theorizing satire is that almost irresistible urge to reify satire, unifying and totalizing a range of often incommensurate impulses and practices. Individual satires are nothing if they are not, to borrow a phrase from Stephen Greenblatt, "localized strategies in particular historical encounters" (714). This means that while certain theoretical generalizations indeed may be useful to a discussion of a given satire, the real work involved in satiric analysis is that of a case-by-case cultural study of the poem. Perhaps no other genre calls out more emphatically for cultural criticism. To impose general laws from without, as would a structuralist, or to confine oneself to intertextual issues, as would a post-structuralist, misses out on the *quidditas*—the messy, earthy whatness—of satire. Thus, while guiding principles and intertextuality are not to be eschewed, it strikes me that for a method of cogent inquiry satire demands intense referentiality. Satire is not a self-enclosed verbal construct. Neither celebrating its structural integrity nor unmasking its internal contradictions adequately accounts for the genre. Satire is a product of a particular person writing at a particular time for a particular audience within a particular society. If we lose sight of this, we have lost sight of satire—and perhaps of literature as a whole.

At the same time, however, I must stress that the historical referentiality being recommended for the study of satire *includes* generic considerations of the form. That is to say, how the traditions of satire—whatever those might be within a given historical time frame—are applied *by writers of that specific era* has everything to do with the type of satire that era will produce. And this, I think, is where so much confusion enters into the attempt to understand satire. Where do we draw the line between legacy and locality? Can we? Should we even try? If one of the obvious dangers of theorizing satire is the tendency to reify the form, to plug it fastidiously into a larger and supposedly ongoing satirical tradition, an equal danger exists in discounting the notion of literary species. Greenblatt's concept of "localized strategies," I feel, is a bit *too* local when it comes to satire. Irrefutably, satire is grounded in "particular historical encounters"; coinstantaneously, however, satire partakes of perhaps the oldest and most self-conscious literary tradition after that of the epic. To slight the leverage of such ancestry is folly.[2] Either critical extreme produces artificial ideas about satire.

Where the analytical waters get so muddy in the case of satire is with the fact that when writers interact with the satiric heritage handed down to them, their consortion with it in effect *localizes* that heritage. Very simply, they make satire their own; they apply its conventions how they see fit and to what they see fit. Nicolas Boileau uses Horace and Juvenal according to his own cultural and personal satiric lights; in turn, the Earl of Rochester uses Boileau according to his. Are these two poets part of a "classical satiric tradition"? Yes they are. At the same moment, neither man seriously tries to participate in the *exact* social circumstances or to re-create the *precise* satiric productions of his predecessor—even if assurances to the contrary are offered. No one writing in any literary tradition ever really does or, for that matter, really can. This metabolizing of genre has the effect of rendering a satiric tradition routinely celebrated as "timeless" and "universal" in fact exceedingly temporal and transitory.[3] Therefore, when examining any given work, the critic of satire is faced with the delicate and puzzling task of segregating the synchronic from the diachronic. However, as indicated before, within the jumble of satire that critic may have considerable difficulty even deciding what is synchronic and what is diachronic. Edward Rosenheim, Jr.'s extremely useful definition of satire as an "attack by means of a manifest fiction upon discernible historical particulars" (31) denotes historicity when it calls attention to satire's assault on recognizably local issues; equally, it implies some manner of generic coding in the phrase "by means of a manifest fiction." "Manifest" means readily perceived, apparent, plain. No matter how intricate the ironic strategy employed by a satirist, in the end the writer wants the reader to know—quite plainly—that satire is the convention at hand. At some level satire must call attention to itself as a form.[4] Recognizable convention, genre, and tradition is vital to the existence of satire. Simultaneously, satiric convention, genre, and tradition constantly shift and change, never remaining the same for very long. The critic must be terribly free from both enthrallment to literary history *and* an overweening fidelity to anecdote or minutiae. We must walk a line between the diachronic and the synchronic without really knowing where that line is.

In this essay I attempt such a high-wire act by examining a climacteric in the chronology of English satire. Over the first half of the seventeenth century, a confluence of literary and cultural forces reshaped the genre. While ancient and novel methods of civil order vied for control of the kingdom, controversialists of the time had both native and foreign genealogies of satire available to them. In this maelstrom of endemic and ecumenical tensions, developments in satire linked vitally with shifts in political circumstances. The outcome was English satire, along with English culture, striking out on a new heading. I believe the crucial change in English satire manifests itself in an observable transition from medieval Complaint to neoclassical satire as the principal poetic mode for political debate.

APPLICATION

However one chooses to define satire, little chance exists of medieval Complaint ever being confused with post-1640 political satire in England. The former is, to modern ears, frequently whiny and distressingly acquiescent, while the latter is predominantly hoarse and universally militant. The two forms share a fundamental concern for public affairs, yet each goes about it in a distinctly different way. Studies on the subject tend to focus on the dissimilarities between the two forms, as well as limit their scope largely to comparisons between later sixteenth-century Complaint and the early Elizabethan satire of the 1590s.[5] Hence issues of style or of Christian versus classical modes predominate. Except in a superficial fashion, none of these studies considers the interaction of these forms much beyond the turn of the century; few involve themselves in the genuine political content of these writings. I propose that a more provocative line to follow when contemplating the move from Complaint to satire is to pursue the period of transition well into the next century. By doing so, our focus shifts from pondering the supposed moral turpitude of the 1590s to inspecting the more telling relationship between the political poetry and the civic turmoil of the early decades of the seventeenth century, the civil war, and even beyond the Restoration of Charles II. Not only did polemicists of this era have two traditions of satire to choose from, but a growing multiplicity of worldviews to negotiate.

It is a commonplace that the seventeenth century presents us with English society undergoing extreme redefinition. In matters of government and religion, England moved reluctantly from, at the century's beginning, a monolithic order to, at century's end, a condition of uneasy plurality. In an impressive instance of content determining form, the radically new social and political climate in England necessitated a radically new voice with which to express dissent. After 1649, Complaint became less workable as a form of political expression. With the execution of Charles I, the paradigm of a monolithic English state was fractured forever. Despite the considerable efforts of parliament, of Cromwell, and of both Charles's sons, functional absolute rule or a single-state religion proved irrecoverable after that event. In this modern atmosphere, medieval Complaint, founded on the unified social and religious order of an era now past, had difficulty flourishing. Conversely, satire based on Roman models found for the first time in England something similar to its original social environs. Growing as it did out of an urban, politically diverse climate, classical satire offered fresh opportunities for invective, topicality, and dialectical techniques that facilitated commentary in the new, more complex, and less secure English political setting. Neoclassical satire innately satisfied the rhetorical shortcomings experienced by its increasingly obsolete predecessor.[6] Naturally, the passage from one pattern to the next was not abrupt. From roughly the 1620s until the outbreak of the civil war, a hybrid of Complaint and satire acts as a kind of transitional marker between the two forms of political verse if not between the medieval and the early modern social paradigms.

Before the changeover from Complaint to satire fully can be grasped, a brief description (as negligible and dangerous as that exercise might be) of the two forms is necessary. While both types protest current policy and urge the reform, or at least the altering, of present conduct in some way, notable contrasts in style and tone, in the use of persona, and in the ultimate objective of the remonstrance divide Complaint and satire. In general, Complaint speaks abstractly, often allegorically. Stereotypical governors, churchmen, nobility, lawyers, doctors, whoever, are rebuked in a plain, ingenuous fashion. Moreover, the upshot of the lecture is distinctly devout. Piety and even charity mark the tone of the discourse, while a certain aura of spirituality—whether real or apparent—characterizes the performance. Critics repeatedly apply the adjective *homiletic* to Complaint. By contrast, satire tends to fasten upon the here and now—the temporal rather than the spiritual. Knavery and folly are given a local habitation and a name; satirists draw a hard-edged portrait of the contemporary setting. Named individuals and groups, rather than general types, are depicted engaged in earthly wrongdoing. Furthermore, this greater sense of tangibility is communicated in a more self-consciously sophisticated style. Guileless intonations of godliness and benevolence are replaced by keen argumentation, which often is pessimistic, grimly humorous, and darkly reflective. At the heart of each form is its narrative persona. Again speaking generally, the medieval complainant usually is a simple, honest, rural fellow epitomized by the "plowman" persona from *Piers Plowman*. In plain terms this narrator addresses plain people on plain matters. He is a kind of Christ figure whose job is to champion a return to Christian social values, particularly mercy and charity. Almost inevitably, the plowman persona acts as the spokesperson for the poor and oppressed of society. Again by contrast, the typical narrative persona of satire exudes educated urban refinement if not courtly savoir faire. Whether emulating the sensible persuasion of Horace, the youthful idealism of Persius, or the righteous indignation of Juvenal, this persona participates in the sophistical struggle to discredit and exclude an opponent. Mercy and piety—except as rhetorical show—are the furthest thing from his mind.

As to the objective of either form, this of course is much harder to generalize, arguably, even to know. Within the manifest fictions of each type, however, certain patterns emerge. Whether the *author* intends it ironically or not, Complaint is predisposed to voicing an imprecise lamentation over the evil of the times. Corruption in high places—civil, ecclesiastical, and judicial—normally occupies the attention of the narrator, and a vague call for reformation at least is implied. However, the plea is long-suffering and at best passive-aggressive in its pursuit of change. With seeming Christian forbearance, the narrator endures the injustices of the great, and apparently through his modest example seeks to shame the greedy and the sinful into a return to the ideal Christian society. Satire routinely takes the opposite tactic. Short-suffering, aggressive, often openly vulgar and abusive, the satiric narrator forcibly identifies and assaults his antagonist without remorse and with little compassion. Instead of sniveling grievances and blurry hopes for amelioration, satire articulates direct action against wrongdoers. Indeed, punishment threatens to overtake reform as a basic motive for much satire. Not by a pious show, but by striking fear into the hearts of the guilty, will the narrator of satire attempt to alter the ways of the unruly. While moral Christianity forms the core pursuit of Complaint, a kind of secular ethical ideology—an adherence to "right reason," however that is defined by the satirist—preoccupies satire. Of course, both forms are intricate rhetorical performances.

By way of examples, consider briefly two separate attacks on the English legal system. The first comes from the anonymous fifteenth-century Complaint *London Lickpenny*. After plodding the halls of justice of the capital city for some time, our plowman narrator abandons his quest for judiciary assistance to return to the countryside. He concludes of his London misadventure:

> Then I conveyed me into Kent,
> For of the law would I meddle no more;
> Because no man to me would take intent,
> I dight me to the plough, even as I did before.
> Jesus save London, that in Bethlehem was bore!
> And every true man of law God grant him soul's meed,
> And they that be other, God their state restore,
> For he that lacketh money, with them he shall not speed.
> (Grigson 4)

Rather than rail openly at lawyers, this Complaint—whether wryly or sincerely—has its rural protagonist sadly shake his head and hope that God can sort out the current state of English forensic enterprise, for surely such a task is beyond mortal endeavors. A very different approach to contemplating the lawyer-client relationship is found a century or so later in Joseph Hall's *Virgidemiae* (Book 2, Satire 3; 1598). In Hall's satire, the narrator articulates virtually the same grievance as the complainant above.

> The crouching client, with low-bended knee,
> And many worships, and fair flattery,
> Tells on his tale as smoothly as him list,
> But still the lawyer's eye squints on his fist;
> If that seem lined with a larger fee,
> Doubt not the suit, the law is plain for thee.

Unlike Complaint, though, Hall's verses do not benignly pray for the emendation of the callous souls of lawyers; instead, solicitors are raked over the coals as "them that would make gain of others' sin." One simile will serve to illustrate this decidedly more aggressive and earthly (not to say earthy) technique.

> So loathly fly that lives on galled wound,
> And scabby festers inwardly unsound,
> Feeds fatter with that poisonous carrion

Than they that haunt the healthy limbs alone.
Woe to the weal where many lawyers be,
For there is sure much store of maladie.
(Grigson 32)

Apparently, where placid chastening failed, frank insult would provoke the desired reform. While one can see how both genres have the potential to be fashioned into viable forms of political dissent, satire happens to be the more pugnacious and, because of its secular nature, adaptable of the two. During the period in question, those qualities held advantages.

Gradually over the first four decades of the century, the conventions of classical satire came to be preferred over those of native Complaint as a means of commenting on issues of statecraft. English political satire—that is, an elementally classical literary matrix accommodating the immediate controversies, events, and personalities of English civil affairs—came into being.[7] Complaint did not suddenly disappear. In the first two decades of the new century, a fair amount of Complaint-like political commentary appeared.[8] However, obfuscation was no longer a desired mannerism for voices of protest—particularly under the increasing censorial pressures applied by James I and even more so under the expanding autocracy of Charles I. By the 1620s, an underground, politically motivated brand of satiric writing had developed. This verse takes as its subject matter the domination of the first Duke of Buckingham in political life at home and the hatred of Spain in political affairs abroad (see also Gibson 272). In displaying the combined attributes of Complaint and satire, it also signals the transformation from the homiletic grievances of the sixteenth century to the new political invective of the second half of the seventeenth century. The best examples of this poetry are found in the manuscript verse dealing with the assassination of Buckingham in 1628 by an irate naval officer named John Felton. Written by a variety of hands during 1628 and 1629 and circulating widely in manuscript, most often anonymously, these poems show that not only was government censorship proving in the long run to be ineffectual, but that the constitution of political poetry was changing markedly.

The number of manuscripts in which copies of the Buckingham poems exist attests both to their popularity and the care with which they were circulated.[9] Rather than housing furtive observation on state matters behind flimsy walls of allegory, these poems brandish detailed criticism of current English affairs. Rather than vaunting deliberate stylistic obscurity and classical affectation, they are written in a direct manner obviously meant for the general reader, not the bookish, university-educated one of the 1590s. Thus the Buckingham poems differ conspicuously from either of their immediate English polemical ancestors—Complaint and Elizabethan satire. Nevertheless, these works also blend those existing forms. Essentially, the poems are an odd mixture of the gist of medieval Complaint placed inside the refined mold of classical-verse satire. In substance, the poems remain rudimentarily Complaint. These are anti-Buckingham verses, not yet anti-Royalist, even though in some instances the implicit criticism of Charles I and his government is strongly present. Like Complaint, the poems deplore the activities of a bad man in a position of power; the poets disapprove of Buckingham's flagrant corruption and abuse of office. However, they do not—indeed, as yet cannot—overtly exalt an alternative theory of government. Unlike later English political writers, the authors of the Buckingham poems do not openly attack one polity and attempt to replace it with another. Hints of this subversive activity occur, but their compositions as yet do not embody fully aggressive calls for direct political action. They simply vilify Buckingham. In configuration, however, these poems constituently are satires. Their narrative personae are not simple plowman figures speaking to an audience seemingly unversed in the mysteries of state. Neither do they plead the case of the lower social orders or appeal for a return to simple Christian values (though the residue of Christian purpose is still present in many of the poems). Equally, while the tone of the narrations is generally straightforward, it is not plain in the sense of being homespun; unmistakable wit and urbanity appear. Moreover, most of the rhetorical techniques employed by the poets are the more complicated ones of satire: witty dialogue, ironic speaker, ghost narrator, as well as the forthright yet sophisticated orator. All are methods used for English verse satire written after 1640 (see Brooks).

Also important, the topics of the Buckingham poems—people, events, issues—all belong to the political topography of the day. For example, in the poem "The Copie of his Graces's Most Excellent Rotomontados, Sent by his Servant the Lord Grimes, in Answere to the Lower House of Parliament, 1628" (28), Buckingham is charged with an amazing array of crimes popularly attributed to him. These include standard accusations concerning Buckingham's fiscal corruption, his holding absolute sway over Charles, as well as the power to dissolve parliament in reality resting in the Duke's hands. They also include more politically sophisticated charges, such as the Duke's being responsible for the loss of the Palatinate and his plotting with Spain and Austria against Charles and England. What's more, the poem inculpates Buckingham on a personal level, claiming he poisoned James I as well as attempting to poison the earls of Southhampton, Oxford, Hamilton, and Lenox. He is even denounced for enlisting the black powers of one Dr. Lambe to keep the king's affections by magic charms and to incite ladies to lust.[10] Only a politically informed audience could appreciate—more than that, wade through—the rich topicality of such a composition. As might be expected, this degree of worldliness necessitated the safeguarding of authorial identity. Like Marvell and Swift after him, the author of "The Duke Return'd Againe. 1627" understood the importance of anonymity.

> Now I have said enough to thee, great George,
> If I were knowne, 'twould make thy radge disgorge
> Its venome on me. (22)

In addition, three-quarters of the Buckingham poems are written in decasyllabic rhyming couplets, the dominant format of English verse satire. The remaining quarter are in octasyllabic rhyming couplets, a close cousin of the longer meter. One poem is even called "A Satyre on the D. of B." All of the above indicators point to a more than a passing effort by these poets to use the conventions of classical satire for political observation.

   Undeniably, much of the topos of medieval Complaint remains in the Buckingham poems. In the poem "To Charles," for example, the narrator is Felton himself. From the outset of his address to the king, he assumes the posture of a simple, humble minion of his sovereign and his savior.

> Syr, I your servant, who have sett you free,
> (Christ's freeman am, your prisoner though I bee.) (72)

Without the country trappings, Felton effectively assumes the tenor of the plowman persona. By imploring Charles to comprehend the national boon brought about by the assassination of Buckingham, Felton portrays himself as champion and deliverer: country, king, and God all have been served by his selfless act. Biblical references and allusions throughout the poem contribute to this aura of narrative piety. By the end of the piece, a Christ-like martyrdom is achieved for Felton, who concludes: "A happie life and death was graunted mee, / To liue for peace, and die for libertie" (74). A significant note of political modernity, however, surfaces unexpectedly with that last word—"libertie." Felton in fact has not striven to realign English society with Christian morality, but in the poet's eyes has improved current English polity. Further indication that the Buckingham poems verge on a modern civil idiom comes from their taking part in embryonic political debate. Included in the collection is a short poem in support of the Duke entitled "Verses Supposed to bee Made by Dr. Corbet, BP. of Oxford: Against the Opposing the Duke in Parliament, 1628" (31). Immediately following it is the poem "An Answere to the Same, Lyne for Lyne" offering meticulous rebuttal to each positive assertion made about Buckingham. In this tirade, Buckingham becomes the king's "darling Absolon" (32). Thus, in germinal form, we see in the late 1620s the blast and counter-blast of post-1641 partisan satire, and even a hint of Dryden and Shadwell's factional satiric debates of the early 1680s.

Perhaps the best description of the Buckingham poems is as the vestiges of Complaint overlaid by the freshly topical and rhetorical. In the poem "Upon the D. of B.," Buckingham is condemned to hell. This sometimes happens to the targets of Complaint.

> O Lucifer, thou must resigne thy crowne;
> For thou shalt meet a duke will put thee downe.
> Hee hath a sinne, besides the deadly seaven,
> More then e're hell found out, to make them eaven:
> For which (O hell-hounds) if you do not graunt
> Him place, you will for ever want
> Your greatest consort. (35)

More than merely gloating about the demise of an amoral figure or a hated power broker, however, a hard political edge accompanies these lines. Beyond Buckingham's indulging in the customary seven deadly sins, he is arraigned as well for the crimes of political intrigue and self-aggrandizement—actions detrimental to the state. The poet relates less of a cautionary tale than exposes a political enemy to ridicule. Similarly, while dialogues are not an uncommon device of Complaint, they tend to lack the element of repartee customary in classical satire. In the Buckingham poems, the technique is amply represented and the banter is distinctly satiric. Sarcasm directed against the Duke is local and political in nature.

> *Charon.* Pish! come, I say: my boate shall stay for none,
> Thy sweet perfumed sinnes will fill't alone:
> If not, thy titles.
> *Duke.* Sure thou'lt stay a while,
> That I may Charles a little more beguile.
> *Charon.* Noe, noe, I can't. Felton, make no delay,
> If thou lou'st Charles, then send proud George away.
>   "Charon and the Duke" (56)[11]

In fact, the real locus of the collection is a character assassination of Buckingham to match his actual assassination by Felton.[12] In a poem written before Buckingham's death, "The Duke Return'd Againe. 1627," the vituperation is specifically designed to damage the Duke's reputation, even if the poet must misrepresent events in order to do so. During the fiasco of the battle for Rhé, Buckingham is accused of having sequestered himself in a small boat well away from the fighting.

> Was't not a noble part and bravely plaide,
> To send a shaddow in thy armes arraide,
> To personate thee in the battle, while
> Thou sat'st environed in a coble vile,
> Discharging sugar pelletts. (22-23)

Tremendous vanity or a shortage of good sense are charges justifiably leveled against Buckingham. Cowardice is not. This passage represents a particularly striking example of the ad hominem strategy so typical of satire.

A close look at two poems reveals best the general drift away from the dated austerity of Complaint and toward the novel complexities of satire. Probably the most medieval of the selections is "Upon the Duke." Written after the style of *A Mirror for Magistrates,* the poem features the spirit of the dead Buckingham delivering an admonitory and moralizing address. The announced purpose of the oration is sacred instruction. The ghost of Buckingham maintains that by heeding his words the listener may know the "better seacrets of my Maker's will" (37).

> Then patiently addresse your eares a while,
> Oh heare mee, not with a remorselesse smile
> At myne extorted plaints; but rather greive
> You are as I. Sonnes of deluded Eve. (37)

Here, Buckingham is used as a solemn reminder of human mortality and, more, as a warning not to pursue the futile path of earthly wealth and glory. Within this context, his assassination is not a secular event with public and political ramifications, but a divine act demanding personal religious contemplation.

> Farewell to favours: bidd them first adieu,
> And then (like shadowes) they will follow you.
> Learne him to feare that can your glories drowne,
> And make you wretched with one cloudie frowne.
> . . . .
> Mount Pegasus: adieu, my clymbing frends,
> How sodainly the soaring larke descends. (46)

Yet even within this homiletic exhortation, particular items of the contemporary political landscape emerge. Mentioned are "Spanish politiques," "some of the Guises tricks," and events where "The commons grieved, and the gentrie mourn'd" (41). When Buckingham recounts his youth and rise to power, he comments: "The straite and narrow path I strove to misse" (38). The narrator of "Upon the Duke" may ask us to repress "a remorselesse smile" while we hear him out, but the author of the poem includes enough touches of a topical and personally damaging nature to Buckingham that we must at least read with tongue in cheek. For all the Christian sincerity mustered by the speaker of this piece, the very fact that it is Buckingham striving to be pious undermines to some degree the excellent sentiments otherwise articulated. Buckingham is simply too hot a political item to make a completely effective profligate-turned-devout. Instead, in "Upon the Duke" we witness an early rehearsal of the ironic or self-damning narrator of political satire as found, say, in Satire 1 and 3 of Oldham's *Satyrs Upon the Jesuits*.

In contrast to the medieval flavor of "Upon the Duke," "A Satyre on the D. of B." represents a self-conscious attempt by its author to withdraw from the motifs of Complaint and relocate amid those of satire. Notably, the poem is written neither with the solemn plainness of Complaint nor the crabbed fashion of Elizabethan satire. Instead, its imagery is ornate; the work exhibits nearly a baroque feel that anticipates English satire to come. For instance, the poet describes Buckingham in much the same manner Swift and Pope portray Walpole a century later.

> The poore were poll'd, the rich were neatly shav'd,
> The dastard mounted, and the stout outbrau'd;
> Blockheads made bishops, when the reverend gowne,
> Like Homer, waited for his smile or frowne.
> Barons bankerupts, and shopmen barons made,
> Knaves knights, the course of auntient knighthood stay'd. (49–50)

In the poem we witness as well the deliberate conversion of guileless narrative lament to willful authorial subterfuge. The narrator seemingly participates willingly in the rationalization of a good king unduly influenced by a wicked minister.

> The yealding nature of a pious king,
> Whose worthie praises through the worlde doe ringe,
> This man's excessive power too much abus'd,
> And by abortive meanes before not us'd,
> That he might mount, favorites honey tasted,
> Whilst others vitall powers by poison wasted. (50)

However, by dint of the sheer number of depreciatory remarks made against Buckingham as well as the ironic tone applied throughout, these lines hardly strike one as being frank. Recalling James I's warning against the satiric stratagem of insincere celebration of the king, this ostensible praise of Charles I masks real censure of a king who permits rascals and knavery to thrive under his rule. Marvell makes similar good use of this ploy against Charles II in *Last Instructions to a Painter*.

The most interesting aspect of "A Satyre on the D. of B.," though, is the author's effort to ally the topicality of the poem with the rational imperative ordinarily found in classical satire. In other words, a deliberate attempt is made to convince the reader that this political condemnation of Buckingham is in fact aligned with the "right reason" of some unspecified—but indubitably correct—ethical system. These philosophical insinuations arise at the end of the piece when contemplating Buckingham's sudden fall from place.

> Oh heavens! what doe I? alas! hee's dead,
> And's burden'd soule untimely from him fledd.
> Burie his faults. I'le say no more then: why?
> Soe much in zeale to warne posteritie
> That all Icarian flights are vaine
> And thundershaken from his waine
> Shall Phaeton slide . . .
> . . . .
> And know promotion at his best,
> Findes death in earnest, not in iest. (50)

Note the heavy irony. Note as well the classical, as opposed to Christian, nature of the imagery. The allusions to Icarus and Phaeton ring loudly in our ears. Like Cleveland, Dryden, and Pope after him, the poet contrives to unite—for the obvious propaganda value it affords—a particular political agenda with a generalized cognitive and behavioral golden mean. Within the fiction of the satire, Buckingham the hated politicaster becomes as well an exemplum of unreason within an indeterminate, more or less pan-human ideological program—one that all right-thinking people pursue. "A Satyre on the D. of B.," then, is just that—a *satire* on a bad man in political power as opposed to a plaint about him. Conspicuously absent is the pontificating of Complaint; medieval elements that do survive are subordinate to the protocol and locality of satire. When weighing the Buckingham poems as a whole, we remark a restyling of political writing in England. This single work in particular represents an early experiment in political satire rather than a late survival of medieval Complaint.

After 1660, traces of Complaint linger in English political verse. However, after the civil war and the thorough politicization of neoclassical satire by poets such as Cleveland and Cowley, these vestiges normally are imbedded within the techniques of satire. An intriguing example of such a remembrance occurs in the anonymous poem *The Chimneys Scuffle* (1662).[13]

Superficially, the piece ventures to be an appeal to Charles II on behalf of the poor suffering from the recently imposed Hearth Tax. Over the first three pages of the poem, more than a passing attempt is made to recapture the demeanor of Complaint. The epitaph announces: "This is no *Libel,* such as *Rogues* disperse,

/ But a poor *Chimney—Plea* in honest Verse" (1). The poet is alert to the fact that, in an age of pasquinade, his composition is likely to be taken for mere political invective. Evidently, he seeks to avoid that stigma by casting the work in the simpler, more virtuous mold of Complaint. He even goes so far as to confer that label on the verses when the narrator begins his protestations.

> But whence comes this *Complaint?* Be pleas'd to hear;
> More's laid upon our *Hearths,* than they can Bear.
> Our *Chimney-Sweepers* may their Hovels keep,
> For now the *Owners* must their *Chimneys* Sweep
> To lessen their *Scrude Tax.* (1–2)

Not surprisingly, throughout the early stages of the poem this narrator has much of the plowman persona about him. His primary theme seems to be the social injustice of the new tax. He asserts that the tariff is a trifle to the rich, or easily evaded,

> Whereas poor *Tradesmen* who live by their Booth,
> Earning no more than serves from hand to mouth,
> With all their Stock can scarce pay Scot and Lot,
> Eating at *night* more than the *day* had got;
> These must be *Smoak'd* too, though their *Chimneys* speak
> "They knew not what Fire *meant* throughout the Week." (2–3)

Thus, the narrator presents himself as a champion of the oppressed speaking directly to the king.

> *Caesar* I beg a boon, and it is thus
> That I may plead *in Forma Pauperis*
> For these weak *Starvelings,* who make't their desire
> "That their Estates may purchase first a *Fire*
> "Ere they pay for their *Chimneys;* and that those
> "Whose *grandeur* by our *Suff'rings* daily grows
> "To such a boundless bottome, as in time
> "Their daring height will threaten a decline,
> "May feel Your *Princely Lash;* and these be many
> "Who ought well to be *smoak'd* as much as any." (3)

However, the term "*in Forma Pauperis*" is significant. In truth, this narrator is a late-seventeenth-century *rendition* of a plowman persona, not the genuine article. Here the narrator speaks not *as* a pauper, but in the *guise* of one. The distinction may be fine, but it is important. In this poem, the plowman pose serves insistently as a deceptive mask deployed by the satirist. While the possibility for irony certainly exists within the plowman fiction of medieval

Complaint, equally, that form of narration can be viewed as a straightforward device of protest and instruction. In *The Chimneys Scuffle,* such a reading is unavailable to us. Furthermore, what emerges in the last six lines of the passage quoted above is the real purpose of the poem: an attack on those *profiting* from the Hearth Tax, not a lamentation for those *suffering* from it. Again, the distinction is subtle but telling. As it turns out, the author will target in his poem an extremely specific and politically controversial group which needs to taste Charles's "*Princely Lash.*" Hence, as this work progresses, the issues and tone of Complaint lessen, mingle, and eventually give way to those of political satire. The climate of medieval social lament proves to be a hook intended to draw us into the poem: planted in the reader's mind is an air of the artless honesty traditionally accorded the plowman figure. This artifice is designed to make the reader more impressionable, if not gullible, to the blatant political message which follows.

Far more than a grievance on behalf of the citizenry, *The Chimneys Scuffle* embodies a factional warning to Charles.

> Awake *Great Prince,* intend your own Affairs,
> Let no light *Dalilah* rob You of Your hairs;
> Those *royal nerves* should now imployed be
> In *Steering* th' *Rudder* of Your Monarchie. (4)

Notably, the tone and concern of the narration at this point also become courtly, stately, even Augustan. Speaking generally, these threatening "*Dalilahs*" are unscrupulous courtiers, MPs, and government officials—"*State Impostors*" (3)—whose only interest lies in self-gain.

> And I must tell You from the zeal I bear
> Unto that Sacred Diadem You wear,
> That those *Court-Burs* who onely set their rest
> On *best-betrust* or on *Self-interest,*
> (For that's prime Game at Cards they daily use
> For their advantage and Your high abuse,)
> Can with a *Spanish-Shrug* complete their Ends,
> And make the world believe they're *Caesar's* Friends;
> "Ingratitude concludes them to be those
> Whom You reward the most be most Your Foes." (3)

What differentiates this condemnation of corruption in high places—a bromide of Complaint—from similar vague medieval admonitions, however, is the fact that the political poet of the 1660s is able and willing to direct his blame more narrowly and within an exact civil context. Generic courtiers and civil servants are not being censured in this poem; rather, the new, modish breed

of Stuart loyalist which emerged *after* 1660 is singled out for special treatment.
The narrator defines them as follows.

> These be those lazy fruitlesse *Droans* who thrive
> By sucking Honey from Your Princely Hive,
> What they ne're wrought nor duly labour'd for,
> And these may rest securely on the Shore;
> While Your *endeered Zelots* who have lost
> Their *Fortunes* for Your sake are hourly crost
> By adverse Winds: Long have these *Starvelings* bin
> Waiting at th' *Pool* in hope to be tane in,
> But some *desertlesse Amorists* of *Fashion,*
> Though really the *Refuse* of our *Nation,*
> Must be admitted to the highest place
> Not by *internal* but *external* Grace. (4)

At last, the narrator reveals himself not to be an unassuming pauper or plowman personality, but an old-style Cavalier in the mold of Clarendon speaking
through that mask—a mask that is now dropped. This Cavalier persona
inveighs not generally against the callous upper crust of society, but specifically against those latecomers to Charles's cause who, without suffering the
hardships of the late wars and exile of the king, now enjoy the fruits of the
Stuart Restoration. While the narrator formerly earned his privilege by virtue
of bluff, honest service to the king, these carpetbaggers are callow fops who
obtain their station via stylish airs, deceptive wit, and litigious skill.

> Shall I draw near Your *Court*? it will aver
> The ranting Courtier *Smoaks* the Cavalier;
> Who though he never fought nor ever will,
> He can prefer a *Suit,* and there's his skill. (6)

Moreover, with this indictment comes tacit but nonetheless unmistakable
criticism of Charles. The king himself bestows preferment on these black-
guards. In the Declaration of Breda, Charles did sell many of his most ardent
followers down the river at the Restoration. Personally, Charles was very like
these fashionable, dissimulative toadies surrounding him. He dressed, com-
ported himself, and counterfeited extravagantly.[14] Despite the frequent loyal
noises made by the narrator, surely the poet counted on his contemporary
readers to recognize such ironies in the poem. In the early 1660s, the realities
of the Restoration settlement were setting in; the issue of who should benefit
from the return of the king was a consuming one. The author of *The Chimneys
Scuffle* obviously found himself on the outside; accordingly, he argues for a
political agenda contrary to the drift of current policy. The poem's core message

may seem idealistic if not simplistic: a plea for honorable service to the king
via a court and parliament tenanted by men without ambitions of their own.
"This is my *Maxim:* they're not *Caesar's* friends / Who mould their *Votes* and
Acts for private *Ends*" (13). Reading between the lines, however, the actual
caveat—almost threat—to Charles is to choose his counselors from amongst
older, wiser, and more stable heads.

From this point onward, the tenor of the poem changes dramatically.
Complaint vanishes altogether; the tactics of censure and exclusion come full
to the fore. The "Starvelings" initially championed by the pseudo-plowman
narrator—that is, the socially underprivileged suffering unfair taxation—no
longer are the poet's care. Rather, that becomes the disfranchised patrician: this
group of "Starvelings" occupies the deliberations of the superseding Cavalier
persona. Accordingly, honest plaint is abandoned; Juvenalian onslaught begins.
Righteous indignation animates the adjusted and irate satiric persona of the
piece. "My Pen ne'r brook'd the Style of *Parasite,* / The World shall see I'll do
each *Office* right" (5). Beside courtiers, those offices admonished by the narrator include the church, lawyers, and "*Commissioners* and *Excisemen*" (see
5–6). All are arraigned for contemporary civil misconduct. The narrator also
engages in satiric theorizing. Like Cleveland, his axioms decisively combine
the Juvenalian with the political.

> I'm bold, but 'tis my *Zeal* that makes me so,
> "Who spares to speak he is Your fawning Foe.
> *Satyrs* who lay true tincture on a Crime,
> Deserve more praise then *Humorists* oth' time.
> 'Tis Charity in Him that shews the way,
> Or lends his *Light* to One who goes a-stray.
> "A Subject to his Prince is such a Debter,
> "The *Plainer* that He writes, he loves him better. (6)

Without question, the narrator has transmogrified from the plain liver of
Complaint to the plain dealer of satire. Whether the word "*Satyrs*" in the third
line of the passage earlier refers to the harsh-tongued sylvan beast or to the
genre of invective poetry (both meanings likely are implied), it is a notewor-
thy shift in nomenclature. Less than midway through a piece the author initially termed a *"Complaint"* and swore abstained from the "*Libel,* such as *Rogues*
disperse," partisan calumny commences on a grand scale. Turning from court
sycophancy, the poet examines a range of state ills. Foremost among these are
the religious controversies of the age. Much of the second half of the poem,
in fact, is spent maligning various sects. As might be expected, in this parade
of knaves and fools the Presbyterians are singled out for particular abuse (see
16). Several formal components of classical satire also appear over the second

half of the composition, such as a crisp exchange between the narrator and an adversarius (10–11) as well as a pair of short satiric codas (16). A safe guess would be that our author was university-educated or otherwise schooled in the craft of classical satire.

Finally, one moment in *The Chimneys Scuffle* strangely crosses the purposes of Complaint and political satire. As the narrator rails against Charles's dandified courtiers, he contends that the sparks at court, in debt for the expensive foreign fashions they wear, in turn become "*Collectors* of our *Chimney Smoak*" (13)—the tax—in order to pay for such luxuries. He remarks:

> And by their *mis-accounting* profit bring
> Gain to themselves in Cheating of the King. (13)

In this couplet convene two worldviews. An older English society grieves for the moral laxity and corruption of persons in authority: Charles's courtiers are not behaving in a Christian manner. At the same time, modern English polity demands the attempted expulsion of a prevailing faction by another currently out of favor: The superior loyalty and experience of the Cavalier persona is designed to supplant the greedy and shallow antics of the young courtiers. In the end, *The Chimneys Scuffle* is not an abstract objection to spiritual turpitude within a social and political system that fundamentally cannot change. Rather, it is a vigorous and detailed attack against material scoundrels who can, perhaps, be ousted. By the early 1660s, then, Complaint—or rather what was left of it—had become yet one more *device* of satire; it served in the satirist's ever-growing rhetorical armory. The author of *The Chimneys Scuffle* uses certain attributes of the older form as a feint to lead the reader into ridicule of an unmistakably virulent, local, and politically dynamic nature. Such circumstance strikes me as definitive testimony to the process of generic transition: what preceded now has been assimilated by what followed.

OBSERVATION

Perhaps the crux of literary history is mapping the turning points in the pursuits and exigencies of literate culture. One recent critic has found the middle of the seventeenth century to be the crucible in which neoclassicism formed. Not only did writers question and strategically revise the inherited grounds of their own cultural practices, but they sought to contextualize and discriminate among ancient sources in an effort to use those sources for their own advantage (Kroll 3, 8–9). I find the transition from Complaint to satire to be an excellent early example of this process. While the native cultural practice of Complaint as a means to dissent against governmental policy and social degeneracy undoubtedly was seen as efficacious by writers of the seventeenth century, the practice evidently came to be regarded as tame and dated as well. The emulation of classical satire, hitherto primarily the odd experiment of literary young men at the Inns of Court, promised better results—but not as it had been applied by Hall, Marston, or Donne. Classical satire needed to be better attuned to the times, specifically the new political circumstances developing in England. Accordingly, political commentators such as the authors of the Buckingham pieces and *The Chimneys Scuffle* poet felt perfectly free to add, subtract, multiply, and divide the genres of Complaint and satire as they pleased. The result of their ingestion of these forms was something entirely new: politicized neoclassical satire. Anyone even vaguely familiar with the course of Restoration and eighteenth-century verse satire will recognize the revolutionary nature and lasting impact of their innovation. Cleveland and Cowley, for instance, soon would apply the technique for vicious propaganda against the Parliamentarians. Pope and Swift would employ it nearly a century later to voice their disapproval of the Hanoverians.

So what is legacy and what is locality in this mess? To be honest, I'm not sure. It is easy, perhaps, to see how express social conditions worked to determine literary transformations in this case. However, can we say the reverse equally occurred? If it is true that to some degree the manner in which we talk about something biases the substance of our talk, does not literary formulation, then, in this instance also determine—even in some small way—social conditions? If English satirists, like their French counterparts, had nurtured Horatian charm rather than Juvenalian militancy, would Charles I have kept his head on his shoulders? It seems unlikely. But already I have strayed into yet another theoretical consideration for satire: the ability of the genre to enact real change in the world. Retreating to the original limits of my discussion, I will close with the comparison of satire to what we used to think was the perpetual motion of a shark (marine biologists, I believe, recently have caught these creatures napping). As a genre, satire ceaselessly moves and feeds in whatever cultural waters it swims. The satiric tradition is a living, omnivorous organism, not a fossilized skeleton of regulations. Satire is *always* in the process of formulating and leaving a legacy to its next generation of practitioners. They, in turn, will do with it what they must given the circumstances that they face.

NOTES

1. A recapitulation of recent critical efforts to define satire is found in the introduction of this book.

2. Satire itself, in fact, may be the example par excellence of Derrida's declaration that "every text participates in one or several genres, there is no genreless text; there is always a genre and genres, yet such participation never amounts to belonging" (65). Structuralist poetics call attention to satire's peculiarity as itself a transgressive form, a genre constituted by transgression against genre and, indeed, as deconstructive even of itself. As Derrida's remarks indicate, however, none of this calls for the absence of genre or generic considerations when studying literature in general or satire in particular. Just the opposite is the case.

3. I believe the more interesting and significant fact is not *that* Boileau or Oldham or Dryden or Johnson imitated Juvenal's third satire, but *what* each author did with Juvenal's poem. Updating the particulars within the original satire and altering its form, each author made the work suitable for the tastes and interests of his contemporary reader. Again, the vital issue is not that these writers participated in a classical satiric tradition—of course they did—but how they adjusted that tradition to coincide with their special cultures, not to mention their personal temperaments or political and literary axes to grind. Each imitation by those four men is altogether different. Simply that each version stemmed from the same Roman model really sheds very little light on the matter at hand. A richer and more useful critical examination of individual poems comes from the study of precisely how each man and age reimplemented the satire of Juvenal's initial design.

4. If it does not, not only does the work fail as a piece of satire, as Oldham discovered with *A Satyr Against Vertue*, but, as Defoe discovered with *The Shortest-Way with the Dissenters,* its author may suffer unpleasant personal consequences.

5. For instance, Peter emphasizes a satiric changing-of-the-guard from a brand of social comment he considers responsible and moral (i.e. Complaint) to one he paints as being unjustifiable and licentious (Elizabethan satire; see in particular chapter four, "The Moral Themes of Complaint," and chapter five, "Renaissance Satire"). In the introduction to his representative collection of Complaint from the sixteenth century, Gransden speaks of the transition from Complaint to satire more in stylistic terms, that is, as a matter of medieval and metaphysical elements slowly being smoothed into heroic couplets. Gransden's purpose similarly is to highlight that form's eventual clash with Elizabethan satire. Much to his credit, Kernan concerns himself with the social realities reflected by the two forms of protest literature; Kernan especially casts an eye toward the very real public ills raised by Elizabethan satire—land enclosure, rank-renting, usury, the uncontrolled growth of London (see in particular chapter two, "The Background of English Renaissance Satire"). Otherwise, for a useful overview of this period of satiric change, see Alden (44–51). Also useful is Tucker; his study undertakes an historical view of the evolution of different types of satiric literature in England from the twelfth century up through 1540. An attempt is made to trace the influence of foreign satire upon the English, and Tucker's work compliments Alden's treatment of satire in the Elizabethan period. Finally, for a brief history of medieval Complaint from approximately 1200 onward, see chapter one, "Political Satire in the Middle Ages," of Previté-Orton.

6. Zwicker notes that with the coming of the civil war literature "assumed increasing importance both as a site for and as a way of giving shape and authority to the conduct of polemical argument." The rise of polemic "can be charted in every quarter of the literary" to include "the development of older modes and the creation of new literary idioms" (10). Although Zwicker's subject is political controversy in literary culture after

1649, he acknowledges of course that the phenomenon shaped works of the late six-teenth and early seventeenth century as well (9–10). I believe that the transition from Complaint to satire is a prime example of this increasing politicization of literary productions in England.

7.   This literary birth was accompanied by complications and pangs; primarily, these took the form of state censorship. The Elizabethan church authorities both banned and burned satire in 1599. The early Stuart monarchs were even less enthusiastic about the form. In three of the last five years before his death (1620, 1623, 1624), James I issued procla-mations warning against the printing of seditious material. The first of these states unequivocally that governmental matters are not "Theames, or subiects fit for vulgar per-sons, or common meetings" and admonishes writers not to "intermeddle by Penne, or Speech, with causes of State, and secrets of Empire, either at home, or abroad." James also displays his literary acumen by cautioning against ironic flattery as a means of dis-guising criticism: "Neither let any man mistake Vs so much, as to thinke, that by giuing faire, and specious attributes to Our Person, they can couer the scandalls, which they oth-erwise lay upon Our Gouerment" (qtd. in Gibson 272–74; see also Wedgwood chs. 1 and 2 as well as Goldberg). Clearly, James sensed the danger of politically directed irony and satire. By and large, he successfully limited the spread of the form. With the ascen-sion of Charles I in 1625 the situation grew worse still. All literature was severely cen-sored (see Hill 98–99). The result of this degree of governmental control was more dramatic than before. From 1625 to the 1640s, no printed satire has survived, and man-uscript satire is rarely to be found after 1630 (see Gibson chs. 8 and 9). However, the consequence of these controls seemed to have the opposite effect of what the govern-ment obviously intended. Before the 1620s, what little satire gets written is predominantly abstract and moralistic (see Wheeler ch. 3). After about 1625, the satire that survives largely is preoccupied with detailed accounts of current events and political personages. The long period of government suppression also primed the fuse for the explosion of political literature after 1641 when official obstacles to publishing were disrupted. For the increase of opposition to early Stuart policy, see Sharpe as well as Cust and Hughes.

8.   Drayton's The Owle (1604), Niccols's The Beggers Ape (written before 1610 but pub-lished after 1627 for fear of government reaction), and Goddard's The Owles Araygnment (ca. 1616) are three prominent examples. Such works took on the general manner of Spenser's Complaints (1590) and Colin Clout Come Home Againe (1595). Cautious of the official attitude to satirical criticism (the 1599 ban on satire remained in place after Elizabeth's death), these authors took advantage of the allegorical nature of Complaint to disguise their political intentions within a symbolic narrative. In fact, even after 1640 the presence of Complaint is felt. John Hepwith's allegorical account of the first Duke of Buckingham's notorious political career, The Calidonian Forest, was written before 1628 yet not published until 1641; at that time it certainly contributed to mounting anti-Royalist feelings (for this, see Gibson ch. 7). Similarly, in the Calendar of State Papers (Domestic Series) for 1644–1645, two long poems appear that attack Archbishop Laud in much the same manner Cardinal Wolsey was attacked more than a century earlier (see entries 34 and 35; 280–81). Thus, while not thriving, neither was complaint totally moribund after 1600. Poets still used the form as it was originally conceived—as a means of cautious political comment.

9.   The main manuscript sources for the Buckingham poems are Malone 23 in the Bodleian Library, and Sloane 363 and Sloane 826 in the British Library. F. W. Fairholt's printed edition of these poems, from which I will quote, comes mainly from the last of these three; all citations are given in page numbers.

10.   See also "A Dialogue Between the Duke & Dr. Lambe" (58), which is another long poem cataloging Buckingham's civic crimes.

11.   See as well two similar pieces in the collection, "A Dialogue Betweene Charon and the D." (56) and the previously mentioned "A Dialogue Between the Duke & Dr. Lambe" (58).

12. The ironic epitaph on the title page of the compilation reads:

> Who rules the kingdom? The king!
> Who rules the king? The duke!!
> Who rules the duke? The devil!!!

13. In Ashmole manuscript 1096 (26) in the Bodleian Library, Oxford; all quotations are from this script and given in page numbers.
14. One need only read portions of Clarendon's account of his king, especially when a youth, to sense the older generation's disapproval of the behavior of Charles I's son.

WORKS CITED

Alden, R. M. *The Rise of Formal Satire in England: Under Classical Influence.* 1899; rpt. Philadelphia: Archon, 1961.

Brooks, H. F. "English Verse Satire, 1640–1660: a Prolegomena." *The Seventeenth Century* 3.3 (Spring 1988): 17–46.

The Chimneys Scuffle (1662). Ashmole ms. 1096 (26). Bodleian Library, Oxford.

Cust, Richard, and Ann Hughes, eds. *Conflict in Early Stuart England: Studies in Religion and Politics, 1603–1642.* London: Longman, 1989.

Derrida, Jacques. "The Law of Genre." Tr. Avital Ronell. *Critical Inquiry* 7 (1980): 55–81.

Fairholt, F. W., ed. *Poems and Songs Relating to George Villiers, Duke of Buckingham; and his Assassination by John Felton, August 23, 1628.* Vol. 29. London: Percy Society, 1850.

Gibson, L. J. "Formal Satire in the First Half of the Seventeenth Century. 1600–1650." Diss. Oxford U, 1952.

Goldberg, Jonathan. *James I and the Politics of Literature: Jonson, Shakespeare, Donne and their Contemporaries.* Baltimore: Johns Hopkins UP, 1983.

Gransden, K. W., ed. *Tudor Verse Satire.* London: Athlone, 1970.

Greenblatt, Stephen. "Shakespeare and the Exorcists." *Criticism: Major Statements.* Eds. C. Kaplan and W. Anderson. New York: St. Martin's P, 1991. 711–37.

Grigson, Geoffrey, ed. *The Oxford Book of Satirical Verse.* Oxford: Oxford UP, 1980.

Hill, Christopher. *The Century of Revolution: 1603–1714.* Edinburgh: Thomas Nelson and Sons, 1961.

Kernan, Alvin. *The Cankered Muse.* New Haven: Yale UP, 1959.

Kroll, R. W. F. *The Material Word: Literate Culture in the Restoration and Early Eighteenth Century.* Baltimore and London: Johns Hopkins UP, 1991.

Peter, John. *Complaint and Satire in Early English Literature.* Oxford: Clarendon, 1956.

Previté-Orton, C. W. *Political Satire in English Poetry.* Cambridge: Cambridge UP, 1910.

Rosenheim, Edward, Jr. *Jonathan Swift and the Satirist's Art.* Chicago: U of Chicago P, 1963.

Sharpe, Kevin, ed. *Faction and Parliament: Essays on Early Stuart History.* Oxford: Clarendon, 1978.

Tucker, S. M. *Verse Satire in England Before the Renaissance.* New York: AMS Press, 1966.

Wedgwood, C. V. *Poetry and Politics Under the Stuarts.* Cambridge: Cambridge UP, 1960.

Wheeler, A. J. *English Verse Satire from Donne to Dryden: Imitation of Classical Models.* Heidelberg: Carl Winter Universitatsverlag, 1992.

Zwicker, Steven N. *Lines of Authority: Politics and English Literary Culture, 1649–1689.* Ithaca and London: Cornell UP, 1993.

·5·

Satyrs and Satire in Augustan England

Richard Nash

Pygmies and Yahoos in Swift, Monsters of Dulness in Pope, all occupy the liminal space defined by Restoration and early eighteenth-century science as monstrous: at once failing to reproduce the same, they are too dangerously similar to be safely classified as "other."[1] They reproduce the stories contemporary science told of the "wild man" or satyr: on the one hand, weak, degraded, diminished, and abject; simultaneously dangerous, threatening, and too free, especially sexually. The monsters of satire, like the constructions of the wild man, are impotent in that word's dual construction—weak and ineffectual, yet given to unrestrained sexual excess and satyriasis. Jonathan Swift's amorous Yahoo repeats (with reversed genders) the common stories of Orangutans (this name meant literally, "wild man of the woods") as Satyrs, marauding the boundaries of forest and society in search of sexual prey. In *Tale of a Tub,* the Moderns are seen to realize the type of those priapic pygmies with enlarged genitalia recorded by Ctesias ("Digression in praise of Digressions"); the "monster breeding" dunces of Alexander Pope's *Dunciad* "get a jumbled race." In the discussion that follows, I want to explore an anxiety at the heart of satire—a concern over the limits and boundaries of what counts as human—and locate that anxiety within a larger cultural framework that includes the emergence of modern science.

At the same time that early modern science sets about discovering in Nature the physical embodiment of the legendary satyr—half-man, half-beast—English literary history marks itself as "an age of satire." The Wild Men, Feral Children, Satyrs, Orangs, and Apes of eighteenth-century natural history represent a dangerous and degraded vision of ourselves against whom we define the category, *Human*. The satirist, metaphorically reenacting the liminal predations of these creatures, subverts this reassuring boundary formation by revealing the bestial within the human. Thus both satirist and satiric victim wind up balancing on the boundary between "human" and "other," and threatening the security promised by such definitions.

In the summer of 1699, there appeared in London, among several other related essays, "A Philological Essay Concerning the Satyrs of the Ancients." In spite of the title, the essay is concerned not with the "satyrs" of Horace, Juvenal, and Persius, but rather with those characters in Pliny and Diodorus Siculus, who "are always represented as Jocose and Sportful, but Scurrilous and Lascivious; and wonderful Things they relate of their Revellings by Night, their Dancing, Musick, and their wanton Frolicks" (46). That is, the subjects of the essay in question are "satyrs," and not "satires." At the same time, although the essay announces itself as philological in method, it is not commonly thought of as a contribution to literary criticism but to medical science. The title of the complete work in which it appears is: *Orang-Outang, sive Homo Sylvestris: or, the Anatomy of a Pygmie compared with that of a Monkey, an Ape, and a Man. To which is added, a Philological Essay Concerning the Pygmies, the Cynocephali, the Satyrs, and Sphinges of the Ancients.*

This oddly titled work would seem to bear no particular relevance to the subject of this book, except perhaps through the folk etymology that once connected a literary form with a mythical creature. That is distinctly not the point of this chapter. What I want to attempt here is to consider the relation of Edward Tyson's "satyr" to those of his literary contemporaries in an attempt to explore new ways of considering literary satire of the eighteenth century, and as a consequence entertain more general ideas about our understanding of the nature of satire. For such a project, Tyson's book commands a special interest, for it is itself what we would term retrospectively a work of "literature and science"—its first half is detailed comparative anatomy; its second half is philological criticism. In this way, it belongs to those distinctly "Modern" contributions to learning that attempted to bring a solid, material basis to the practice of philological criticism. In this respect it is of a piece with those antiquarian projects so well characterized by Joseph Levine in *Dr. Woodward's Shield.*

Such an odd, hybridized quality defies easy generic classification in a way that is itself related to the practice of satire.[2] Tyson's work is an anatomy; both in that word's principal sense of a dissection of the body, and in the secondary (and more literary) sense of a logical dissection or analysis of a body of knowledge. In this latter sense, it belongs to a tradition, popularized in the seventeenth century by Richard Burton's *Anatomy of Melancholy,* that is frequently identified with Menippean satire. We should note that the difficulty in classifying Tyson's book reflects the difficulty in classifying the subject of that book, and also is reflected by the persistent problem of classifying satire within the realm of literature.

Together, the various claims of Tyson's titles reveal his project as consisting of three interrelated activities: a comparative anatomy, a taxonomy, and a philological essay on the myth and literature of the Wild Man. The comparative anatomy is "hard science," the philological essay is literary criticism, and the taxonomy is the hybridized act of naming the world that underwrites not only this, but so much of eighteenth-century science. However much Tyson attempts to position literary criticism ("philology") as a supplement to the pre-existing scientific discourse of "comparative anatomy," the two enterprises are in his narrative mutually reinforcing, drawing upon each other for support, and subordinating both to the unidentified privileged discourse of taxonomy.

Tyson's title provides us with six nouns, names that are to be compared with one another not as words, but as bodies: *Orang-outang, Homo Sylvestris, Pygmie, Monkey, Ape,* and *Man.* The first term, from which the modern-day *Orangutan* is derived, is a Malayan word meaning, literally, "wild man of the woods." It was first employed in Europe by the Dutch physician, Nicolaas Tulp (the central subject of Rembrandt's *The Anatomy Lesson),* and was used generically to refer not only to creatures found in Borneo, but to what are now referred to as "anthropoid apes." On one hand, it is important to recognize that Tyson uses the term in this generic sense; he is not confusing the creature he anatomizes with an orangutan. At the same time, we must also recognize that the very concept of "generic" in the Linnaean sense that we now use the term is anachronistic when applied to Tyson. While taxonomies existed before Linnaeus, nothing approaching the rigorous system he developed was familiar to Tyson. When he uses *Orang-Outang,* he refers not to "anthropoid apes," but to all creatures commonly referred to as some kind of "wild man of the woods." Thus, his first subtitle, "sive Homo Sylvestris," provides the proper scholarly Latin alternative name, "or Man of the Woods." If, for Tyson, *Orang-Outang* and *Homo Sylvestris* are synonymous terms, so too are *monkey* and *ape,* as they will continue to be for Samuel Johnson fifty-six years later. Our current practice of using *ape* to refer primarily to the five so-called great apes—man, chimpanzee, gorilla, gibbon, and orangutan—and using *monkey* to refer primarily to the lesser primates had not emerged. Of the two remaining terms, Tyson consistently uses *Man* in one of the widely accepted usages of the day, "as distinct from beast"; *Pygmie* is used in the sense provided by Johnson, "one of a nation fabled to be only three spans high, and after long wars to have been destroyed by cranes." *Man,* in this usage, is a term of science, locating a creature in the scale of beings; while *Pygmie* is opposed to it as a fabulous term of mythology. What Tyson is about to do is relocate the figure of myth in the discourse of science, position that figure between man and ape as a liminal figure of science, and then denying the possibility of liminal status, demote it to the status of ape.

Tyson's work, in short, is a study of "man" that proceeds by focusing attention on instances of monstrous alterity.[3] It is, quite literally, a cataloging of identity and difference that aims to fix and establish the boundaries of what constitutes the human. In this respect it mediates between the mythic role of its subject— the satyr—and the literary role of the satire. For the legendary figure of the satyr, half-man and half-beast, is a figure of (especially sexual) predation lurking in the shadows of the forest who polices the boundary between civilization and the wild, threatening to carry off those women and children who do not participate in their own domestication. Satire, too, performs a kind of border work, and does so repeatedly by invoking an antithesis between the social and the animal. It is one of the important paradoxes of satire that the figure of the satyr describes both the satirist and the object of satire. The satirist, often characterized as a figure of rage and violence, serves through his attacks the social function of establishing the limits of social behavior. At the same time, his attacks repeatedly take the form of stripping away the civilized veneer of social respectability to reveal a bestial nature at the core. In the various descriptions of "primate" behavior between Tyson and Linnaeus, and in the contemporary satiric contributions of Pope, Swift, and Dr. Arbuthnot, one can find a similar impulse: a constructive projection of self-loathing onto those who threaten by resembling too closely.

In what follows I want to pay particular attention to an intercourse, a boundary crossing, that was clearly at work in the early eighteenth century and that is frequently obscured for late twentieth-century readers. Today we are likely to treat as separate and isolated episodes narratives of gorillas, chimpanzees, pygmies, wild men, etc., but as Tyson's account and other works of natural history make clear, there was an extensive traffic in representations of such creatures. All such creatures belonged to the class of Orang-Outang, a figure differing in degree but not in kind from man. Daniel Beeckman's voyage to Borneo (published in 1718) articulates the relationship of man and Orang-Outang in some detail:

> The monkeys, apes, and baboons are of many different sorts and shapes; but the most remarkable are those they call Oran-ootans, which in their language signifies men of the woods: these grow up to

be six feet high; they walk upright, have longer arms than men, tolerable good faces (handsomer I am sure than some Hottentots that I have seen), large teeth, no tails, nor hair but on those parts where it grows on human bodies; they are very nimble-footed, and mighty strong; they throw great stones, sticks, and billets, at those persons that offend them. The natives do really believe that these were formerly men, but metamorphosed into beasts for their blasphemy. They told me many strange stories of them, too tedious to be inserted here. (108–09)

This troubling and problematic kinship provides the central anxiety as well as the crucial joke in An Essay of the Learned Martinus Scriblerus, Concerning the Origin of the Sciences.[4]

Pope described the design of this satire to Joseph Spence as being "to ridicule such as build general assertions upon two or three loose quotations from the ancients" (126), and that has usually suggested to critics that it is principally directed towards a chief antagonist of the Scriblerians, Dr. Woodward, whose Remarks upon the Ancient and Present State of London, Occasioned by some Roman Urns, Coins, and Other Antiquities lately discovered (1713) would nicely model such practice. If so, it would suggest that the essay was composed about 1714, which is not unlikely although it was not published until 1732. While such a target may well have been in Pope's mind, there is no specific mention of Woodward, and the essay does explicitly allude to Tyson's anatomy. I am less interested in substituting Tyson for Woodward as the focus of satire, and more interested in exploring the work's relation to his anatomy—a relation that has tended to be obscured by reading the essay as an attack on Woodward.

Pope's characterization of the general design of the satire is born out by the title and opening line of the essay: "Among all the inquiries which have been pursued by the curious and inquisitive, there is none more worthy the search of a learned head than the source from whence we derive those arts and sciences which raise us so far above the vulgar, the countries in which they rose, and the channels by which they have been conveyed" (360). As one can see readily enough in Pope's other writings (notably, his preface to Homer), this view represents a fundamental perversion of what he considers an appropriate respect for "the Ancients." Those whose interest in the Ancients was nothing more than a diligent search for the most ancient, missed entirely the aesthetic point that one should value the works of the Ancients because of their merit, not their age. This conceit leads Scriblerus to seek the ultimate origin of Arts and Sciences: "It is universally agreed that arts and sciences were derived to us from the Egyptians and Indians; but from whom they first received them is yet a secret" (360).

That secret is soon revealed through the mediation of Tyson's anatomy. Appended to the anatomy proper, Tyson had included "A Philological Essay Concerning the Pygmies, the Cynocephali, the Satyrs, and Sphinges of the Ancients." His purpose was to argue that these fabulous creatures had no real existence but were the distorted representations of such subhuman creatures as the one he had anatomized. In doing so, he sought to bring the light of science to the shadows of myth and legend. At the outset of his preface, he explicitly identifies his project with eclipsing the explanatory power of mythic narrative with that of scientific discourse: "I have made it my Business more, to find out the Truth, than to enlarge in the Mythology; to inform the Judgment, than to please the Phancy." By proclaiming his essay "philological," he aligns himself with Richard Bentley and those other "verbal critics," who by seeking to establish the study of literature on a material basis, challenged the aesthetic criterion of taste and judgment long accorded to the poets. His philological essays consist almost entirely of "loose quotations from the ancients" strung together, so that he may then establish that whatever creatures the ancients may have been referring to, they were not men.

Like Tyson, Scriblerus begins his essay with references to accounts of "Pygmaeans . . . in Homer, Aristotle, and others" (361), and like Tyson, he quickly takes up Diodorus's description of the Satyrs encountered in Ethiopia. Where the entire force of Tyson's anatomy and philological argument had been directed to distinguishing man from these liminal figures, however, Scriblerus's use of Tyson's materials is to solidify the bond between humans and the monstrous other. Thus, Scriblerus takes from Diodorus precisely the same passage that Tyson extracted, and ties the description even more tightly to Tyson: "He met . . . a sort of little Satyrs, who were hairy one half of their body, and whose leader Pan accompanied him in his expedition for the civilizing of mankind. Now of this great personage Pan we have a very particular description in the ancient writers; who unanimously agree to represent him shaggy-bearded, hairy all over, half a man and half a beast, and walking erect with a staff, (the posture in which his race do to this day appear among us)" (361). Tyson had reasoned that his creature's natural posture was erect, but that his illness had left him to weak to stand unsupported for long; as a result, he had provided him with a staff in the accompanying illustration: "Being weak, the better to support him, I have given him a stick in his Right-hand" (16). Subsequent illustrators perpetuated the trope of the walking staff in eighteenth-century illustrations.

In opposition to Tyson's attempt to distinguish his creature from civilized humanity, Scriblerus finds this creature the very source of human civilization by pairing this quotation from Diodorus with another selected from Homer: "And, since the chief thing to which he [Pan] applied himself was the civilizing of mankind, it should seem that the first principles of science must be received from that nation, to which the Gods were by Homer said to resort twelve days every year for the conversation of its wise and just inhabitants" (361). In the pages that follow, Scriblerus traces the lineage connecting Tyson's fabulous references to sub-humans to the flourishing of Classical Greece. Socrates, for example, is known to have had "an uncommon birth from the rest of men," to have demonstrated his lineage in his physiognomy, "being bald, flat-nosed, with prominent eyes, and a downward look," and to have shown a penchant for the writings of Aesop "probably out of respect to the beasts in general, and love to his family in particular" (363). This discussion continues through the ages and for several pages, culminating as it must in Tyson's own anatomy: "Nor let me quit this head without mentioning, with all due respect, Oran Outang the great, the last of this line; whose unhappy chance it was to fall into the hands of Europeans. Oran Outang, whose value was not known to us, for he was a mute philosopher: Oran Outang, by whose dissection the learned Dr. Tyson has added a confirmation to this system, from the resemblance between the *homo sylvestris* and our human body, in those organs by which the rational soul is exerted" (366).

Now, the first thing to keep in mind here is that Scriblerus makes use of Tyson's findings in a way that is precisely opposed to Tyson's intent. I belabor that point because Montagu, Tyson's twentieth-century champion, has taken this passage as a tribute from Arbuthnot: "Arbuthnot makes serious reference to Tyson's work" (404). The reversal here (keeping in mind it is Scriblerus, and not Arbuthnot or anyone else speaking) is accomplished so blandly that it may escape notice. Tyson—maintaining proper scientific objectivity—considered only the material body, but his concern in being able to distinguish human from other must have been in no small part motivated by concerns about "the rational soul," especially in one who was renowned as "a strict Adherer to the Doctrine and Discipline of the Church of England." Nonetheless, in his summary list of attributes wherein "the Orang-Outang or Pygmie more resembled a Man, than Apes and Monkeys do," number 25 reads: "The Brain was abundantly larger than in Apes; and all its parts formed like the Humane Brain" (92). Scriblerus thus turns Tyson's observations to his advantage, blurring the very boundary Tyson intends to establish.

This reversal highlights the problematic role of impersonation on which so much satire depends.[5] Scriblerus, a "solemn fool" modeled on Don Quixote, embodies those aspects of false learning—particularly prevalent in the new science—that the Scriblerians set out to ridicule. He is, in this manifestation, a parodic alter ego to Tyson, the grave, studious scientist whose attention to the body is subordinated to the pleasures of the mind. Not least significant here is the rhetorical affinity between Martin and the proponents of the "New

Science." In one of the few critical discussions of this work, Lester Beattie calls attention to the persistent use of modest self-effacement:

> This tentative idiom of the overconfident scholar is employed in all its known forms: "I cannot but persuade myself"; "if I should conjecture . . . it ought not to seem more incredible than . . ."; "nothing is more natural to imagine"; "it should seem that the first principles of science must be received from that nation"; "I am much inclined to believe"; "India may be credibly supposed"; "I make no question that there are remains." (228)

Recently, historians of science have begun identifying the crucial role this "literary technology" of modest reporting played in the establishment of modern science. In describing the various means by which Robert Boyle lobbied for his reader's belief, Steven Shapin and Simon Schaffer identify the form of the essay itself as calculated to emphasize the credibility earned by modesty: "The essay . . . was explicitly contrasted to the natural philosophical *system*. Those who wrote entire systems were identified as 'confident' individuals, whose ambition extended beyond what was proper or possible. By contrast, those who wrote experimental essays were 'sober and modest men,' 'diligent and judicious' philosophers, who did not 'assert more than they can prove'" (65). Moreover, within these essays, Boyle consciously adopted the rhetoric of modesty parodied by Martin, informing his son: "in almost every one of the following essays I . . . speak so doubtingly, and use so often *perhaps, it seems, it is not improbable,* and such other expressions, as argue a diffidence of the truth of the opinions I incline to, and that I should be so shy of laying down principles, and sometimes of so much as venturing at explications" (qtd. in Shapin and Schaffer, 67).

The satire in Martin's essay will be effective precisely to the degree to which the parodic characterization transgresses the boundary that separates it from the original. To the extent that such an impersonation is successful, Scriblerus's argument—like Tyson's—will appear learned, leading to an equation between modern proponents of science and their pygmie originals. It was Tyson, after all, who after diligent examination was unable to distinguish his own brain from the pygmie's. Finally, such a successful impersonation also licenses a displacement, for it is ultimately not Tyson, but his pygmie, who is revealed as "the great . . . philosopher." If Tyson's triumph was, by introducing scientific method to popular spectacle, to establish an inviolable barrier between man and beast, the satirist by challenging those barriers subverts the very logic of domination on which they depend. Here, then, is a particularly compelling convergence of the two senses of *satyr,* for both figures, dwelling on the boundaries of society, are committed to challenging our constructions of what it means to be human.

I have discussed elsewhere the relation of this work and Tyson's anatomy to *The Memoirs of Martinus Scriblerus* with respect to the scientific attempt to appropriate from the carnivalesque space of the fair the marginal human as a subject for knowledge construction.[6] Such an appropriation seeks to domesticate the subject by locating it within the social space of the Royal Society, transforming it from "mindless spectacle" to a curiosity for speculation. The traffic in knowledge construction between Court society and fair-booth, modulated by the participation of Royal Society and coffeehouse, contributes to the dynamics Jurgen Habermas alludes to as the "genesis of the Bourgeois Public Sphere" (14). Here, I wish to allude briefly to a separate but related movement with respect to another form of knowledge construction regarding a liminal human. Again the link occurs through Scriblerian satire and the general rubric of *Orang-Outang*. That term loosely applied, throughout the early eighteenth century to any creature that could be considered a wild man of the woods, including Peter, the Wild Boy discovered in the woods near Hanover and brought to London in 1726.[7]

Peter's arrival occasioned a barrage of newspaper accounts, poems, sermons, and pamphlet literature, serious and speculative as well as satiric. In most accounts, Peter is represented through his potential, the promise of upward mobility he offers. In the satires, however, the Scriblerians deploy Peter as a sign of collapsing boundaries, the location where man and beast, courtier and commoner, share an intermingled identity that comments adversely on each. The satire bites both the credulous mob at Bartholomew Fair and the equally credulous beau monde at Court.

What is most important in their treatment of Peter is the way in which Peter becomes a sign, capable of multiple—even inconsistent—interpretations, one that can consequently serve the purposes of the satirist: to ridicule the folly of those who credulously believe the unfortunate Peter to have been raised by animals, and simultaneously to expose the corruption that lurks beneath the polish of the Court. Peter draws together in common folly the mob and the King, but where in mass culture folly is ridiculous, among the powerful "cultural elite" its corruption is dangerous. The satire on Peter, like that on Tyson's "Orang-Outang," collapses the boundaries between high and low culture, revealing the necessary complicity of the curious and the credulous, the knave and the fool. It is the very liminality of the satyr figure of the wild man that licenses the transgressive challenge to boundaries that characterize the activity of satire.

NOTES

1. I am using "liminal" here in the sense articulated by Victor Turner as a state of transition "betwixt and between" firm identities; see "Betwixt and Between: The Liminal Period in Rites of Passage," *Betwixt and Between: Patterns of Masculine and Feminine Initiation*. Eds. Louise Carus Mahdi, Steven Foster, and Meredith Little (LaSalle, Ill.: Open Court Press, 1987).
2. Here I would call attention to the affinities between my local argument about satires and satyrs and Bruno Latour's larger argument about the "Modern Constitution." According to Latour, "Modernity" (which in this usage corresponds roughly with the enlightenment) depends on the strict division of the world into human and non-human (culture and nature) and the simultaneous proliferation of, and refusal to recognize, the hybrids such a division requires.
3. As Donna Haraway reminds us, "*monsters* have the same root as *to demonstrate; monsters signify*" (333). Early modern science is very much located in the space of wonder where monsters became demonstrations, as spectacle is transformed to intellectual, as well as economic, speculation.
4. See also my discussion of this work and the social space(s) of knowledge construction in "Tyson's Pygmie: The Orang-Outang and Augustan 'Satyr'" in *Ape, Man, "Apeman": Changing Views 1600–2000*, eds. R. Corbey and B. Theunissen, Leiden University Press, 1994.
5. Maynard Mack's influential essay on "The Muse of Satire," *Yale Review* 41 (1951): 80–92, details the importance of "personation."
6. "Tyson's Pygmie."
7. In the discussion that follows, I want only to sketch out some of the issues raised by the literature surrounding Peter; I hope to grant the episode the fuller treatment it deserves in a larger study currently in progress. One indicator of the fluidity of these categories is to note that it was not until the tenth edition of Linnaeus's *A General System of Nature* (1758) that the term *primate* was first deployed in its current scientific sense, and that throughout the various editions of Linnaeus's *General System* a special rung was always assigned to *Homo Sapiens Ferus*, as illustrated by various examples of feral children, including Peter.

WORKS CITED

Arbuthnot, John. "An Essay of the Learned Martinus Scriblerus, Concerning the Origin of Sciences" *Miscellanies in Prose and Verse*. London, 1732.
Beattie, Lester. *John Arbuthnot*. New York: Russell & Russell, 1935.
Beeckman, Daniel. *A Voyage To and From the Island of Borneo in the East Indies*. London, 1718; rpt. in John Pinkerton, *Voyages and Travels*. London, 1812.
Habermas, Jurgen. *The Structural Transformation of the Public Sphere*. Cambridge, Mass.: MIT P, 1992.
Haraway, Donna. "The Promises of Monsters," *Cultural Studies*. Eds. Lawrence Grossberg, Cary Nelson, and Paula Treichler. New York: Routledge, 1992.
Johnson, Samuel. *Dictionary of the English Language (Abridged)*. London, 1756.
Latour, Bruno. *We Have Never Been Modern*. Harvard UP, 1993.
Levine, Joseph. *Dr. Woodward's Shield*. U of California P, 1974.
Mack, Maynard. "The Muse of Satire," *Yale Review* 41 (1951): 80–92.

Nash, Richard. "Tyson's Pygmie: The Orang-Outang and Augustan 'Satyr.'" *Ape, Man, 'Apeman': Changing Views, 1600–2000.* Eds. R. Corbey and B. Theunissen. Leiden: Leiden UP, 1994.

Shapin, Steven and Simon Schaffer. *Leviathan and the Air-Pump.* Princeton: Princeton UP, 1985.

Spence, Joseph. *Anecdotes, Observations, and Characters, of Books and Men.* 2nd ed. London, 1858.

Swift, Jonathan. *The Correspondence of Jonathan Swift.* Ed. Harold Williams. Oxford: The Clarendon Press, 1963.

Turner, Victor. "Betwixt and Between: The Liminal Period in Rites of Passage," *Betwixt and Between: Patterns of Masculine and Feminine Initiation.* Eds. Louise Carus Mahdi, Steven Foster, and Meredith Little. LaSalle.: Open Court Press, 1987.

Tyson, Edward. *Orang-Outang, sive Homo Sylvestris: or, the Anatomy of a Pygmie compared with that of a Monkey, an Ape, and a Man. To which is added, a Philological Essay Concerning the Pygmies, the Cynocephali, the Satyrs, and Sphinges of the Ancients.* London, 1699.

Woodward, *Remarks upon the Ancient and Present State of London, Occasioned by some Roman Urns, Coins, and Other Antiquities lately discovered.* London, 1713.

·6·

From Cheated Sight to False Light: Analogy in Swift and Churchill

Jon Rowland

INTRODUCTION

The tenor of the following argument, that analogy becomes both increasingly important to and problematic in satire of the eighteenth century, requires the recognition of the relatedness of panegyric and satire as twins of one branch of rhetoric—the epideictic. Epideictic is that kind of writing concerned with the nobility or the ignobility of present things; panegyric may be regarded as one branch, satire the other. While opposite in the character of their subject matter, as "display" rhetoric the two branches have many things in common, foremost among which is their use of analogical "vehicles" to help the reader imagine their respective moral "tenors." Borrowing from Richards's *The Philosophy of Rhetoric, tenor* stands for that part of the analogy that is the *meaning* to be explained and illustrated, and *vehicle* for that part that does the explaining and illustrating.[1]

Curiously, while analogy has long been thought of as the appropriate means of approaching knowledge of absolute goodness, it has never been given its due as an even better means of approaching knowledge of evil. I hope to show how far this critical neglect lags behind the practice of satirists such as Jonathan Swift and Charles Churchill.

Analogy is traditionally a "second best," as a means of approximating knowledge of what is ultimately unknowable; yet, second best is the best, as Martin of *A Tale* demonstrates, in his willingness to tolerate his brother Peter's gew-gaws on his coat, as the price of having a coat at all. The kind of satire that distinguishes the eighteenth century depends on a conscious acceptance of this second best as the best possible. To be dissatisfied with tenors' somewhat distorting vehicles is to begin to doubt and thereby undermine the authority on which such satire is based; to be too readily satisfied or *unconscious* is, of course, to be proud, self-sufficient, and foolish.

ANALOGY IN SWIFT'S ODES

When he wrote his odes in the 1690s, Swift was heir to a tradition of English panegyric that began with Samuel Daniel's *Panegyrike Congratulatory* of 1603 and included both the epic treatments of John Dryden and Edmund Waller and the heroic, Pindaric versions of Abraham Cowley. More immediately, like his Whig contemporaries, Joseph Addison, Matthew Prior, and William Congreve, he inherited the challenge of reconciling past panegyrical excess to the need for "a new mode of praise suitable to a constitutional polity since the extravagant rhetoric and figuration of Gallic and late Stuart panegyric evoked absolutist views of kingship incompatible with the moderate principles of Whig and Tory loyalists" (Williams 57). While analogy tends to be unsatisfactory in itself, recent political developments (including the Glorious Revolution of 1688) would have made it potentially embarrassing. The association of panegyrical excess with both the recently deposed Stuarts and the absolutist monarchy of Louis XIV, would have helped make analogy, like figurative language generally, unpatriotic as well as politically reactionary.

The title of this chapter, "From cheated sight to false light" (from the "false mediums [that] cheat our sight" of line 147 of "Ode to Dr. William Sancroft" to the "*Artificial Mediums,* false Lights, refracted angles, Varnish, and Tinsel" of p. 172 of the "Digression on Madness" in *A Tale*) describes the change in the perception of the ideal and the transcendent as we move from Swift's odes to *A Tale,* from panegyric to satire. Insofar as the panegyrist accepts the existence of the ideal, he will understand the problem of transcendence in terms of *cheated* sight: there is something there, you just cannot see it. The satirist will tend to discount the ideal and treat the problem of transcendence differently: there is *nothing* there and *that* is what you cannot see.

The perception of the ideal (negative or positive), in any absolute sense, is impossible; we require some kind of *analogy* to approximate it. Swift's analogies succumb to gravity; they tend to illustrate vice rather than virtue. Edward Rosenheim remarks this problem in the "Ode to Sancroft," and describes Swift's attitude as "perverse Platonism": "For Swift, on the contrary, human 'knowledge' as it appears in this ode is the product of an active distortion and inversion of Truth—to such a degree that our 'truth' resembles its original only enough to foster our deluded belief in our own wisdom" (33). The analogies that should help us to understand transcendent virtues like "truth" either don't work or work in reverse, by illustrating falsehood and vice.

The entire "Ode to the King" may be regarded as one of Swift's unsuccessful vehicles of the good, since rather than the goodness of William III (which it is clearly intended to convey as its tenor) it suggests rather a chasm between such goodness and the man himself. While the poet's function is to confirm the King's "delight of doing good," which is "fixed like fate among the stars," the problem is how that "delight" gets translated on earth. Considering the first lines of "Ode to the King,"

> Sure there's some wondrous joy in doing good;
> Immortal joy, that suffers no allay from fears,
>   Nor dreads the tyranny of years,
> By none but its possessors to be understood: (1–4)

it is hard not to translate "joy in doing good" into joy in plain *winning*, especially when Swift seems to translate it thus, a little later in the same strophe: "What can the poet's humble bays / . . . Add to the victor's happiness?" (8–11). The empty pageantry of the first strophe already suggests the divorce between the ceremonial thing that kingship ought to be—in theory or "among the stars"—and the gritty, bloody reality, a split that panegyrists (according to Garrison and others) have traditionally tried to mend.

There is also, as John Irwin Fischer argues, a split between two versions of William that split the poem itself: "The subject of the first is a king who is beyond death, fear, and even time itself, but who is unknowable. The subject of the second is a king whose deeds and character are significant precisely because they are referable to a providential design that is not only beyond his control but beyond his very understanding" (17). A problem with transcendence has fragmented even the subject of Swift's poem.

Part of the tension, which leads Fischer to read the ode as *two*, is between the apparently permanent nature of the "joy in doing good" (by which the poet means, essentially, the *thesis* that we always derive joy thus) and the nature of William's enjoyment of such joy, which is clearly impermanent and dependent on "*valour*," but that also *seems* to be more permanent than it is, coming as it does in contrast to a passage whose theme is transitory pomp. It is as if Swift would have us take (or *mistake*) for an ascription of permanence to William what, upon examination, is really an ascription of permanence to his *thesis*. In the "Ode to Dr. William Sancroft" the problem of transcendence is treated explicitly as one of analogy. Swift asks Truth in the second strophe, "But where is even thy image on our Earth?" (17) and suggests why men can't see it:

> foolish man still judges what is best
> In his own balance, false and light,
> Following opinion, dark, and blind, (54–6)

That the problem is analogical becomes explicit in Swift's obvious embarrassment at his own analogy between what the Jews did to Christ and what Sancroft's contemporaries did to him (the effect of which is to make Sancroft Christ (if not Christ Sancroft):

> And though I should but ill be understood
> In wholly equalling our sin and theirs,
> And measuring by the scanty thread of wit
> What we call holy, and great, and just, and good,
> (Methods in talk whereof our pride and ignorance makes us use)
> And which our wild ambition foolishly compares
>   With endless and with infinite;
>   Yet pardon, native Albion, when I say
> Among thy stubborn sons there haunts that spirit of Jews
>   That those forsaken wretches who today
>   Revile his great ambassador,
>   Seem to discover what they would have done
>   (Were his humanity on earth once more)
> To his undoubted master, heaven's almighty son. (121–34)

There are, in fact, at least two Sancrofts. The regular one "moves too high / To be observed by vulgar eye" (149–50) while the irregular one only appears so because of our own "cheated sight" (147). The tendency in this poem is for the worse to prevail.

While the two poems discussed address the difficulty of analogy, the "Ode to the Athenian Society" develops this difficulty of analogy into a theme nearly identical to its own difficulty of interpretation. The poem's elusive, transcendent tenor may in fact be its meaning. John Irwin Fischer sees in the poem another illustration of "the human dilemma that what is perfect in itself is necessarily blank to us" (21). In terms of panegyric, in which the poet occupies a middle position between the ideal and the real, the poet replaces the real with his own pleasant—and in the poem wildly far-fetched—imagination of it. What we end up with is a solipsistic version of a public form in which the effort to translate transcendence is supplanted by subjective daydreaming. That the almost *necessarily* nebulous Athenians, really a group of Grub Street hacks led by the notorious journalist, John Dunton, have replaced some significant figure like a king, is manifest from the number of panegyrical topoi addressed to them: the "sun" topos for the renewal of learning in 22-24, the restoration topos, with its "prius, nunc" pattern, the "Nile" topos, with its idea of the limitation of monarchical power to describe the recovery of England after the war, et cetera.

The first strophe of Swift's poem is complicated by the fact that, while the whole may be regarded as one vehicle, it contains arbitrarily designated sections of tenor and vehicle in a 21-line analogy whose "::" (or "so" in a construction "as the sun is to day, *so* the moon is to night") is stated precisely in the middle at line 11: vital heat, flood, mountain, universal main, primitive sailor in the designated vehicle; learning, household, sacred ark, philosophy, and dovemuse in the tenor. The tenor appears to comprise lines 11-21, the gist of it being that after turmoil (war) learning revives, helped by philosophy; the vehicle appears to comprise lines 1-10, and uses the story of the resettling of the waters after the flood and the landing of the ark on Ararat. In fact, both sections of the strophe should be designated "vehicles" for a "tenor" that is nowhere stated and is, after all, rather cliché. As if Swift himself were doubtful of the "tenor," he *laminates* it with vehicles that still fail to convince us, not only of the *good* that is there, but that there is anything there at all.

The country in the second strophe looks "As if the universal Nile / Had rather watered it than drowned" (42–43). The Nile in turn provides an important, pivotal connection to analogical cruxes that seem to be at the center of the poem, insofar as it has one. In Swift's day the most important thing about the Nile after the fact of its regular and benign flooding was the obscurity of its source and man's fascination with the same. Thus it can be seen as, however obliquely, connected to the young poet's "wild-excursions," his sometimes prurient curiosity, the rather cynical and debunking curiosity of the vulgar "crowd" (87), and the consequently necessary obscurity of the "Athenians," all of which are developed in the third and subsequent strophes.

There Swift remarks that praise and blame are but different effects of the same cause, "want of brains" (85). Apparently we cannot understand even wit by its effects, since opposite effects may be achieved by the same cause. In the fourth strophe, the wits themselves can, on a more important level, see no relationship between effects and cause: "Do own the effects of Providence, / And yet deny the cause" (109–10). What Swift leads to, I think, is ultimately the problem of understanding a transcendent (in his case a "cause") by its effect, or, in terms of this discussion, a tenor by its vehicle. While Swift fears that knowing the Nile to be caused by "a little inconsiderable head" (147) might damage that river's reputation, the fact that the source of the Nile was still unknown suggests that the main concern is for the way whatever cause or tenor we imagine reflects not the effect but a prior subjective judgment of it, which it subsequently reinforces. Similarly, atheists who wish to see no cause but "eternal seeds . . . jostling some thousand years" (128–29) first decide that their effect is not "wondrous wit" but "atoms jostling in a heap" (127). Cause and effect then alternate as vehicle and tenor without external reference.

Just as the "wits" deny major causes, they deny minor; thus, in the fifth strophe they will fail to see any relationship between the Athenians and their effects, between them and their magazine, and will "deny you to be men, or anything at all" (120). From God as cause to John Dunton is too great a leap. While the atheistic wits who doubt the existence of God seem intended to function as vehicles for those who doubt the existence of the "Athenians" (really of John Dunton and his hacks), it is hard to avoid a rather embarrassing reversal, implicitly an identification of John Dunton with God. The fears about atheistic "wits" in the fourth strophe, about the way the difficulty of arriving at the tenor can cause us to deny that there is one, may well represent the tenor of the poem, and the cynicism of such "wits" about the Athenians in the fifth strophe may be the "vehicle" for such ideas, but it is very easy for the two to be reversed, and either way the discrepancy between the "tenor" and "vehicle," between skepticism about God and skepticism about rather nebulous "Athenians" (who are after all only Grub Street hacks) is too great not to be damaging. One *effect* of the discrepancy is to bring *analogizing* itself into disrepute, and indirectly to *deny* that a cause, at least an *important* cause, can be deduced analogically from its effect—any more than a tenor from a vehicle, the tenor of this poem especially. In the process of attempting to solve the problem analogically, Swift actually indicates its insolvability—an indication that is itself a kind of solution—by means of the poem's "tenorless vehicles," which are themselves "causeless effects." While Swift finally appears to settle for something like agnosticism in the sixth strophe,

> But as for poor contented me
> Who must my weakness and my ignorance confess
> That I believe in much, I ne'er can hope to see; (132–34)

turning from rage at what others see to "contentment" at not seeing anything himself but believing regardless, the nagging problem remains: our attitude to the Athenians and our belief in God have become hopelessly confused.

FROM PANEGYRIC IN THE ODES TO SATIRE IN *A TALE OF A TUB*

Panegyric, in the rhetorical and generic sense elaborated by Garrison and others since the mid-seventies remains one of the least explored aspects of *A Tale of a Tub*. Although when the word is used it usually connotes praise, the sections of *A Tale* repeatedly exploit conventions common to the genre. An awareness of these conventions, thematic and formal, and the way they are exploited helps us to account for certain currents of increasingly solipsistic analogizing that come to a head in "Section IX."

The dedications to Somers and Prince Posterity reproduce the triadic arrangement common to panegyric of poet, people, and prince. In the first piece the poet is supplanted by the Bookseller (in several senses, since the Bookseller seems to have the writers entirely under his control), the Prince by Lord Somers, and the people by the reader; in the second, the poet becomes the Grub Street hack, the Prince "Posterity," and the people the faction of moderns the hack is promoting. Swift reproduces many of the conceits of the earlier odes (in particular of the "Ode to Temple") in the first dedication. The Bookseller refers to the topics of praise as "an old beaten Story" (25) but lists the typical virtues anyway, by means of parasepiopesis, stating something while pretending not to.

The second dedication is notable for the way the conventions of panegyric are systematically violated to discredit the hack. Perhaps the most important violation, that to which the others are tributary, is of *ethos,* the proof that depends on our impression of the moral character of the speaker and that, as Aristotle indicates in his *Rhetoric,* helps to convince us that what the speaker praises really is praiseworthy (17). The hack's very language tends to undermine this; he frequently uses words that are traditionally to be avoided or at least to be used more cautiously in panegyric: "before the next *Revolution* of the Sun" (33) and "What *Revolutions* may happen before it shall be ready" (36) are typical slips of this sort. Elsewhere he refers to the "murderers" of the moderns as authors, thereby deflecting some of the blame onto himself, as the most conspicuous author present. Worse, he continually states things negatively— modern works are "never-dying" rather than "always-living"—and in defending himself he usually just states his enemies' case—his own kind of parasepiopoesis, perhaps.

The conventions of panegyric—and their violations—can be traced throughout the body of *A Tale.* In "Section I" the "people" of the triadic arrangement become "the crowd." Poetry is represented by the ladder—"a symbol of faction and poetry"—in reality a gallows, which is clearly a violation of the reconciliation topos. The poet himself is depicted as a kind of usurper "climbing up by slow Degrees" (62). In "Section III" the hack writes a mock-panegyric to critics, invoking the traditional topics to praise the true critics, distinguished by their inability to praise. Peter, in "Section IV," is referred to as the "hero of the play," and in "Section VI" as a hero who "by gradual steps" rises to a throne. We are reminded of the uneasy combination of the heroic and the panegyric introduced by Cowley and continued by Swift himself, especially in "Ode to the

King," discussed earlier. Clearly Peter is a kind of king, and the description of his adventures comprises a kind of mock-panegyric in prose.

ANALOGY AND *A TALE*

Of course, not all of the problems with analogy in the odes need be a problem for satire, which in treating the "bad" also uses analogy; if analogy is approximate or irresistibly reductive, so much the better. Brian Vickers indicates that Swift's earlier works reflect the influence of a seventeenth-century tradition in which writers such as Bacon figured prominently. For example, Vickers compares typical Baconian analogies, like "it is in praise as it is in gains" (*Essay* "Of Ceremonies"), to Swiftian imitations, "It is with *Wits* as with *Razors*" (1): "The beginning of the analogy . . . is formal, and the reader thinks it is going to continue seriously—he begins to assent to the proposition—and then the trap springs" ("Swift and the Baconian," 103).

Unlike these analogies, which are what Nilli Deingott calls explicit, the main analogy of *A Tale* slides almost immediately into identification; man is not like a suit of clothes, he *is* a suit of clothes. This fact, and Swift's comments on St. Paul's "allegories" and how they are wrongly converted into "articles of faith" (IX, 262; 66), suggest to Vickers that what Swift most dislikes about analogical language is the ease with which it slips from comparison to identification. The clothes analogy clearly works on the order of identification between microcosm and macrocosm, between man and the world, the very mistake that Vickers remarks ("Analogy Versus Identity") that Aquinas and like-minded thinkers, including, much later, Bacon himself, wanted to avoid: "Man has 'some' similarity with the world and, therefore, is called a microcosm; but he [Aquinas] does not say that man is, strictly speaking, such a microcosm" (102).

"The peculiar Talent" of the Modern, of "fixing Tropes and Allegories to the *Letter,* and refining what is Literal into Figure and Mystery" (189–90), is just this confounding of analogy and identification. Moreover, the tenor of analogies tends to become just other vehicles (i.e. "letters") rather than the tenor they are supposed to help us understand (i.e. "the spirit"). According to John R. Clark, this is the essence of the knave and fool configuration in *A Tale;* the modern knave is an allegorist, or analogist, of the "letter" or of vehicle rather than the tenor. Consequently there is really no distinction between knave and fool in *A Tale.*

Deborah Baker Wyrick, in *Jonathan Swift and the Vested Word,* calls the clothes analogy in *A Tale* "the book's root metaphor" (31). She see in it "the problem of how and by whom or what an investiture—the word as the clothing of thought, or feeling, or intention—is given meaning" (20). Surely this remains a problem beyond the scope of particular religious and social disputes over materialism and preferment (though still a part of these): moreover, a narrow attack on materialism (Harth 76–77) would not account for or even be consistent with Martin's acceptance not just of clothing but even of "corrupt" clothing in order to have any clothes at all.

Wyrick's indication in the analogy of the role of intention in determining meaning on a fairly abstract textual level remains pertinent on other levels. Where Martin "draws the line" in preserving the coat on one hand, and ridding it of corruptions on the other, depends entirely on good faith, on his good intention to preserve never entirely disinterested meaning. He must decide with himself what the tenor of the coat is, deliberately distorted vehicle that it is. The reader, for that matter, must do exactly the same thing when he comes to the clothes analogy or any other part of *A Tale*. He must establish with himself, his conscience, his judgment, a tenor for this vehicle "encrusted" not just by Swift but by generations of not-so-disinterested critics. The temptation for the "latest" critic is no less than it was for Jack, to hate the encrusting vehicles more than he loves their tenor.

If, as Wyrick puts it, "Swift's lyrical tableau of investiture" lacks "satiric bite" (32), an opinion she shares with Edward Rosenheim and Kathleen Williams, it must be both for the reason she gives, that "the metaphor of investiture serves the concept of authoritative order," which Swift believed in, and because the bad that is the target of the satire is inseparable from the good that is not. Not unlike Martin with his coat, Swift is willing to accept a degree of corruption and distortion in order to preserve the "fabric" of his church. Finally, Swift's satire of clothing "lacks bite" because clothing for Swift is necessary even when partly corrupt and therefore good even when bad, like the very vehicles it is itself a vehicle for. Implicit in his (and Martin's) tolerance of corrupt clothing is the conscious tolerance of bad even in the act of blame; to say that the satire lacks "bite" is perhaps only to restate something that Swift himself felt keenly and expressed better.

That authority, as Wyrick argues (supported, I should think, by critics like Michael Seidel), is also paternal suggests another connection with panegyric. The problems with worldliness, preferment, institutionalization, and meaning, to name but a part of the tenor of the clothes analogy, arise from the death of the first authority, God, the "willing" father of *A Tale*. His absence, the uncertainty (to say the least) surrounding those figures like Peter and Jack who attempt to fill it, and the resulting confusion and vertigo of *A Tale*, are all presented in terms of the corruption and even violation of the conventions of panegyric, especially of its tripartite relationship (now between writer, authority, and readership; originally between poet, prince, and people). John R. Clark suggests that it is surely no coincidence that analogical disorder occurs in the context of the loss of authority in *A Tale*; such disorder can be seen as one consequence of "The revolt of the Renaissance and Reformation against medieval authority" (69).

The frenzy of Jack, trying to get at the tenor in the very act of destroying the vehicle, hating his brother's usurpations more than loving his father's authority, appears then to be a metaphor for the danger that continually confronts the reader (no less than the preferment-seeker), the risk that the book repeatedly takes of irreparably separating vehicle from tenor, of meaningless vertigo or, to use its own phrase, "perpetual turning." At its most agreeable such disjunction seems merely fanciful, the "playfulness" remarked by Rosenheim, when a fiction "gleefully expanded, loses its analogical dimension and acquires the character of robust comic fantasy" (*Satirist's Art* 133). At such moments the tenor is no longer a particular satiric target, Rosenheim suggests, but something else—perhaps just story—constructed "on the well-established foundations of anti-Puritan satire" (135). I believe, however, that the most important moments of *A Tale* are *not* playful and agree with John R. Clark that "one might well question an examination of the *Tale's* serious artistry that is resolved by implying that playfulness in itself is the work's end or purpose" (67). At such moments his vehicles seem to be intentionally sabotaged—as opposed to unintentionally in the odes—so as not to go, or not to go very far before breaking down (or sinking). The Grand Committee itself cannot arrive at a suitable tenor: *A Tale* is supposed to divert schemers, but in the analogy "whales, tubs, and even the Grand Committee itself are all so many schemers, dangerous to government; and the reader finds himself in perilous and confusing waters" (67). Clark finds a similar metaphorical confusion in the definition of wisdom, which finally suggests that wisdom, "that something of value beneath the rind, after all the pains of the journey, is in reality valueless, offensive" (59). I suggest that such an unpleasant nothingness lurks behind all the significant analogical vehicles of *A Tale,* including, of course, the "Carcass of *Human Nature*" as it is read (dissected) by the hack. This *nothing* is paradoxically *something* in the context of so many panegyrical schemes and topics, a surprisingly *negative* fulfillment of the nebulous addressees of the odes.

THE RANGE OF ANALOGIES IN *A TALE*

The analogies of *A Tale* range from the extended allegory of the three brothers and their coats to the concentrated analogizing in the emphasis on names and naming. These include analogies that work through inversion or reversal, through inappropriateness of the vehicle (usually due to a disturbing difference in kind or quality), through a gradual development that seems to cause the tenor to change or reverse itself from a good thing to a bad. Such kinds are by no means distinct, and nearly all of the analogies of *A Tale* work through the identification of a vehicle with a tenor on the basis of a partial or irrelevant or even mistaken similarity, which is after all a type of reversal.

The clothes analogy seems to have infiltrated the "Apology" of *A Tale* and even established colonies. Swift accuses the *"weightiest* Men in the *weightiest* Stations" of conniving in their humorlessness at "pulling up those very Foundations wherein all Christians have agreed." This "pulling up" is similar to Jack's ripping and tearing and perhaps similarly motivated more by hatred for other brothers (Catholics) than love for the Father. While not exactly Jack they are certainly his abettors: "The Abuses in Religion he proposed to set forth in the Allegory of the Coats and the three Brothers, which was to make up the Body of the discourse. Those in Learning he chose to introduce by way of Digressions" (Apology, 4). It is curious that after speaking of the brothers' bodily garb he refers to their story as a body. The book or "discourse" clothes their story just as their coat clothes their bodies, as their church "clothes" their lives. *A Tale* is itself implicitly a coat, a "vehicle." This early emphasis on surfaces helps prepare us for the "findings" of the sect of "tailor-worshippers" of "Section III," which all stem from an abuse of analogical relationships. In their preference for clothes, for the surfaces of things, for vehicles over tenors, all they appreciate is the superficial aspect of things. Thus their findings disturb not just because they are false but because they are incomplete. Their failure to arrive at knowledge, or worse, to arrive at *true* knowledge, stems from a greater failure to understand the inherent nature of analogy. Partial knowledge mistaken for complete knowledge makes for a tremendous falsehood worse than plain ignorance. Thus the wrongness of their assertion that the universe is "a large *Suit of Cloaths"* derives from taking as complete the incomplete knowledge provided by an analogy between the way "the Earth is invested by the Air; the Air is invested by the Stars" and the way the body is covered by layers of clothing. They consistently, like the hack himself, identify the vehicle with the tenor. These postulata being admitted, as the hack says, or allowing a whole series of identifications to be made on the basis of slight similarities, it is possible to remake man as a kind of sartorial Frankenstein, patched together out of a whole series of stolen parts, but considerably less viable than even that monster.

Still, one's sense of the impropriety of the hack's procedure is probably complicated and maybe even blunted by having encountered just such monsters in positions of authority and respect. It is hard not to implicate one's self in the hack's obviously foolish mental processes, especially given this element of truth that they *seem* to discover. But this, one senses, occurs on a height miles above the hack himself, who remarks with an air of cheerful, uncritical discovery that "so, an apt Conjunction of Lawn and black Sattin we intitle a *Bishop*" (Section 2, 79). The hack can no more *feel* the truth of this than the falsehood. He himself resembles the tailor-worshippers; could even be one in his own obvious preoccupation with the surfaces of things. Some of the uneasiness one feels reading the hack's description of the sect stems from the impression created by his presentation there and elsewhere that he is in some ways himself a member; one readily perceives through his dark mystifying prose the obvious that he never does, that the "idol" is in fact a tailor.

The description of the tailor-worshippers' analogical abuses is itself a vehicle, of course, for the similar abuses perpetrated by the brothers on their coats. They proceed the same way, identifying vehicle with tenor on the basis of slight and arbitrary similarity. Their procedure is complicated somewhat by the existence of the father's will, but this proves no major obstacle once they begin. Just as the tailor-worshippers eventually assemble a man from the pieces, the vehicles of violated analogies, they assemble a word (S.H.O.U.L.D.E.R.) from the letters of other words. Like the tailor-worshippers' soulless man, this word, in terms of the father's will at least (which comprises after all, all the terms that matter), has no tenor. Eventually they obtain desired vehicles from other less legitimate sources, or get rid of undesirable vehicles by giving them false tenors, as when they ignore the injunction against fringe by deciding that fringe means broom-sticks—another false identification based on partial similarities.

The hack's procedure with *critic* is not unlike the brothers' with *fringe*. He too dispenses with the obvious tenor ("such Persons as invented or drew up Rules for themselves and the World, by observing which, a careful Reader might be able to pronounce upon the Productions of the critic *Learned*" (Section, 92)), but substitutes for it one by virtue of which the, in some ways like a collector of faults, becomes indeed "*a Discoverer and Collector of Writers Faults*" (Section 3, 95). By a typical reversal of tenor and vehicle, the "true critic" actually becomes the faults, or "an *Abstract* of the *Criticisms* themselves have made" (Section 3, 96). The hack can now read history exactly as the brothers read the will, by ignoring obvious meanings and substituting others derived from faulty procedures. The brothers and the hack treat all texts as their own.

Such treatment, selfishly motivated substitution of obvious tenors by abstruse ones derived from the vehicles-become-tenors of other analogies, mentally prepares us for the reversals of the ancients v. moderns controversy (as when, in "Section V," he criticizes Homer for not having read the moderns and so effectively makes *them* the ancients and Homer the modern) and all the other "great revolutions" (Section 4, 50) of *A Tale,* which include such diverse events as the hack's despotic placement of a preface (Section V) in the middle (in a sense the tenor) of the book, Peter's overthrow of Constantine and Jack's overthrow of Peter and, finally, "great" men's overthrow of their reason.

The brothers' sartorialism seems to be reflected in the hack's obsession with outerness (always disguised as a desire for innerness and profundity), as when he remarks, "I have some Time since, with a World of Pains and Art, dissected the Carcass of *Humane Nature,* and read many useful Lectures upon the several Parts, both *Containing* and *Contained;* till at last it *smelt* so strong, I could preserve it no longer. Upon which, I have been at a great Expence to fit up all the Bones with exact Contexture, and in due Symmetry, so that I am ready to show a compleat Anatomy thereof to all curious *Gentlemen and others*" (Section 5, 123). The hack's vehicle of a dissecting session for his analysis of human nature suggests that human nature, at least for him, is a rotting corpse. For us the analogy suggests, among other things, both the offensiveness of the hack's version of humanity and the offensiveness of his treatment, his technique. The vehicle is surprising in that, as *dissection,* it suggests inwardness and meaningfulness, which I identify with the tenor, at the same time it is consistent with all the other analogies of the hack in its overemphasis on exuberant and even runaway presentation. The vehicle is also, I think, highly paradoxical in that it employs a vehicle for depth (of sorts) in what is after all a most materialistic and therefore (in that sense) superficial presentation of human nature.

Of course, the hack has probably confused things by mixing metaphors or mixing analogies. He has used a vehicle for a movement from inside to outside for a movement from physical to spiritual; consequently, what ought to suggest spirituality or spiritual things (the essence of human nature) suggests instead just more internal physical things.[2] Similarly, the skeleton that he reassembles after his analysis suggests not the essence that he supposedly was after but instead something reductive and even grotesque. What he offers as the final result of this dissection, the old cliché about instruction and diversion, is neither. And he forces this into the same inside outside vehicle as the spiritual and the physical, a kind of Horatian sandwich: "with a *Layer* of *Utile* and a layer of *Dulce*" (Section 5, 124).

The tailor-worshippers' use or abuse of analogy anticipates the wind-worshippers or Aeolists of "Section VIII"—indeed, provides an intratextual vehicle for them. The spirit of the world may in some ways be like wind, but it is not wind. The Aeolists' wind is the madmen's vapors in "Section IX"—though I admit this is itself an identification based on similarity. But the madmen's zeal of "Section IX" should be compared to Jack's in "Section VI." It is their zeal that leads the madmen to innovate and form schools and philosophies, just as his leads Jack to found the Aeolists. And their zeal is "in things impossible to be known" (Section 9, 166) or "Things Invisible" (Section 9, 169), like Jack's for a pristine coat, a tenor he can never arrive at, or like those things (such as goodness), which are traditionally the object of analogy. Like the sartorialists, like the Aeolists, like the hack himself in his analyses, the madmen seem to have constructed whole systems out of partial and indeed slight similarities. Swift demonstrates considerable skill at analogizing, through a character singularly inept at it, even though it is something he consciously endeavors to excel at: "[T]he *Grubaean* Sages have always chosen to convey their Precepts and their Arts, shut up within the Vehicles of Types and Fables, which having been perhaps more careful and curious in adorning than was altogether necessary, it has fared with these Vehicles after the usual Fate of Coaches overfinely painted and gilt; that the transitory Gazers have so dazzled their Eyes, and fill'd their Imaginations with the outward Lustre, as neither to regard nor consider, the Person or the Parts of the Owner within" (Introduction 66). The hack complains about the overemphasis on presentation, on the vehicular side of things, with a vehicle that has clearly got away from him (though not, of course, from Swift). He is clearly not the one for the task he has undertaken, of "untwisting and unwinding" Grub Street works. His confession that he is "somewhat liberal in the Business of Titles" refers not just to paratextual matters like the "Treatises written by the Author" at the start of *A Tale,* but also more generally, I think, to his preference for names, indeed for all aspects of signification over things signified.

The arbitrariness of these analogical procedures is not unlike simple naming, a theme of *A Tale* anticipated as early as the "Apology" where Swift complains that, while out of respect he forbears to name his hoped-for protectors and actual detractors, they "fix a Name upon the Author of this Discourse" (Apology 6) and to works that he never wrote. This concern with names, part of the larger concern with arbitrary signification and imbalanced presentation pertinent to analogy, is carried over into the Bookseller's arbitrarily use and abuse of titles both literary and aristocratic, since he cares no more for Lord Somers the dedicatee of *A Tale* than for the book itself, of which he admits "I am altogether a Stranger to the Matter" (23). Similarly the hack's list of subscribers' names tends to become just a series of "tenorless vehicles" as the poets' works and the poets themselves are forgotten by time: "I am preparing a Petition to *Your Highness,* to be subscribed with the Names of one hundred thirty six of the first Rate, but whose immortal Productions are never likely to reach your Eyes" (33). His manipulation of names and titles is as arbitrary as the bookseller's, only less successful, and certainly less *profitable.* His one solution for modern obscurity, validating their titles by limiting them to the immediate present, is clearly no solution at all, in a piece addressed to posterity: "what I am going to say is literally true this Minute I am writing" (Posterity 36).

This foundation of truthfulness on the sheer *assertion* of its signification should be counted among the "common Privileges of a Writer" claimed by the hack, like the "understanding" that "whatever word or Sentence is Printed in a different Character shall be judged to contain something extraordinary either of *Wit* or *Sublime*" (Preface 47). In other words, meaning may be affected (even *effected*) by typeface. *That* the text means is all it indicates, never *what*. The latter is arguably the writer's jurisdiction, the former the reader's. He abnegates one to usurp the other. Meaning's reduction to a matter of the writer's assertion establishes the validity of self-praise as merely a form of *self-assertion*. The absence or presence of any quality can be asserted just as the absence or presence of meaning itself: "when an Author makes his own Elogy, he uses a certain Form to declare and insist upon his Title, which is commonly in these or the like Words, '*I speak without Vanity*'" (Preface 47). The hack's vehicle for the modern right to self-praise is a sum of money, or "Fee-Simple," that has been bought out by those who formerly received just the interest from it. Modern self-praisers are to their praise what recipients of their own money are to their own money. Such beneficiaries acquire complete control at the expense of *what* they control. The analogy brings us back to the hack's initial and indeed fundamental dilemma, of making meaning entirely a matter of assertion, or arbitrary signification, of "that" he means without regard for "what."

It is important that all this analogical abuse occurs in the context of much discussion of panegyric and satire, praise and blame, blame delivered as praise and vice versa. Indeed, the confusion over good and bad indicated by *these* inversions has much to do with the inversions of tenors and vehicles described earlier. For one, the analogical abuses create an atmosphere of topsy-turviness in which one *expects* other reversals. Moreover, Swift seems to imply that where such analogical reversals occur others *ought* to be expected. Indeed, when identification is based on spurious similarities it is extremely easy to make the bad the good or *vice versa*. One simply bases the identification on a spurious similarity to the appropriate vice or virtue—the Aeolists' wind, the madmens' vapors. No doubt the sheer epistemological uncertainty created by Swift's manipulation of analogy also creates an uncertainty about the possibility of knowing good and bad, but such uncertainty is entirely in the reader. The point may be that one *ought* to be uncertain, whereas the hack is not only certain about good and bad but convinced that what he is writing contains not "one grain of Satyr intermixt" (Preface 48). At its most abstract level Swift's satire seems to be of the very epistemological certainty of good and evil on which satire is based.

Whereas the "cheated sight" in the odes seems merely to have rendered old virtues less accessible, false light and delusion discover new virtues—really just kinds of "unpleasant nothingness"—by means of analogy. In "Section I" the procedure of great clerks and philosophers is to "force common Reason to find room" (57) for the particular tenet they choose to make a virtue of, in their case the number three. This process involves finding threes everywhere—especially where they are not—and excluding everything else where they can't be found. In "Section II" the tailor-worshippers proceed by analogy, or rather by *abuse* of analogy, similarly "reducing, including, and adjusting every *Genus* and *Species* within that Compass, by coupling some against their Wills, and banishing others at any Rate" (57). Religion and honesty may be equated with vanity. The earth may be lauded as a "suit of clothes" and an injunction not to wear silver fringe may be construed as an injunction not to wear broomsticks (thereby dispensing with the original "tenor" and allowing for silver fringe). On one hand analogy enables the Aeolists to elevate belching to "the noblest art of a rational creature," and on the other to reduce learning to "nothing but wind" because *"Words are but Wind; and Learning is nothing but Words"* (153).

The Aeolists' elevation of wind to a virtue in "Section VII," like the tailor worshippers' elevation of clothes or the philosophers' elevation of triadicity, facilitates the treatment of princes whose presence the panegyrical language of *A Tale* leads us to expect and, ultimately, causes us to miss. As the "unpleasant nothings" are elevated into virtues, nonentities do not merely become great while great men become nonentities, but men deemed great before are seen to be so precisely for *nothing,* indicating that something more sinister than a simple inversion has taken place. In fact, as in some of the earlier examples, the tenor of virtue itself changes, changing the tenor of "princes" along with it. Thus the princes of panegyric are exposed as madmen, "Persons, whose natural Reason hath admitted great Revolutions" (162), who should not be surprised at revolution in their states. The assassination topos, so negative in panegyric, here becomes at least a necessary remedy, a cure for the "nothing" in Princes that drives them to bother their subjects: "In the midst of all these Projects and Preparations; a certain *State-Surgeon,* gathering the Nature of the Disease by these Symptoms, attempted the Cure, at one Blow performed the Operation, broke the Bag, and out flew the *Vapour;* nor did anything want to render it a complete Remedy, only, that the Prince unfortunately happened to Die in the Performance" (164). The reconciliation kings were expected to achieve is replaced by madmen each with "Parties after his particular Notions" (171), as exclusive, chauvinistic, and arbitrary as the other system-makers of *A Tale* or as "Learning" seems to be in the "Ode to the Athenians" for that matter: "Learning's little household did embark / With her world's fruitful system in her sacred Ark . . ." (12–13). Finally, the ceremonial, public aspect of panegyric, the feeling of spaciousness, of poet addressing a head of state before some vast national gathering, seems to be deliberately frustrated in the microcosmic Bedlam, with its representative "officers in a state, ecclesiastical, civil, and military," no longer strictly an analogy at all, but an identification.

1730: "DIRECTIONS FOR A BIRTHDAY SONG"

Analogy continues to be an issue in Swift's later poetry and in the poetry of many of his satirical successors, in particular Charles Churchill. Swift's encomiastic poems to Stella read like panegyrics deflected from public to private, like Dryden's *Eleonora,* which Dryden considered a satire on the times. His "Directions for a Birthday Song" continues to exploit, in the late 1720s, many of the same panegyrical topoi encountered earlier, as well as the habit of self-conscious analogizing, here even more extreme, closer to the kind of epistemological breakdown at which satire becomes (I believe) impossible. The "Directions," with their advice-to-the-artist convention, reproduce at one significant remove the advice element of panegyric and hark back to Andrew Marvell's painter-poem satires of the 1660s, while they anticipate the way Churchill's "Gotham" advises an artist who is, moreover, the poet himself.

As Laurence Eusden, George's "real" laureate (and, therefore, poetical advisor), had died in 1730, it is not hard to see Swift's "Directions" as advice to Eusden's successor, a parody of the panegyric ("Threnodia Augustalis," for example) that would be written on the death of a monarch to his successor, written to his laureate instead. Notes in Rogers's edition indicate that the poem may have been written as early as 1729 or as late as 1733, and that the addressee was probably one Matthew Pilkington, who wrote a birthday ode to the king in 1730. A. B. England, when he states that "There is a central theme in the poem, of course, which has to do with the falsity of Eusden's odes" (108), actually does the poem an injustice, I think, because its theme is so much more, signification itself, everything and nothing at all. Like much "late" eighteenth-century satire, its lateness is largely a function of its rather cerebral, analogical, and even *epistemological* themes.

I divide the "Directions" into four sections: (1) a list of gods dealing, as more-or-less unsatisfactory vehicles, with George II (1–104); (2) a passage on encomium or, more precisely, *mock*-encomium (105–50); (3) lines on Caroline and Frederick, Prince of Wales (151–208) in which the King's relatives appear to have "usurped" the tenor of the poem; and (4) a passage on names (Hanover, George, Brunswick, Hesse Darmstadt, Guelph, Caroline, Sabrina, Medway, Thames, Albion, Nassau, Walpole, etc.) (209–82). In other words, the whole poem is organized around problems of signification, in particular *naming*. It has been described as "rambling" in the manner of Restoration satire, but one could easily argue that its structure reflects something contingent, catch-as-catch-can, about its subject, which is both George and his dynasty and how to praise George and his dynasty. At the same time its four sections describe a carefully plotted, thematic movement away from

George and Caroline, the King and Queen, toward G, E, O, R, G, E, C, A, R, O, L, I, N, and E.

In other words, as in the Brothers' construction of vehicles for which there is no tenor (like S.H.O.U.L.D.E.R), in the "Directions" there is a similar movement away from sense toward nonsense, from words as representations of reality to words as representations of the stuff of which, in a reductive sense, reality is made—or just of representations.

After a suggestion that George might have been born without a mother ("And should it be your hero's case / To have both male and female race" [5–6]) the first section busies itself about finding a signifier, a god that can represent George. Gods seem to pass by in burlesque theatrical review ("Your hero now another Mars is / Makes mighty armies turn their arses" [29–30] or "Dismissing Mars it next must follow / Your conqueror is become Apollo" [57–8]) but, like even words themselves eventually, none of them is seen to be adequate (that is, sufficiently inadequate) to express George's virtue.

When Swift advises the "birthday bard" how to praise Queen Caroline and other members of George's family ("breed"), quantity is used to remind us of absent quality. Goddesses like Venus are said to be six thousand years old when in fact they are immortal and ageless; this gives the poet the chance to remark that Caroline "hardly fifty odd is" (162), as if what were nothing to a goddess were not "middle aged" to a woman. The repetition of three is a similar joke: "she hath graces of her own: / Three graces by Lucina brought her, / Just three; and every grace a daughter" (164–66). The real graces (Anne, Amelia, and Caroline) were notoriously ugly. The comparison of Mary and Louisa to Hebe ("patterns of youth and beauty") is a negative reflection on Caroline, as Hebe's mother, Juno, was fat. As a Cynthia unwholesomely married to her brother Apollo, she has usurped George's obviously very weak sun.

The poem's steadily mounting tensions between vehicle and tenor, signifier and signified are brought near to breaking in the last section, which reads like a mock-panegyric addressed to Caroline (and other members of George's family), until one remembers that the George and Caroline addressed are not rulers or even people but names, and that this section is therefore a panegyric to certain combinations of letters that will sound (one cannot say good) in the "birthday poet's" poem (or in a musical setting by "Mister Handel"). Their very names are inimical to poetry and therefore inexpressible in it: "A skilful critic justly blames / Hard, tough, cramp, guttural, harsh, stiff names" (209-10). The good old English names are also worn out: "Albion's cliffs are out at heel" (244), but in this exhaustion there is a telling correspondence, since the country itself is exhausted. The Queen's name is analyzed phonetically, then addressed in lieu of Caroline herself: "May Caroline continue long, / Forever fair and young—in song" (233–34). What words are in Caroline's song is no more than what her body is in decomposition:

> What though the royal carcass must
> Squeezed in a coffin turn to dust;
> These elements her name compose
> Like atoms are exempt from blows. (235–8)

Caroline "sung" will continue as long as Caroline "dung," because her song itself has been decomposed into phonetic elements as eternal as chemicals and as nugatory.

1760: CHARLES CHURCHILL

Roughly thirty years after Swift's panegyric, the genre was renewed by the peculiar circumstances of the start of George III's reign—the facts that George was perceived by Churchill as a would-be despot, and that his principal advisor was a Scot and a Stuart. In reviving this kind of writing Churchill inherits not only its rhetorical topoi and formal arrangements, but also its preoccupation with aspects of signification, with analogizing and naming. These continue to have political as well as epistemological implications.

Like the last lines of Swift's "Directions," the first few lines of *Gotham* (1764) are about *naming*, and the arbitrary—and proprietary—effect of it. Imperialists' claim to the New World is no less shaky than Churchill's claim to England for naming it Gotham. The name is significant in other ways, of course, since (a footnote tells us) "Gotham is a parish six miles south of Nottingham, proverbial for the simplicity of its inhabitants, a simplicity that is said to have been simulated in order to avert the anger of a king" (n. 308).[3] There is then, at the outset of the poem, in the preoccupation with naming, in the concern with the arbitrariness of the relationship between signifiers and their signifieds, an *epistemological* focus to Churchill's panegyric that is characteristic of latter-day epideictic writing and which leads to a rather bewildering confusion of tenors and vehicles, revolving around the idea of kingship. Already it is unclear whether Churchill's king is a vehicle for the abstract goodness of kingship (the *optimus* of princeps), for George III, for the native chiefs who sell their people's country "for a bit of glass" (44), or for Churchill himself.[4]

Perhaps the ultimate in arbitrary signification (with all the appropriate political connotations) is the colonizers' planting of Christ's cross, "his royal master's name thereon engraved" (19), upon an island they wish to enslave. There is nothing Christian about the process of colonization, and there is nothing of the royal colonizer about Christ. As a flattering vehicle or an insulted tenor, the cross stands for both the arbitrariness that imposes and the arbitrariness that is imposed on, that is *both* vehicle and tenor. Obviously, in some ways it too is just another vehicle for George III, as the last constitutional monarch to really reign, himself something of an imposed on imposition. That there might be nothing kingly about capitalist exploitation or capitalistic about George, would only make him more instrumental for capitalism.[5]

Along with a counterfeit cross and crown go pastors who cannot read or write; subsequently, the gospel itself has lost its proper tenor and become just another vehicle of oppression:

> Pastors she [Europe] sends to help them in their need,
> Some who can't write, with others who can't read;
> And on sure grounds the Gospel pile to rear,
> Sends missionary felons every year. (69–72)

The gulf between signifiers and signifieds will eventually be bridged by revolutionary violence, when the virtues will, from the standpoint of the oppressor, return as the daemonic inversions or vices of the "ten times more the sons of Hell" (88), because directed against themselves. Prudence, wisdom, and faith will return but as cunning, resentment, and stoic resolve all directed against those who banished them initially, who created and subsequently exploited the gulf between their appearance and the reality.

While one can argue that Churchill discredits European claims to the New World by likening them to his own arbitrariness in calling England—or some never-never land—Gotham in order to make himself king of it,[6]

> Europe discover'd India first; I found
> My right to Gotham on the self-same ground;
> I first discovered it . . .
> . . . .
> With Europe's rights my kindred rights I twine;
> Hers be the Western world, be Gotham mine. (103–10)

one can argue the other way, that Churchill substantiates his personal arbitrariness by seeing it as established on the same footing as no less than half the globe. Churchill seems to confirm *his* private willfulness at least as much as he denies *their* public arbitrariness. Epistemological acts of violence seem to be as good for individuals as they are bad for states. Thus, after discrediting Europe, he proceeds to credit himself, and for nearly the same things:

> All instruments, self-acted, at my name
> Shall pour forth harmony, and loud proclaim,
> Loud but yet sweet, to the according globe,
> My praises, whilst gay nature, in a robe,

> A coxcomb doctor's robe, to the full sound
> Keeps time, like Boyce, and the world dances round. (153–58)

The refrain merely insists on the point. The subsequent passage, a kind of temporal procession poem uniting praise from different age groups, continues to develop this theme of positive naming and even delightful arbitrariness:

> Infancy, straining backward from the breast
> Tetchy and wayward . . .
> . . . .
> Shall murmur forth my name, whilst at his hand
> Nurse stands interpreter through Gotham's land. (165–72)

His arbitrariness stands for that arbitrariness in all of us, which is universally an expression of freedom and therefore a good thing in itself. The troubling thing throughout is that this celebratory freedom or freedom worth celebrating is never too distinct from the kind of arbitrariness that obviously deserves deploring.

The second part of *Gotham* develops the theme of signification by dwelling at first on problems of poetic composition and craft or, as Churchill puts it (rather nicely),

> when to use the powers
> Of Ornament, and how to place the flowers,
> . . . .
> To make proud Sense against her nature bend,
> And wear the chains of Rhyme, yet call her friend. (17–28)

He divides poets into those who stress vehicles at the expense of tenors, or what he calls "sense,"

> Who make it all their business to describe
> No matter whether in or out of place;
> Studious of finery, and fond of lace . . . (30–32)

and those who stress tenors, who "depend / On sense to bring them to their journey's end" (55–56). The first he likens, again with characteristic reference to a panegyrical topos, the union of ceremony and power, to "idle monarch boys":

> Neglecting things of weight, they sigh for toys;
> Give them the crown, the sceptre, and the robe,
> Who will may take the power, and rule the globe. (50–52)

and the second he compares to monarchs who, though they may have power, lack popularity (so may not have power long):

> Sense, mere dull, formal Sense, in this gay town,
> Must have some vehicle to pass her down;
> Nor can she for an hour insure her reign,
> Unless she brings fair Pleasure in her train.(73–76)

Though it is often confused with the austerity of its presentation, virtue itself, which ought ultimately to be the poet's subject, is neither austere nor otherwise but "acts from love" and finally seems to require no vehicle: "In her own full and perfect blaze of light / Virtue breaks forth too strong for human sight" (107–08). Churchill at times seems painfully conscious of the fact that he is dealing with moral absolutes (for I think the same could implicitly be said for vice), which can only be approximated by analogy. The ideal for what epideictic might do is *Christlike*, a kind of ultimate in terms of word made flesh: "Like God made man, she lays her glory by, / And beams mild comfort on the ravish'd eye" (113–14). The more practicable model is that of the greatest English writers who "held the golden mean" (144) between sense and grace, tenor and vehicle. Churchill finds himself, not surprisingly, among those whose fail conspicuously at such a compromise, whose thoughts often fail to get adequate expression so are likened, significantly, to children who may not live long enough to be baptized, or in other words to get a name.

Increasingly, though, in the second book of *Gotham* Churchill appears to side with the tenor over the vehicle, with the things named against the act of naming itself. Rather than be bound up with the words themselves, his meaning seems to transcend them as the freedom and wildness bound up with "loose Digression" (205) and "gay Description" (211). Of course, it is arguable that this apparent siding with the tenor over the vehicle is really no such thing, just a siding with different tenors of different vehicles. But clearly there is at least an important change in the nature of the vehicle from the word to something else, larger and harder to pin down. And clearly whatever side Churchill is really on, he wishes to come out strongest for meaning over whatever means, as when he describes his own poetry (with rather precise naming, one must note): "Materials rich, though rude, inflamed with thought, / Though more by fancy than by judgment wrought" (227–28).

This preference of tenor over vehicle is identified with detestation of George III's minister, the Earl of Bute, since that—he tells us finally—is really his meaning (and it excuses all).[7] Thus the whole second half of the book compromises a kind of reprise of Stuart history, and a revision of the kind of poetry associated with it, as Churchill "pays back" the Stuarts for all the lies told about them in panegyrics, in another panegyric addressed (ostensibly) to himself. Of course, this is also a screen for getting at George III, as Churchill himself, as king of Gotham, becomes a vehicle for the King of England, and Churchill's detestation of Bute an example for George to follow: "Cursed be the cause whence Gotham's evils spring, / Though that cursed cause be found in Gotham's king" (275–76).

The arbitrariness of naming is given its strongest political corollary in Churchill's seemingly double vision of Charles I. On one hand Charles is king so "could do no wrong" (536); on the other he is clearly a liar and a wrongdoer of the first order. The arbitrariness of this act of naming is best understood historically, and indeed the violent discontinuity of the king's name or vehicle with the king's tenor or real self seems a direct consequence of that other violent discontinuity that separated his head from his body: "hadst thou laid down in death / As in a sleep, thy name by Justice borne / On the four winds, had been in pieces torn" (542–44). Not inappropriately, arbitrary naming here defends arbitrary rule, and even moves that other arbitrary namer, Charles Churchill, who regarded Charles I as a martyr even though he knew better.

Finally, when he usurps George III as Gothamite King, naming is obviously tinged with the absurdity of presumption: "Will I, or can I, on a fair review, / As I assume that name, deserve it too?" (51–52). The crown is itself a deceptive vehicle that "glistens" (106) but is "lined with thorns" (112), and the king worthy of the name must be Christlike in more ways than one:

> Be it my task to seek, nor seek in vain,
> Not only how to live, but how to reign,
> And to those virtues which from reason spring,
> And grace the man, join those which grace the king. (219–22)

He must avoid being a tenorless vehicle, a "royal cipher" (260), a disgrace of "All that is royal in his name" (316), the effect of which is to make other names equally arbitrary and unsuited, especially "Rebellion" (303), which then becomes a bad name for a good thing, for an act that is not rebellion at all but rather national conservation. One way to avoid this is, apparently, to read this poem, since he tells us (561–65) that as Patriot King history will become his special study. While he must not forget that "monarchs are for action made" (474), he must also demonstrate an ability to deal successfully with the very epistemological problems posed here; he must do generally what he says he must do with religion: "let me find out there / What's form, what's essence" (581–82).

If these are the things the Patriot King must do, then Churchill by his own admission possessed of a marked preference for tenor over vehicle, for meaning over means, would be too radical and, in a specific sense, arbitrary for the job. Careful sifting of the wheat from the chaff is clearly not for Churchill; of the three brothers of *A Tale,* he is closer to Jack than Peter or even Martin. The impartial reading of history would have been similarly inimical to him, as he might have expected us to notice. It would be splendid to name oneself Patriot King, but how could one know? Yet, as Bertelsen indicates, knowledge is offered as the panacea for the ills of monarchy.[8] His response is a significantly more offhand (and even positive) version of Swift's Hack's "promise" to the "truly learned" reader everywhere that *here* he will "find sufficient Matter to employ his Speculations for the Rest of his Life": "Something I do myself, and something too, / If they can do it, leave for them to do" (187–90).

Panegyric has finally been revised by having its conventional analogical machinery reversed. The poet whose whole poem should in analogical terms serve as a vehicle for the king, has become the meaning of his poem; vehicle has become tenor. Vincent Carretta's point (in his recent *George III and the Satirists*) about the distinction that continued to be made in the eighteenth century between the king's body natural and body political ties in neatly with these analogical reversals that characterize epideictic writing (increasingly satirical) in general and this poem in particular (Carretta 1–40). Instead of the body natural embellishing the body political, the body political illustrates a body natural increasingly gross and material. Instead of helping us to comprehend spiritual goodness, analogy enables or forces us to fathom physical depravity. Churchill mockingly accouters in all the old spiritual panoply, not the king's body natural but his own more grossly natural body that, given his notorious bearlike ugliness and ill-health, lends a suitable (and I think typical) ambiguity to the form of "constitutional" monarchy expressed here.

From panegyrists and satirists alike Churchill inherits a tradition of epistemological satire, of self-conscious and arbitrary analogical signification to which he is at least ambivalent. While Churchill himself manifests some of the hack's (even Jack's) potential for arbitrariness, he indicates nothing of his capacity for certainty. Arbitrariness of signification is positive for Churchill precisely because it is, almost paradoxically, a free act (for the namer; it may be Churchill's innovation that *anyone* can be a namer), whereas with the hack it seems to be imposed from without, part of some crazy and inhumane gnostic system in which most of us would only be disciples.

Epistemological satire is concerned with important sources of knowledge like analogy, and ultimately, by virtue of being satire, with an important kind of knowledge, knowledge of evil. The disadvantages of analogy, its reductiveness and its approximateness, truly disadvantages in terms of knowledge of the good, become—at least for a time—advantages in terms of knowledge of evil, which is characteristically reductive—and nebulous—anyway.

In an essay dating from the mid-seventies Irvin Ehrenpreis argues that eighteenth-century writing is characterized by what amounts to an ease and confidence of analogizing, a "conception of style as the frame of meaning or (even worse) as ornament applied to meaning" (5). This is truer of early eighteenth-century satire than of later, when ease and confidence appear to have degenerated into their opposites. The self-conscious analogizing of Swift and Churchill exhibits both an impatience with its own epistemology, and a failure to discover a better alternative. Satire, according to Leon Guilhamet and many others, typically expresses dissatisfaction with the very arrangements it is nostalgic for. Eighteenth-century satire ridicules the conventions of a discredited genre, panegyric, while exploiting them to expose current abuses. The object of its ridicule and the object of its nostalgia are briefly, curiously one, and its expression as part of the same kind of writing, is only sharper for this awareness: a self-reflective art form, written in obvious awareness of the full implications of its subject matter and of the strengths and limitations of its characteristic means of representation.

NOTES

1. See Keith J. Holyoak, "An Analogical Framework for Literary Interpretation," *Poetics* 11 (1982): 105–26. His terms *target* and *base* roughly correspond to Richards's *tenor* and *vehicle*.
2. See Michael McKeon, *The Origins of the English Novel 1600–1740* (London: Century Hutchinson Ltd, 1987) 61. McKeon remarks that the hack's "dismay at superficial and deep reading alike is one version of the central problem of the *Tale*, the untenable choice between being a fool and a knave." Such distinctions are misleading since for him "deep" reading is the identification of the tenor with a vehicle to which it is only superficially similar. He pretends to offer two alternatives, but really offers only one.
3. See Bertelsen, *The Nonsense Club*, 224.
4. See Peter M. Briggs, "'The brain, too finely wrought': Mind Unminded in Churchill's Satires'," *Modern Language Studies* 14 (1984): 39–53 for a discussion of Churchill's "wavering epistemology, a faltering ability to grasp his satiric objects *and* his own values firmly" (40).
5. Many of panegyrical topoi can be found in *Gotham*, particularly in "Book III." More generally, and more significantly, panegyric is about the proper relationship between prince and people. According to Lance Bertelsen in *The Nonsense Club: Literature and Popular Culture, 1749–1764* (Oxford: Clarendon P, 1986), this is the subject of at least two books of *Gotham*: "a discussion of the proper relationship of the monarch, his ministers, and the people." In his treatment of what he terms "middling culture" (4), Bertelsen should give more acknowledgment to the specific rhetorical contribution, as many of the topoi and formal arrangements of panegyric get translated into popular culture by writers like Churchill.
6. As does Ronald Hatch in his "Charles Churchill and the Poetry of 'Chartered Freedom'," *English Studies in Canada* 15 (1989): 277–87.
7. Bertelsen calls this "a rather unimpressive transition" (228), but I imagine it would have worked with the contemporary audience for whom the Earl of Bute was a real concern.
8. See Bertelsen, *The Nonsense Club*, 230.

WORKS CITED

Bertelsen, Lance. *The Nonsense Club: Literature and Popular Culture, 1749–1764.* Oxford: Clarendon P, 1986.

Briggs, Peter M. "'The brain, too finely wrought': Mind Unminded in Churchill's Satires," *Modern Language Studies* 14 (1984): 39–53.

Carretta, Vincent. *George III and the Satirists from Hogarth to Byron.* Athens: U of Georgia P, 1990.

Clark, John R. *Form and Frenzy in Swift's "Tale of a Tub."* Ithaca and London: Cornell UP, 1970.

Deingott, Nilli. "Analogy as a Critical Term: A survey and Some Comments." *Style* 19 (1985): 227–41.

England, A. B. *Energy and Order in the Poetry of Swift.* London and Toronto: Associated UP, 1980.

Fischer, John Irwin. *On Swift's Poetry.* Gainesville: UP of Florida, 1978.

Garrison, James D. *Dryden and the Tradition of Panegyric.* Berkeley: U of California P, 1975.

Grant, Douglas, ed. *The Poetical Works of Charles Churchill.* Oxford: Clarendon P, 1956,

Harth, Phillip. *Swift and Anglican Rationalism.* Chicago: U of Chicago P, 1961.

Hatch, Ronald. "Charles Churchill and the Poetry of 'Chartered Freedom'." *English Studies in Canada* 15 (1989): 277–87.

Holyoak, Keith J. "An Analogical Framework for Literary Interpretation." *Poetics* 11 (1982): 105–26.

Lockwood, Thomas. *Post-Augustan Satire: Charles Churchill and Satirical Poetry, 1750–1800.* Seattle and London: U of Washington P, 1979.

McKeon, Michael. *The Origins of the English Novel 1600–1740.* London: Century Hutchinson Ltd, 1987.

Richards, I. A. *The Philosophy of Rhetoric.* Oxford: Oxford UP, 1936.

Rosenheim, Edward W. "Swift's Ode to Sancroft: Another Look." *Modern Philology* 73 (1976): S24–S39.

———. *Swift and the Satirist's Art.* Chicago: U of Chicago P, 1963.

Smith, Raymond J. *Charles Churchill.* Twayne's English Authors Ser. 197. Boston: G. K. Hall & Co., 1977.

Swift, Jonathan. *Jonathan Swift: The Complete Poems.* Ed. Pat Rogers. New Haven and London: Yale UP, 1983.

———. *A Tale of a Tub.* Eds. A. C. Guthkelch and D. Nichol Smith. Oxford: Oxford UP, 1958.

Vickers, Brian. "Analogy Versus Identity: The Rejection of Occult Symbolism, 1580-1680." *Occult and Scientific Mentalities in the Renaissance.* Ed. Brian Vickers. Cambridge: Cambridge UP, 1984.

———. "Swift and the Baconian Idol." *The World of Jonathan Swift.* Ed. Brian Vickers. Cambridge: Cambridge UP, 1968.

Williams, Arthur S. "Panegyric Decorum in the Reigns of William III and Anne." *Journal of British Studies* 29 (1981): 56–67.

Wyrick, Deborah Baker. *Jonathan Swift and the Vested Word.* Chapel Hill and London: The U of North Carolina P, 1988.

·7·

English Academic Satire from the Middle Ages to Postmodernism: Distinguishing the Comic from the Satiric

Christian Gutleben

From a puristic point of view, satire and comedy can comfortably enough be set apart because they belong—or at least used to belong—to two different generic spheres, namely and respectively, poetry and drama. Speaking of the satiric and the comic hugely complicates the problem of differentiation insofar as these terms no longer refer to a genre or a form but to a mode or even a mood.[1] Since there are no formal markers specifically ascribed to the comic or the satiric, the distinction between the two necessitates then an intricate analysis of modality, tonality, and narrativity.

In twentieth-century postmodernist fiction, the generic field in which the satiric and comic modes are predominantly embedded is naturally the novel, whose hegemony seems ever-increasing. The novel, which originally derives from comedy and satire, has now altogether appropriated the two modes. The inborn subversive, hence satiric, potential of the novel has fully realized itself in the postmodern era, which violates the ultimate taboos and flaunts the chaotic nature of the postmodern condition—including the chaotic nature of the postmodern novel. But the fiction of postmodern times is also fundamentally playful both in its production and in the task it sets for the reader; as such it partakes of a literature of enjoyment that touches on the comic.

The contemporary campus novel (also called academic or university novel), appears as an ideal field for the exploration of the relationships between postmodernism and the combination of the comic and the satiric because the co-presence of both modes seems inscribed in this genre written by academics about academics. Indeed the disclosure of the foibles of a secluded world appears to link up with the denunciatory aspect of the satiric mode, and the pure funniness of self-derision as well as the ludic exploitation of language seem to correspond to the emphasis on laughter associated with the comic mode. The association of comic and satiric elements in the campus novel creates an ambiguous and polyvalent tension that, partially at least, accounts for the formidable success of the genre,[2] and that can be traced to its origins where pure comedy and formal satire both stand out prominently.

If academics can be assimilated to the learned and to scholars, then their mockery in literature seems at least as old as classical Greek literature since Plato in *Republic* (Book IV) and in *The Symposium* stresses their uselessness and their corruption. Scholars are also debunked in *The New Testament*, and, more to the point, they were already the butts of Old Comedy, as in Aristophanes' *The Clouds*, as well as of formal satire, as in Horace's *Satires* and *Epistles*. Interestingly, the mood does not appear to be directly dependent on the genre, since Aristophanes' play turns out to be more satirical in tone than Horatian satire.

In the British context of fiction dealing with academics, in order to assess the relative importance of the comic and the satiric, the difference has to be established between literature stemming from without universities and literature produced from within universities. In the former case, the point of view being external and the purpose being to expose academics' follies, the episodes concerning the university acquire almost automatically the accusatorial coloration of satire. Two series of tales, *The Jests of Scoggin* (1565) and *The Merie Tales of Skelton*, epitomize this treatment of Oxford and Cambridge in these typical statements: "Heere a man can see that money is better than learning" (Hazlitt, II, 68) and "A Mayster of Arte / Is not worthe a Farte" (Morris 38). The taste for caricature shown in the latter quotation is not the least of the hereditary traits transmitted by the original university fiction tinged with satire.

In these instances, the satiric must needs be restricted to the mood, since, as the titles indicate, the works are written in the formal mode of the tales. In addition, as can also be inferred from the titles, the satiric tendency is matched by a comic tendency inasmuch as the overall purpose aims at "jest" and merriment. When the comic and the satiric cohabit, the former inexorably softens the latter. In the case of fiction dealing with academics, the detailed lingering on vices and excesses seems a fictional tool used for the sheer amusement of the reader. The lot of the academics, cloistered as they were, was beyond the public's concern; the desire for satiric amendment or reform was therefore never a temptation for literature proceeding from outside the university.

As regards the few traditional comedies referring to academe, the dominant comic mode seems even more to exclude satiric objectives. Nevertheless, the mocking tinges of the satiric mood stand out vividly in Shakespeare's portrait of the pedant Holofernes (*Love's Labours Lost*) and in Jonson's caricature of the ineffectual student Fungoso (*Every Man out of his Humour*). Here again though, the concentration is on eccentricities (of speech and of behavior) not on ideology; the result is increased laughter not fundamental questioning. Considering that the university as a system is never taken up, let alone challenged, and that the main concern is the disclosure of the academics' cranks and pranks, the satire of early university fiction appears restricted to a satire of characters while the comic remains the paramount goal. The satiric as tonality seems subservient to the comic as modality.

Not so in the case of formal satire. When it deals with the idleness and the fatuity of the well-to-do of academe, as in Satire 6, Book II of Joseph Hall's *Virgidemiarum, Sixe Bookes* (1597–1598) or in John Marston's *The Metamorphosis of Pigmalion's Image and Certaine Satyres* (1598), formal satire becomes bitter and sardonic in the manner of a Juvenalian model whose ruggedness and ruthlessness was conceived to proceed from satire's link with uncouth satyrs.[3] Formal satire, though short-lived in England, nevertheless left a lasting imprint on subsequent university fiction, which adopted its unpolished and indeed obscene tones. Moreover, campus novel narrators seem closely akin to the persona of the Renaissance satiric speaker as characterized by Alvin Kernan: "It was fairly standard for Elizabethan and Jacobean authors to present their satirists as men who in their younger days had been overly curious scholars and who on entering the world discovered that their bookish wisdom was of no value. They react by becoming parasites, flatterers, and satirists" (148). The traces of pure satire that can be found in today's university fiction appear to be specifically expressed in the disillusionment of the narrative (and/or authorial) voice.

In the case of literature about the university produced from within the university, that is, in the case of endogenous literature,[4] there appears in the sixteenth century a series of intramural productions in which the satiric becomes ironic partaking as much of self-praise as of self-criticism. Indeed, these academic comedies[5] never were intended for the general public: written by academics about academics, they were also performed privately for academics. When the addressers and the addressees form a coterie of initiates, self-derision and self-parody come to be the dominant modes and the satiric seems to be invalidated. In such a case, self-mockery becomes self-flattery and the satiric becomes panegyric.

The main feature of these academic plays, namely their enactment behind closed doors, is also encountered in another academic entertainment, the vastly underrated college saltings. Because the tradition was oral and very few transcriptions have been discovered,[6] college saltings have so far not been taken into account in the genesis of university fiction. Yet these jocular ceremonies performed in the colleges of Oxford and Cambridge, which "are recorded from as early as 1510 to as late as 1639" (Nelson 732), must have prepared more than one young man for the writing of witty literature about the university. This practice consisted of both initiators and initiatees improvising pithy verse on the topic of college life. The full description of the ritual is owed to the pioneer work of Roslyn Richek:

> A salting is an initiation of freshmen or sophomores into their college by a senior. . . . All the undergraduates of the college holding the initiation were assembled in Hall, where certain senior sophisters were selected as "Fathers." Each Father . . . enacted a kind of burlesque with his Sons of the public exercises and subscriptions to the various oaths required for admission to the university. . . . Because of the many references to college life and the quibbles on what is rather esoteric material to many of us today, we must conclude that the initiates would not only understand these allusions but find humour in them. . . . Because saltings are shows which by definition do not follow any classical rules of genre, it is not surprising to find a variety of styles in this patchwork of oratory in which the Father uses the unifying framework of naming his Sons after dishes while he shows his wit and talent for entertaining by frequent digressions and by as many allusions to the immediate past and present as he can manage. . . [Available] saltings are incomplete, perhaps because some of each speech was *extempore* and because the Son's spontaneous responses could not be included (Richek, 105; 110–12).

Those who did poorly at this rhetorical exercise were compelled to drink a quantity of salted beer, which according to Richek explains the name *salting*, but Nelson maintains that "they probably owe their name to the Latin *sal*, meaning wit, facetiousness, sarcasm, more than to the literal use of salt in the ceremony" (Nelson 996). It appears from this explanation that the saltings prefigure university fiction not only through their main theme (the parody of university customs) and some of their techniques (wit and esoteric quibbles), but also, and fundamentally, through their self-centeredness and self-reflexiveness that forebodes the essential narcissism and metafictionality of the campus novel.

The satiric, in the saltings, is confined to the personal in the form of the ritual scoffing to which each student is submitted. Here again though, the mockery is tinged with the sense of elitist approbation and the satiric vanishes into convivial comedy. A community of initiates has nothing to accuse itself of, nor to denounce to itself, therefore, the literature it produces for itself cannot be accusatory nor denunciatory, in which case it cannot be satirical. Because they are directed inwardly and because they have no divulgation purport, the saltings and the academic comedies turn out to be positively antisatiric subgenres. It appears then that literature cannot be satiric without a public that can be made indignant. Consequently, one of the conditions for literature to be satiric is that it must needs be centrifugal, or, in other words, the satiric is incompatible with centripetal literature.

Unlike saltings, the campus novel would be disseminated into the general public and so departed from the intramural type of literature. It maintained the tradition established by formal satire of forcibly caricaturing its characters and of writing in an unceremonious style. On the other hand, the campus novel did, after the fashion of the saltings, go on exploiting self-parody and arcane playful language; it also seems to have retained a sense of self-satisfaction.

➤┅╫╫┥   ┝╫╫┅◄

In the course of the seventeenth and eighteenth centuries fiction dealing (still partially) with the university concentrated on sparkling descriptions of Oxford and Cambridge debauchery—which, according to the historical documents on the subject, was at its peak at that time.[7] The passages dedicated to the subject followed the examples of formal satire and of character-writing since they revelled in caricatured portraits of dissipated academics. As can be inferred from the most famous examples—Stephen Penton's *The Guardian's Instruction, or, The Gentleman's Romance* (1688), Henry Fielding's *The History of Tom Jones, A Foundling* (1749), Francis Coventry's *The History of Pompey the Little* (1751), Tobias Smollett's *The Adventures of Peregrine Pickle* (1751)—the treatment of the university was dominated by a satire of characters. I wish to insist though that the satiric was never extended to the fundamentally ideological in the works of fiction,[8] and it consisted mainly in using academics as laughingstocks, thereby reinforcing the diverting quality of the works in which it was exploited.

But a gallery of satiric portraits cannot in itself constitute a novelistic framework; the lack of dramatic evolution, increased as it was by the closed and static quality of college setting, had to be compensated by a structural dynamism for the campus novel to be born. This impetus was to come from the utilization of romance. Indeed, the first true university novel, John Gibson Lockhart's *Reginald Dalton: A Story of English University Life,* originated in 1823 from the coupling of romance and satire. The satiric is obvious in the detailed accounts of student Chisney's uproariousness. The framing presence of romance is particularly apparent in the structure of the novel that aptly describes "the cyclical movement of descent into a night world [here the nightmare of university dissolution] and a return to the idyllic world, or to some symbol of it [here the marriage]" (Frye 54). This final phase of anagnorisis recalls of course the dénouement of comedy, which follows a similar movement from discord to harmony. The structure of reconciliation, which is common to romance and comedy, conveys then to *Reginald Dalton* and to the early campus novels built on this model a conservative coloration that is much closer to the conformism of the comic than to the subversion of the satiric.

Not only the structures but also the objectives of romance and comedy seem to intersect: at the heart of both can be found the purpose of entertainment. By adopting the mode of the romance, the first campus novel and its followers moved away from the sharply satiric and converged toward the divertingly comic. Indeed, when the overall design of a work is recreational, satiric revolt dissolves into comic acceptance and we reach the paradox that the satiric moods sustain and increase the comic mode.

The comic mode of later nineteenth-century academic novels accentuated itself in two further ways: the organization of the themes and the choice of the narrator. Clearly, the mishaps and misdemeanors of college life made up the thematic body of the university novel, which soon became a loosely connected series of practical jokes. A boyish humor therefore characterized its comic mode, manifesting itself through a sequence of farcical episodes including set scenes such as this typical chapter heading from the most famous comic university novel of the period, Cuthbert Bede's *The Adventures of Mr Verdant Green, An Oxford Freshman (1853):* "Mr Verdant Green endeavors to keep his spirits up by pouring spirits down."

To the comic modality secured by the set of themes corresponds a comic tonality induced by the figure of the narrator. Far from condemning the students' licentiousness, the narrator reproduces it in his/her own narration, which becomes itself festive. The thematic unrestraint is then transposed at the level of discourse and the quest for pleasure contaminates both the form and the content. As the narrator of one of the pioneering novels explains, the narrative is intended "for my own pleasure and to gratify—I don't conceal it— that vanity to which as an Oxford man, I have a right to lay claim" (Hewlett I

130). Transformed into a trickster of narration, the narrator plays with the narratee, the characters, and even kindred works of fiction. Thus, in Reade's *Liberty Hall, Oxon,* the narrator mockingly introduces a character as a double of Verdant Green: "Tims, likewise freshman, was a contrast *verdant* and vivid. I cannot pretend to follow him through all the mishaps into which he was flung by his own folly, and by the childishness of others. . . . Such incidents have been penned by a genius [Cuthbert Bede, of course] whose brilliant versatility I should tremble to compete with" (Reade, I, 91). When narrative playfulness extends into intertextuality, the ludic postmodernism of twentieth-century fiction seems very proximate indeed.

The evolution towards an increasing narrative jocularity can best be seen in Max Beerbohm's *Zuleika Dobson* (1911). In that outstanding academic novel the comic originates in the thematic (i.e., the havoc wreaked among Oxford students by femme fatale Zuleika Dobson), and is entirely contained in the wit and irony of the narrative presentation. Primarily language-conscious, as is befitting, the narrator sarcastically comments on the (im)propriety of his/her characters' speeches, as in the following instance when young Clarence has to inform his sister that her beloved Duke has sacrificed his life (in the honor, naturally, of Zuleika): "'The Duke, he's drowned himself,' presently gasped the Messenger. Blank verse, yes, so far as it went; but delivered without the slightest regard for rhythm, and composed in stark defiance of those laws which should regulate the breaking of bad news" (212). The unorthodox mocking of one's characters and the presence of a pointed linguistic analysis within the language of the narrator both engage in the sort of game with the very material of fiction that would be played by any postmodernist novel. In a similar instance, the narrator exposes the landlady's language, adding this time an ironic suggestion of self-flattery: "In some such welter of homely phrase (how foreign to these classic pages!) did Mrs Batch utter her pain" (190). To the rhetorics of self-advertising the narrator adds the rhetorics of enticement, guiding the "sensitive reader" through the narrative and explaining each step thereof: "I am loath to interrupt my narrative at this rather exciting moment—a moment when the quick, tense style, exemplified in the last paragraph but one, is so very desirable. But in justice to the gods I must pause to put in a word of excuse for them" (207). Playfulness seems at its peak here with the teasing of the narratee, the provocative delaying of the story, the stressing of the stylistic skill, the disruptive self-reference of the narrative act, and the facetious boastfulness of the godlike narrator. The obvious satisfaction the narrator finds in his narrative creation endows the latter with a sprightliness that seems definitely wide apart from the dissentious satiric.

Another precursory game played by *Zuleika Dobson* is the deliberate blurring of illusion and reality. The narrator discusses and mixes with the gods

(Clio and Zeus personally give him the gift of omniscience) and as such becomes a figure of myth. But s/he also recounts an actual meeting with "a writer, a Mr Beerbohm" (76), which suggests a change of ontological level. Finally, s/he steps into the diegetic world and sits next to the heroine to analyze her state of mind—not unlike *The French Lieutenant's Woman's* narrator in chapter fifty-five of John Fowles's postmodernist novel par excellence. Gods, people, and characters, along with myth, reality, and fiction, are combined to create a new illusion, the illusion of the narrative sleight of hand.

Finally Beerbohm's novel foreshadows later university fiction in its revitalizing use of parody. *Zuleika Dobson* plays not only with its own material but also and foremost with the whole tradition of sentimental novels. This parodic text—or, to use Genette's terminology, the hypertext—harnesses, distorts, and remodels the parodied texts—or hypotexts—in order to convert stale conventions into a refreshed work of art. Parody works according to the ludic system,[9] *Zuleika Dobson* exacerbates the mawkishness of sentimental novels to the degree where the melodramatic swings over to the comic. It is this taste for literary ludism that later university fiction chooses to develop.

⇥⊹⊹⊹⊹⫷   ⫸⊹⊹⊹⊹⇤

After World War II the British campus novel enters the era of postmodernism and becomes associated with some of the distinguished practitioners of the new aesthetics: Malcolm Bradbury, David Lodge, David Caute, William Golding, David Benedictus, A. S. Byatt, Andrew Davies, Stephen Fry, Christine Brooke-Rose.[10] But the conception of postmodernism as a historical period is by far too restrictive ("postmodernism cannot simply be used as a synonym for the contemporary," [Hutcheon 4]), it has to be associated with "a style or a sensibility manifesting itself . . . in any creative endeavor which exhibits some element of self-consciousness and reflexivity. Fragmentation, discontinuity, indeterminacy, plurality, metafictionality, heterogeneity, intertextuality, decentering, dislocation, ludism: these are the common features such widely differing aesthetic practices are said to display" (Smyth 9). For our purpose it must be added that postmodernism is "inescapably political" (the phrase is Linda Hutcheon's) and that its fundamentally dismantling and decentering action seems resolutely satiric in nature. Lance Olsen demonstrated, for that matter, that when postmodernism is combined with the comic it becomes particularly subversive: "At the core of the comic vision . . . is a subversive impulse toward the dominant culture. Postmodernity, then, is a radically skeptical state of mind whose impulse is to decenter, detotalize and deconstruct. Because both the comic and the postmodern attempt to subvert all centers of authority and because they both ultimately *deride* univocal visions, toppling bigots, cranks, and pompous idiots as they go, they tend to complement each other well" (Olsen 23; 27; 31).

At the same time, and contradistinctively, postmodernism when it applies to the novel is illustrated by metafictional hide-and-seek, by metaleptic red herrings, by narrative snakes and ladders, by linguistic riddles, in short by literary ludism, which inclines toward a formal refinement that seems more akin to the enjoyable comic than to the disquieting satiric. In the case of the contemporary English academic novel the conflict between ludism and subversion within postmodernism seems to be settled in favor of the former mainly because of the absence of any radically postmodernist exemplar.

Indeed, even the most innovating English campus novels comply to a certain degree with the nonsubversive structures of reconciliation or at least of continuity. In David Caute's *The Women's Hour* the narrator ostentatiously uses some of the techniques of postmodernism, now putting the narratee in a position of narrative power ("the reader must decide whether Sidney has pocketed the book contract or not"), now defiantly contradicting her/his own narrative account by first telling the death of the protagonist and then bringing him back into the story: "you all thought I was savaged to death by two rottweilers, eh? Bad luck—alternative ending. May as well post-modern the postmoderns" (186; 269). The most prominent self-reflexive non sequitur appears in the end when the narrator sums up the unresolved enigmas of the plot and answers, tongue in cheek, by listing a series of totally unrelated facts such as the extinction of certain species of butterflies. Admittedly then, the narrator postmodernistically short-circuits the narrative closure of the novel, but the mere absence of conclusion does not transform the whole work into a radical gesture. Far from undermining the novel's basic center of authority, *The Women's Hour* unfolds in the tradition of the detective novel (with a clear progression from one focus of suspicion to another) and then progressively shifts to rather conventional slapstick comedy with tomato throwing, bottom spanking, and the magical intervention of an Arabian sheik—as rich in pounds as his English is poor. The structure of the novel reveals no narrative upheaval and no ontological questions; it is organized for the reader's entertainment—postmodernism being just the main tool used for this purpose. The disruptive course of postmodernism is then limited to the logicality and the finality of the *plot,* while the bulk of the novel is actuated by a traditionally comic, albeit derisive, *narrativity.*

In the case of Christine Brooke-Rose's *Textermination,* the most venturesome novel of its kind, the decentering and dislocation of fiction lies at the heart of both plot and narrativity. The frame of the novel is constituted by the Annual Convention of Prayer for Being (a clear parody of the huge MLA conferences) where academics meet hundreds of famous characters from all sorts of fictions to discuss the future of fictional characters. The (self-)deconstruction of the notion of character occurs then in the very course of the diegetic speeches as in this complaint voiced by Emma Woodhouse: "We are not read, and when read, we are read badly, we are not lived as we used to be, we are not identified with and fantasized, we are rapidly forgotten. Those of us who have the good fortune to be read by teachers, scholars and students are not read as we used to be read but analyzed as schemata, structures, functions within structures, logical and mathematical formulae, aporia, psychic movements, social significances and so forth" (25–26). Furthermore, the uncertain status of a character is literally illustrated in the story when some of the characters are suddenly dropped because they appear already on the lists of forgotten characters.

If the characters vanish under the reader's eyes, the same happens to the intradiegetic narrator who finds her name on the same list: "She can't go on. She doesn't exist" (105). The story of the novel's narration demonstrates then the precariousness of fictional status: character, narrator, and fiction in general, all depend upon the reader to exist; they have no ontological status of their own. Instead of allowing the reader to lapse into the comfort of reading a realistic story, *Textermination* confronts the reader with the disturbing mirror of her/his own responsibilities.

Again though, the structure of the novel conveys a sense of continuity that lightens the postmodernist disruption. In the closing chapter all the famous characters depart from the convention in pairs in a close parallel to the opening chapter where they arrived in the same company (Clarissa Harlowe with Lovelace, Emma with Mr. Elton . . .). In addition, these concluding pages are verbatim copyings from the initial pages, thus not only underlining the idea of a reproductive circle but even suggesting an absence of change, an immutability—at least for the characters who belong to the canons of literature. The identical extremities of the novel, both describing incongruous pairings of fictional characters, envelop *Textermination* into a sort of parenthesis that appears more analogous to a joyous hiatus than to an undermining project.

What is true for experimental novels such as *The Women's Hour* and *Textermination* is even more true for Bradbury's, Lodge's, and Byatt's more traditional university fictions, which flirt with but never embrace the postmodernist aesthetics. Lodge's *Small World: An Academic Romance* (1984) and Byatt's *Possession: A Romance* (1990) ostentatiously display structures of reconciliation that may serve the purpose of the romance parodied by both novels but that also impart the harmlessness propitious to the comic. In Bradbury's *The History Man* (1975) it is the narrator's ironic voice that ensures the structural unity and guides the reader through the various plots set up by the characters. Once again, that narrative constancy keeps the novel clear from the radical dissem-ination of more avant-garde texts.[11]

As *The History Man* proves with its sarcastic portrait of academic self-interest, these novels are not devoid of satirical tendencies; it is just that the satiric remains thematic and does not contaminate the discourse of the novel. From postmodernism the campus novel does not retain the radical concep-tion of fiction: it appropriates only the constitutional playfulness that it then enacts in both narrated and narrating worlds.

In the game of fiction academic characters are of course particularly skill-ful players. As men of letters these Don Juans of eloquence love to pay trib-ute to language as often as possible. In Lodge's *Small World,* for example, two scholars illustrate the comic potentiality contained in the juxtaposition of lit-eral and figurative acceptations through a discussion on different languages: "For instance, this mutton we're eating. In French there's only one word for 'sheep' and 'mutton'—*mouton.* So you can't say 'dead as mutton' in French, you'd be saying 'dead as sheep,' which would be absurd.' 'I don't know, this tastes more like dead sheep than mutton to me'" (23). The arbitrariness of the signifier (particularly in an idiomatic expression) is here both explained didac-tically and used comically. Language is the academics' magic hat from which they draw all sorts of funny birds.

Analyzing the origins of a venereal disease, which "spreads a damn sight faster than post-structuralist poetics" (166), Jock the campus doctor in Davies's *A Very Peculiar Practice* remarks: "Arts Faculty produced the largest number of cases, predictably. Idle sods, too much time on their hands. Modern Languages don't seem to have heard of French letters" (172). The neat paral-lel between 'Modern Languages' and 'French letters' with a shift from literal to liberal meaning in the second phrase produces a comic linguistic clash based on lexical connection and semantic opposition. In this and the above-men-tioned example words are used as seduction instruments inasmuch as they are brandished to show a mastery of their comic and polysemous interest. To the foregrounding of words correspond a feast of the form, a celebration of the enunciation, a staging of the signifier. The ludic preoccupation with the sur-face of the text seems at variance with the satiric impulse.

Even more instrumental than the characters in the playfulness of the cam-pus novels are the narrators, the tricksters of discourse. In Lodge's *Nice Work* the narrator plays at faking an argument with her/his academic protagonist, Robyn, "a character who, rather awkwardly for me, doesn't herself believe in the concept of character" (39). The narrator first lets the protagonist expose her views on the illusory and antihumanist nature of character and then, quite iron-ically, states: "I shall therefore take the liberty of treating her as a character, not utterly different in kind . . . from [traditional] Vic Wilcox" (41). The teasing rapport established by the narrator with her/his protagonist is carried to the point of mimicry as in the following instance where s/he derisively reproduces Robyn's academic idiolect to describe her conception and practice of sex: "Where else would the human subject have sex but in the head? Sexual desire was a play of signifiers, an infinite deferment and displacement of anticipated pleasure with the brute coupling of the signifieds temporarily interrupted. Charles [her lover] . . . seemed to approach sex as a form of research, favoring techniques of foreplay so subtle and prolonged that Robyn occasionally dozed off in the middle of them, and would wake with a guilty start to find him crouched studiously over her body, fingering it like a box of index cards" (57). The blatant irony of the rhetorical question, the obvious excess and displacement of academic jargon, the sportive extended metaphor assimilating a practical human activity to a theoretical mental activity, the comic suggestion (through Robyn's "doze") of the inefficiency of the transfer from the textual to the sexual, all contribute to build up a rhetoric of ludic derision that endeavors to engage the reader into laughing *with* the narrator *at* the characters. The formal ludism displayed by the narrator partakes of an aesthetics of seduction and of the seduction of aesthetics. The ludic (just like the comic) inclines toward an entertaining communication that seems to rule out the satiric.

Extending the playing zone from the correspondences between signifiers and signifieds to the disposition of the text, the narrator in David Benedictus's *Floating Down To Camelot* epitomizes the ludic quest. In order to suggest the funny diversity of thoughts that are concomitantly entertained during a lecture, the narrative instance divides the page into two columns, transcribing in one column the teacher's talk (in the following example the reading out of Tennyson's "The Lady of Shalott") and in the other the students' private reactions:

PROFESSOR LEEKS
Goes by to towered
   Camelot;
And sometimes
   through the mirror   Helen
   blue.
The knights come
   riding two and   "I live in a tower with
   two: a casement. And a
She hath no loyal   mirror. She hath no
   knight and true,   loyal knight and true,
   The Lady of Shalott.   that's really sad. But
                       who has these days?
                       Margaret Thatcher?" (34)

The comic principle of startling parallelism is here visualized, the unexpected verbal associations are mimicked by the daring spatial juxtapositions, the funniness of coincidence is materialized by the boldness of disposition, incongruity is substantiated by typography. Clearly, the comic arising from this technique tends to turn against the students and therefore to merge into the satiric, now mocking their philistinism (as in that interplay between the mention of "bold Sir Lancelot" and the reaction of "A Peterhouse Hearty": "Isn't there a rugby song about Sir Lancelot? I bet there is. Roll on the trials" (36), now pillorying their lack of linguistic finesse (as in the concordance between the line "He flash'd into the crystal mirror" and the semantic mistake of "A Girl From Surrey" exclaiming to herself: "Another Cambridge flasher!" (38). But the emphasis is so ostentatiously on the comic process rather than on the derided target that the ludic seems to eradicate the satiric. The dressing up of the page and the muddling up of the space stem from, and aim at, a playful use of the presentation. The production and the reception of such a text come necessarily within the scope of an essentially ludic literature.[12]

In the contemporary British campus novel, then, postmodernism embraces comedy. As a consequence, the desire to charm appears stronger than the will to challenge, the propensity to entertain outweighs the need to disquiet, the urge to provoke laughter prevails over the ambition to arouse thought. Still, the laughter has to be turned against something or somebody (the time of fundamentally benign and sympathetic humor in the manner of Sterne seems definitely in the past) and the satiric keeps therefore a foothold in the genre—albeit on the thematic periphery. Restricted as it is to the caricature of the various academic representatives, the satiric appears deprived of its ideological dimension and seems both to reside in, and to foster, stereotypical representations.

   The knell of the truly satiric has been tolled by the postmodernist celebration of the aesthetics of ludism. One may indeed wonder whether the games of signifiers, the tricks of narration, the enjoyment of the enunciation, the pleasure of the text that are gleefully displayed within the genre are at all compatible with the referential emphasis of satire. The comic playfulness of the contemporary campus novel can also be traced in the essentially parodic nature of the genre— parody being after all a sophisticated form of intertextual ludism. While the parodic quality of university fiction has not been examined in this chapter, it would be fruitful to examine if, and to what extent, parody excludes the satiric.

NOTES

1. To use Allan Rodway's definitions: "The moods are a matter of tone—the spirit in which he [the writer] deploys his methods. The modes represent the final effect." He goes on to explain that in a comic satire the mode would be satirical and the mood comical; conversely in a satiric comedy the mode would be comical and the mood satirical. See "Terms for Comedy," *Renaissance and Modern Studies* 6 (1962): 106–07.

2. For the post-World-War II period Kramer (*The American College Novel: An Annotated Bibliography,* [New York: Garland, 1981], and *College Mystery Novels: An Annotated Bibliography,* [New York: Garland, 1983]) lists 439 American campus novels! In Great Britain, also after 1945, Ian Carter (*Ancient Cultures of Conceit: British University Fiction in the Post-war Years,* [London and New York: Routledge, 1990]) enumerates 189 academic novels, a figure to which I have been able, so far, to annex 47 additional titles in the course of my research.

3. Witness the title of Marston's work; witness also this remark of Alvin Kernan: "The idea that poetic satire had its origin in a dramatic form distinguished for its viciousness of attack and spoken by rough satyrs was the basis of nearly all Elizabethan theories of satire" (*The Cankered Muse: Satire of the English Renaissance,* [New Haven: Yale UP, 1959], 55).

4. Joseph Hall's aforementioned work is also endogenous, it having been produced while he was a student at Cambridge, but its concern being only minimally academic, it could not be integrated into this chapter.

5. Here are the main examples: Thomas Mudde's *Comedy Satirizing the Mayor of Cambridge* (1582–1583), Thomas Randolph's *The Drinking Academy* (1626–1631) and the anonymous *The Return from Parnassus* (1601–1602), *Heteroclitanomalonomia* (1613?), *Risus Anglicanus* (1614–1618), and *A Christmas Messe* (1619?).

6. For the details concerning the available transcriptions of saltings, see chapter 1 and appendix 1 of the work I am presently writing on the subject of university fiction.

7. See particularly Anthony à Wood, *The History and Antiquities of the University of Oxford,* Oxford: Clarendon P, 1786, and also V.H.H. Green, *A History of Oxford University,* (London: B. T. Batsford Ltd, 1974, 24; Jan Morris ed., *The Oxford Book of Oxford,* 39; 58.

8. The ideological debate, when it is broached, appears in the form of pamphlets, treatises, or essays as in Thomas Hobbes's *The Leviathan* (Part IV, Chapter 46), Abraham Cowley's *Proposition for the Advancement of Experimental Philosophy* (1661) and John Milton's *Of Education* (1644). In these cases the purpose and the goal are really satiric considering that they attack the system and aim at reform.

9. See Gérard Genette, *Palimpsestes: la littérature au second degré,* Paris: Collection Poétique, aux Editions du Seuil, 1982. 35–37.

10. This is even more true in America where the campus novel was explored by some of the most eminent representatives of postmodernism: John Barth, Vladimir Nabokov, Bernard Malamud, Philip Roth, and Raymond Federman.

11. Patricia Waugh comparing *The History Man* with John Barth's *The Sot-Weed Factor* (1960), a novel taking up the same theme of internal plottings, shows the comparative constancy of the British example and the radical overturning of the American work of fiction where "there is no such area of narrative stability" (*Metafiction: The Theory and Practice of Self-conscious Fiction,* London and New York: Routledge, 1984. 51).

12. For the fundamental ludic attitude required from a reader of postmodernist texts, see Michel Picard, *La lecture comme jeu: Essai sur la littérature,* Paris: Editions de Minuit, 1986.

WORKS CITED

Beerbohm, Max. *Zuleika Dobson.* 1911. London: Penguin Books, 1988.

Benedictus, David. *Floating Down to Camelot.* London and Sydney: Futura, 1985.

Bradbury, Malcolm. *Possibilities: Essays on the State of the Novel.* Oxford and New York: Oxford UP, 1973.

Brooke-Rose, Christine. *Textermination.* Manchester: Carcanet, 1991.

Carter, Ian. *Ancient Cultures of Conceit: British University Fiction in the Post-War Years.* London and New York: Routledge, 1990.

Caute, David. *The Women's Hour.* London: Paladin, 1991.

Davies, Andrew. *A Very Peculiar Practice.* London: Coronet Books, 1986.

Fry, Stephen. *The Liar.* London: Heinemann, 1991.

Frye, Northrop. *The Secular Scripture: A Study of the Structure of Romance.* Cambridge and London: Harvard UP, 1976.

Genette, Gérard. *Palimpsestes: la littérature au second degré.* Paris: Collection Poétique, aux Editions du Seuil, 1982.

Hazlitt, William Carew, ed. *Shakespeare's Jest Book.* London: Willis and Sotheran, 1864.

Hewlett, Joseph. *Peter Priggins, The College Scout.* 3 vols. London, 1841.

Hutcheon, Linda. *A Poetics of Postmodernism: History, Theory, Fiction.* New York and London: Routledge, 1988.

Kernan, Alvin. *The Cankered Muse: Satire of the English Renaissance.* New Haven: Yale UP, 1959.

Kramer, J. *The American College Novel: An Annotated Bibliography.* New York: Garland, 1983.

Lodge, David. *Nice Work.* London, Penguin, 1989.

————. *Small World: An Academic Romance.* London: Penguin, 1986.

Morris, Jan. *The Oxford Book of Oxford.* Oxford: Oxford UP, 1978.

Nelson, Alan H., ed. *Records of Early English Drama: Cambridge.* 2 vols. Toronto: U of Toronto P, 1989.

Olsen, Lance. *Circus of the Mind in Motion: Postmodernism and the Comic Vision.* Detroit: Wayne State UP, 1990.

Picard, Michel. *La lecture comme jeu: Essai sur la littérature.* Paris: Editions de Minuit, 1986.

Reade, William Winwood. *Liberty Hall, Oxon.* 3 vols. London, 1860.

Richek, Roslyn. "Thomas Randolph's *Salting* (1627), its Text, and John Milton's Sixth Prolusion as Another Salting." *English Literary Renaissance* 12 (1982):102–31.

Rodway, Allan. "Terms for Comedy." *Renaissance and Modern Studies* 6 (1962): 102–24.

Saintsbury, George. *MacMillan's Magazine* 77 (1897): 334–43.

Sheppard, Richard. "From Narragonia to Elysium: Some Preliminary Reflections on the Fictional Image of the Academic." *University Fiction.* David Bevan, ed. Amsterdam and Atlanta: Rodopi, 1990. 11–48.

Smyth, Edmund J., ed. *Postmodernism and Contemporary Fiction.* London: B. T. Batsford Ltd., 1991.

Waugh, Patricia. *Metafiction: The Theory and Practice of Self-Conscious Fiction.* London and New York: Routledge, 1984.

Part Three

Satire and Society

·8·

Early Modern Complex Satire and the Satiric Novel: Genre and Cultural Transposition

Christiane Bohnert

Traditional theories of genre demand a relationship between a certain form and a certain content. If traditional genres, such as tragedies, sonnets, and novellas, resemble a well-regulated forest, then satire is the lawless and irrepressible poacher within, the genre that has no consistent form, but comes as verse satire, satiric epic and drama, satiric short and long prose. In 1784 Karl Friedrich Flögel called satire a "Proteus" (294), a shape, or rather form-shifting genre, that is, a generic anomaly. So does Worcester in 1940 (1). The "best short summary of what we know of satire today" (Kernan 4) by Elliott in the *Encyclopedia Britannica* opens with the bald statement "'Satire' is a Protean term" (vol. 23 [1989], 182). Calling satire a "Proteus," or "Protean term," signals a certain resignation. It is descriptive and accepts satire as an anomaly, an attitude Elliott advocated in 1962 (cf. Elliott, *Definition,* passim).[1]

By contrast, German scholars have taken to calling satire a "mode of writing"; that is, they see primary genres, such as novels, comedies, and poems, adopting "the satiric" as their style. While this German view denies satire any generic reality, a recent book speaks of it as "semi-genre," claiming that satire has no generic "substance," no "in-itself" (Snyder 11). Satire is supposed to be "perceptual" in that it is "neither a matter of form nor of function but a matter of the way both of these are perceived in particular contexts by particular people" (Kuiper 459). Accordingly, satire would be in the eye of the beholder, a matter of subjective awareness rather than objective existence. The terms "Proteus" and "Protean" imply regret as to satire's changeability. Its definition as a "mode of writing" or a "semi-genre" suggests that it lacks something essential to a genre, and that a genre is superior to whatever satire may be. Indeed, eighteenth-to-twentieth-century critics usually understand literary genres and, consequently, satire in terms of aesthetics. They note satire's relationship to reality as an aesthetic feature, that is, mimetically transformed.[2] The literary quality of satires is thought to depend upon the ability of their authors to camouflage their real-life points of departure and to transcend them toward "timeless validity" (*Römische Satire* 58, on Horace), conciliatoriness (Weinbrot 1, on Dryden), and serene humanity (Martini 157-58; Jacobs 195-96, on Wieland). The aesthetic perspective sees Horace, Dryden, and Wieland in exactly the same light.

Against their dwelling under the one roof of "satire," common sense might argue that literature is part of a culture, and that, culturally, a Roman from the first century B.C., a Briton from the seventeenth, and a German from the eighteenth century have hardly anything in common at all. If one views satire from the vantage point of culture, Kuiper's observation that "particular people" and "particular contexts" influence the making of satires gains a new and positive meaning. Furthermore, satire's change of form, its "Protean" quality becomes a function of its dependence upon the culture surrounding the genesis of particular satires. Seen historically and culturally, the genre of satire reconstitutes itself by transposing its basic trait, the attack upon cultural norms inimical to its own culture(s), into each new cultural environment.[3]

Satire came about in a cultural climate that saw the form of literature in the service of its didactic intent. Horace summarizes the classical view of literary texts: a poet wants to be useful to readers and to entertain them (*aut prodesse volunt aut delectare poeta, The Art of Poetry* 1:333). Thus, literary texts per se incorporate didactic intent. Among the genres, satire expresses its truth mockingly (*Satires* 2:1), and its variety continues to reflect the first use of the term *satura* for a collection of stylistically and topically different poems. Medieval theorists concur that a satire is to display topical variety and substantial content (*thematischen Reichtum und inhaltliche Fülle*, Kindermann 36). Thus, they limit the genre to complex satire that targets the whole universe rather than merely one facet of it. Form does not feature in their theories. Roman and medieval cultures focus on content with little or no regard for form (cf. *Römische Satire* 23; Haug 19–21).

Enlightenment cultures take the opposite approach. Form is everything, and model examples for each genre are listed in works on aesthetics. In accordance with their cultures, writers of satiric novels must pay some attention to form in their satiric endeavor. Rather than understanding this Enlightenment obsession with form as a cultural imperative particular to the Enlightenment, today's scholarship on satire tends to turn the aesthetic approach into a universal imperative valid for every text supposed to be a satire wherever and whenever it may have been composed. Thus, it unintentionally deprives many pre-Enlightenment satires of their own cultural realities by subjecting them to Enlightenment standards. Instead of viewing them in their own light and by their own merits, medieval and early modern satires are put into the Procrustes bed of Enlightenment aesthetic theory that, contrary to previous aesthetics, created a niche for art and literature separating them from everyday reality and partisan or tendentious ends. When Weinbrot credits Dryden with having turned a previously "rude," uncouth genre into a polite literary reminder inoffensive to the reader, he implicitly transfers his own post-Enlightenment aesthetic standards to pre-Restoration satires that followed different rules. They were written in a world that did not clearly distinguish between aesthetic or literary and nonfictional, didactic, or entertainment concerns.

Such a universal approach results from the principle of uncertainty as regarding history. If we are not extremely careful in examining our own culture in relationship to the target cultures of our analyses, we fall victim to a distorted view of these target cultures. Our impressions are blurred because space, time, and mentality, that is, the culture in which we operate, refract, and filter our observations of past cultures or those simultaneous to our own. We cannot completely escape these distortions, since the laws of our own culture governs our every observation. The cultural filter allows us to build models of past cultures. We must be careful, however, not to claim absolute truth for them (Williams 286). They are true inasmuch as they are built in accordance with scholarly methodology.

This approach is consistent with what Wellbery terms "cultural hermeneutics" (383). Its models of past cultures derive from texts and thus do not escape the hermeneutic circle, that is, the tautology of choosing the texts from which one proves one's theory, and using this proof as an argument for the grouping of texts one did first. Accepting the hermeneutic circle, one must recognize that concepts of genres and cultures under this semiotic, or any model, are "heuristic tool[s]" (Rosmarin 25) rather than objective truths apart from the observer.

A *culture* consists of interdependent systems of signs, or as Lotman's "working definition" has it, it is "the totality of non-hereditary information acquired, preserved, and transmitted by the various groups of human society" (213; cf.

Uspenskij 6.0.0.; I. Winner 106–07). Different cultures within the same society come about with different groups processing "non-hereditary information" differently, and thus creating a different frame of reference.

A corresponding definition of *genre* places the emphasis on the generic "program" that, in each text, "becomes the constructive law . . . and gives rise to the form of the content and the form of the expression" (Corti 107). A genre changes its "form of the content" and "form of the expression" in accordance with the culture that supports its program at a given moment. It is relatively rather than absolutely true. If a genre is incorporated into another culture, its sign system, or program, will be transposed. Transpositions create an intertextual interdependence (cf. Kristeva 111) and thus make a genre historically viable.

In a culturally semiotic model of satire, texts present their own cultural signs as encoded by an author and decoded by a reader, both of whom refer to their similar or different cultures. If a satire is decoded from the viewpoint of a different culture, the text may shift genres. Thus, *Gulliver's Travels* turned into a children's classic when its references to Georgian court society and early eighteenth-century culture became obsolete (cf. Traugott 128–31). The same can happen when a satire is transferred from one culture to another, simultaneous one.

The reason for satire's instability as a genre is its forms of content and expression. Rather than engaging in an ideal communication, that is, permitting a true exchange of opinions and ideas by inviting open responses, satires express an ideology by means of manipulation. In terms of communication, an ideology presents its argument in order that the addressee will accept half-truths or selective truth. Ideologies "sell" as true reality what in fact is only a part of it. Every ideological sign implies one or more lies of omission, which need not be intentional: an ideologue may well believe in his or her own creation, having fallen victim to whatever form of manipulation is employed. Manipulation initiates a disturbed discourse in which an issue is sneaked past the reader, so to speak, rather than presented in a manner that would invite a response. The addressees are not familiarized with the issue at hand and cannot make informed choices about their preferred realities. Rather, they are railroaded into accepting the choice made for them. In a satire, the text's culturally determined norms clash with the norms of other cultures perceived to be inimical to the satire's own culture(s). Readers who know a satire's culture(s) of origin can identify with the ideology represented, and the resultant criticism, whereas others either reject the satire out-of-hand, or do not understand it at all.

As distinct from other manipulative genres, such as commercials, satire challenges cultural perceptions rather than affirming them. Even medieval satire, which didactically represents Christianity, that is, something like an official doctrine, opposes sinfulness as the at present dominant attitude toward life. Thus, medieval satire affirms a prescribed code of behavior for the human being by challenging a dominant way of life that ignores it. The satire's entertaining aspects aid the manipulation and obscure the ideology. The satirist's "choice of a certain interpretive model of reality" (Corti 117; cf. T. Winner 262–64) is based upon his or her own culture and its relationship to other cultures that may become the object of the satiric attack.[4]

In the following discussion, I will demonstrate my cultural approach by exploring three satires: Brant's *Ship of Fools* (1494) from the medieval humanist culture,[5] Wieland's *Die Abderiten: Eine sehr wahrscheinliche Geschichte* ("The Abderites: A Very Probable Story," Book one and two, 1774) from the utopian Enlightenment[6] culture, and Wezel's *Belphegor, oder Die wahrscheinlichste Geschichte unter der Sonne* ("Belphegor, or The Most Probable Story Under the Sun," 1776) from what one might call skeptical Enlightenment culture.

Sebastian Brant's "prologue" to his *Ship of Fools* introduces the author by his name, title, and hometown, rather than leaving us guessing as with most medieval authors. Sebastian Brant was a scholar and university professor in Basel, a humanist and famous lawyer of both secular and canonic law. His *Ship of Fools* (1494) was the first best-seller written in the German vernacular and came to be translated into all the major European languages (cf. Manger 85–92). Brant's fellow humanist, Trithemius, who translated the *Ship of Fools* into Latin, called it a "divina satyra," thereby relating it to Dante's *Divina Comedia*. Trithemius' praise places *The Ship of Fools* within the canon, and recommends it to the notice of his and Brant's fellow humanists.

The prologue presents the satire's opening arguments along a clear cut rhetorical disposition, complete with introduction, narration, argument, and peroration. Like a lawyer's plea at court, it deals with justice and injustice, accusation and defense, past and present, the satire, the fool, and the world around them. Brant uses both traditional and humanistic topoi to lay out his purpose, his hoped-for readership, and his satiric object—the fool.[7] The very first lines introduce us to the satire's universe.

> All lands in Holy Writ abound
> And works to save the soul are found,
> The Bible, Holy Fathers' lore*
> And other such in godly store,
> So many that I feel surprise
> To find men growing not more wise

---

* *Ler* meaning "teaching."

> But holding writ and lore in spite.
> The whole world lives in darksome night,
> In blinded sinfulness persisting,
> While every street sees fools existing
> Who know but folly to their shame,
> Yet will not own to folly's name.
> Hence I have pondered how a ship
> Of fools I'd suitably equip—[8]

Brant's satire starts with a bang: the *Ship of Fools* is to convey divine truth as a light in the darkness. It is to do nothing less than enhance the effectiveness of the Holy Scriptures in counteracting folly.

Brant's figure of the fool, albeit a novelty in terms of the genre of satire, is well known from one of these Holy Scriptures, the biblical book of Proverbs,[9] one of the most popular in those days. Brant's opening statement, though more pleading in tone, reflects the opening of Proverbs, which adjures the fools "To receive the instruction of wisdom, justice, and judgment, and equity" (1:2). In Proverbs, the term *fool* appears synonymous with "the wicked" and "the sinner." It refers to forsaking God rather than to any individual flaws of understanding or reason. Correspondingly, a wise person is also "righteous." "The fear of the LORD is the beginning of knowledge: but fools despise wisdom and instruction" (1:7). "The wise shall inherit glory: but shame shall be the promotion of the fools" (3:35). Brant's satiric intent is modeled after the dogmatic intent of the biblical book of wisdom. Both also share the allusion to the law court, the pursuit of justice for all—divine justice.

Accordingly, the satire's entertaining aspect, its laughter, must be seen in relation to its usefulness, the reminder it gives of the judgment "wisdom" (1:20), the voice of God, pronounces over the fools.

> Turn you at my reproof: behold, I will pour out my spirit unto you,
> I will make known my words unto you. / Because I have called, and
> ye refused; I have stretched out my hand and no man regarded; / But
> ye have set at nought all my counsel, and would none of my reproof:
> / I also will laugh at your calamity; I will mock when your fear
> cometh; (1:23–27)

The fools' laughter may yet come to stick in their throats. A text that challenges a secular culture in the name of a Christian one is not a laughing matter, however much its seriousness may be leavened by amusing images of fools who ramble past the reader in what could be referred to as a variety-show format.

Satire is enveloped by a spiritual context that interprets the genre and signifies its importance. Words are typologically or figuratively conceived and have several layers of significance. Interpretation, or in the Bible, exegesis, uncovers the eschatological sign beneath the surface sign (cf. Haug 18–19, cf. also Auerbach, Danielou). A God has inspired the teachings of the Bible and the Church Fathers, and empowers them as cultural points of reference. Their empowerment in turn suspends intentions and character of the satirist.

Sebastian Brant draws on both Roman and medieval traditions of satire, emphasizing usefulness, entertainment, and complexity. His prologue is situated within an early modern urban culture (cf. Bohnert, "Narrenschiff" passim).

> Here you will find of fools no dearth
> And everything you wish on earth,
> The reasons why you're here are listed,
> Why many fools have ay existed,
> What joy and honor wisdom bears
> And why a fool in danger fares,
> The world's whole course in one brief look—
> Are reasons why to buy this book.
> In jest and earnest evermore[*]
> you will encounter fools galore.[10]

Zuo schympff vnd ernst vnd allem spil renders Horace's prodesse et delectare. Its literal translation would be something like "adhortation, seriousness, and amusement." The German word spil is ambiguous. On the one hand, it means "play" and might be taken to refer to the variety of fools with 111 chapters ranging from "forsaking God" to bad table manners. On the other hand, spil means "gambling," one of the favorite recreations of the fool (e.g. Prologue 92, chapter 77), and a reminder that the entertaining side of the satire must not distract from the underlying seriousness of its object, the fools whose habits endanger their souls.

Along with Horace's description, Brant also alludes to the medieval demand of complexity. He promises "thematic variety and richness of content" by declaring that his satire features the "whole course of the world," a comprehensive rather than representational depiction of fools. Amusement comes from the variety of fools presented. Capital sins like greed (chapter 3) appear in between chapters on good council (2) and newfangled ideas (4). The survey's scope ranges from apocalyptic visions of the Antichrist being at the gates (99, 103) to a neighboring lengthy complaint about bad table manners (110a) that features a new figure, the lout (Grobianus), who sparked a literary fashion in sixteenth-century German literature.

---

[*] This line reads Zuo schympff vnd ernst vnd allem spil.

Brant extends the concept of complexity to the audience. He names, or implies, three groups of addressees, a general audience that might be interested in the image of the ubiquitous fool (Prologue 57–58), those who need the woodcuts because they find reading difficult (25–28), and his fellow humanists whom he lures with a wealth of allusions and quotations from Greek and Roman sources in addition to traditional references to the Bible.

The satire is to present the whole world to the whole world, thus emphasizing the collective acceptability of its satiric object and purpose. In real life, early modern readership was limited to the educated and moneyed classes. Hence, the function of the woodcuts was probably to enhance the adhortative effect of the satire (cf. Manger 55). Those who cannot read in the sense of not understanding correctly may be the ones who need it most, and the woodcuts—of unusual quality compared to other incunables—make them sit up and take notice.

The prologue also addresses the reader as a prospective buyer, a reference to the mercantile culture that had engulfed bookmaking in the wake of the invention of the printing press.

> The world's whole course in one brief look—
> Are reasons why to buy this book.

"Thematic variety and richness of content" not only legitimize the satire generically—they also form the basis for a sales pitch. The satirist profits from his text spiritually as well as financially, an individual and secular perspective apart from the divine territory ploughed at the beginning of the prologue.

The individual component of writing a satire is also apparent in Brant's emphasis on his humanistic merits.

> In truth I've slaved laboriously
> That 'mongst these leaves these idiots might
> Foregather; I have worked at night
> While snug in bed they slumbered tight
> Or gambled, freely drinking wine,
> And never thought of me and mine.[11]

Having labored hard and worked at night signals to humanistic readers that the author is erudite. The allusion to the author's scholarship in turn enhances the authority of the text (cf. Lemmer, passim). Divine inspiration is augmented by human merits, notwithstanding the human being's disclaimer, his very proper show of modesty (86–87). In early modern culture, the text's authority is the result of a cooperation between a God and his creation in that divine and human sources, the Bible and classical secular writings, provide the inspiration. In retrospect, this humanistic emphasis on human merit marks the very first, hesitant steps toward God's death about 250 years later.

Culturally, the *Ship of Fools* fuses signs of medieval Christianity and Renaissance humanism. The early modern mercantile culture is the satire's main object of attack. Greed is the most serious capital sin by far, the one that is at the root of all others (cf. Bohnert, "Narrenschiff" 626–28, 633, 644). Considering that Brant himself is not above a little sales promotion, the satire rejects the pervasiveness of greed rather than the mercantile culture as a whole. The fool is the one who is prone to excess like the sinner in Thomas Aquinas's *Summa theologiae* (cf. Bohnert, "Narrenschiff" 623).

Brant transfers the sign /fool/[12] from the *Book of Proverbs* into his satire, and retains the referent /sinner/. With some sins, such as *gula* that Brant depicts as excessive drinking, the /fool/ is also a /stupid person/ whose overindulgence leads to physical problems. In fact, most capital sins and other ungodly attitudes primarily refer to the late medieval culture while secondarily suggesting a secular significance. Given this hierarchy, it is not a secular frame of reference for which the satire claims power. The *Ship of Fools* is not subversive or carnivalistic. Rather, it asks its readers to follow a marked trail illuminated by the divine spirit and His designated authorities toward an eschatological truth.

In the eighteenth century, individuals are on their own. Both utopian and skeptic Enlightenment cultures repudiate the concept of the human being as subject to divine direction. Utopian Enlightenment satire challenges them to re-create themselves in accordance with their innermost potential. Its readers are to blast a trail into a future that coincides with their share in humankind. The human potential is epitomized by a small elite, called "cosmopolites" by Christoph Wieland and "Freemasons" by Lessing.[13] Average individuals are to follow their examples in order to escape "their self-induced immaturity," as Immanuel Kant puts it in his *Answer to the Question: What is Enlightenment?* (1784). By contrast, skeptic Enlightenment culture rejects any kind of utopia and sees the individual's fate up to a chance-ridden history.

In accordance with the individual focus, literary texts are to be self-reflexive, that is, they create their own universe based upon a mimetic relationship to nature. The novel, for instance, is to offer its readers insights into the *condition humaine* by imitating nature, that is, staying true to human psychology and keeping plots within the realms of probability, as Wieland demands in his *The History of Agathon* (1767). Wieland (1733–1813) stakes out the parameters of the modern German novel by emulating English authors, such as Laurence Sterne and Henry Fielding.

Like the novel, each genre has its own niche within the literary universe, and form becomes more important than content for the definition of a genre. Complex satire as defined by content turns into satiric novel in answer to the new cultural imperative. The basic secret of this transposition is to wrap the satire, its ideological signs, manipulative designs, and satiric object, in a mantle of narration that will suggest universality.

The change from self-declared advocacy to insinuation is based upon the cultural turn from a God to the individual as the major point of reference. Modern satirists stand as individuals against other individuals, their opinions uttered at their own peril rather than warranted by a God or societal tradition. They employ poetic forms rather than culture-given points of reference to manipulate the reader, submerging their satires in other genres. Their "borrowed" forms serve multiple purposes of which parody (cf. Paulson 7) is one and that of a cover is another. They make satirists invisible. This subtle conveyance of satiric criticism prevents the individualities of satirist and reader from becoming polarized in a personality conflict that might distract from the truth of the satire.

As the satirists' judgments are their own rather than a reiteration of known truths, satiric criticism is unenforceable. Readers who dismiss satiric criticism as playful, or as not applying to them, may frustrate the satirist; they will not incur the wrath of a God. Therefore, satiric strategies rely on stealth for their impacts, the usefulness being hidden under an invitation to laughter, ridicule, or intellectual puzzles, for example, allusions to other texts.

The plot of *Die Abderiten* demonstrates the modern strategy of stealth. Wieland transposes an ancient Greek setting to represent eighteenth-century Germany and gives his contemporary satiric object an historical sheen. He takes his image of Abdera from Greek stories that contended its Thracian citizens were stupid by definition, an antique precursor of today's ethnic jokes. Democritus, "the laughing philosopher," was born there. In the satire, he escapes the Abderitian mind-set by his natural gifts and twenty years of travel during which he acquires knowledge, and even more important meets all the best and brightest scholars of other countries. This transposition adds some intellectual spice for the educated reader and enhances the universal appeal of the novel that conceals a satire.

The text introduces the Abderites, represented by their social and political leaders, as "antipodes" to the "cosmopolites" (cf. 230-32) as epitomized by Democritus and, in the second book, also by the physician Hippocrates. A narrator describes the Abderites' lack of common sense and reason, their resistance to any meaningful education, their lack of taste and morality, and their preference for the letter of the law over its spirit.

By insisting that if ever a wise man were to be born in Abdera, the Abderites would not in any way contribute to his wisdom, Wieland polarizes his two groups of characters, the cosmopolites as utopian Enlightenment representatives, and the Abderites as epitomizing the old order (132-36). The modern concepts of folly and wisdom become apparent in the narrator's comment on the disdain the Abderites feel for Democritus and his views.

> The true reason why the Abderites did not pay much attention to their fellow citizen Democritus was this: they did not think him—— a wise man. / "Why not?" "Because they could not." "And why could they not?" / Because they would have had to think of themselves as blockheads, if they had. And to do that, even they were not contrary enough. (137)[14]

This passage establishes the leitmotif of Wieland's satire: the true and false meanings of wisdom and folly. Democritus knows that he is wise, and the Abderites are fools, whereas the Abderites know the reverse to be true. Wieland's sign /fool/ is devoid of any transcendental connotation. Instead, the interpretant of /fool/ is /lunatic/, and the authority behind this frame of reference is the potential of humankind that the utopian Enlightenment culture vests in each individual. Wieland's /fool/ is responsible for blocking the progress of humankind rather than disturbing the divine peace. The antonyms of /fool/ in Brant and Wieland's satires, the /wise man/ and the /cosmopolite/, reflect the cultural change. Whereas Brant's /wise man/ was righteous, Wieland's /cosmopolite/ is right, and the narrator's comments throughout the text make sure that the reader does not forget it.

The foreword to *Die Abderiten* is part of the readers' manipulation into accepting the text's ideology. The foreword depicts the satire as a part of an artistic universe derived from nature. The Abderites, regardless of their stereotyped appearance, are to be taken as characters whom the reader could encounter in real life. "A painter can paint idols, pictures, or grotesques, as it pleases him; but idols and grotesques are not pictures; and if it is true that they resemble somebody, then one must probably blame nature or chance. It is difficult to think of a degree of beauty that significantly surpasses that which is most beautiful in nature; but perhaps it is completely impossible to invent a caricature that does not resemble any of God's creatures" (729).[15] Thus, the relationship to reality that aesthetic theories of satire notice is part of a pretense at mimesis in many modern satires. Alluding to nature as the source of the mimetic portrayal, Wieland accomplishes the transformation of complex satire into satiric novel. Wieland's narrative comments on the Abderites throughout the text come under the heading of common sense, although in reality they turn the text partisan. The satirist hides behind his plot, and his very emphasis on the natural occurrence of Abderites make the reader focus on the inequities of the satiric object.

Wieland calls his text "a modest contribution to a history of human reason," adding the judgmental aspect of satire to the mimetic quality of the novel. The very mention of nature and reason obliquely legitimizes the satire. As divine law backs Brant's satire, so natural law upholds Wieland's.

Wieland camouflages the typecast nature of his opposites by depicting both the cosmopolites and the Abderites as individuals. The narrative structure of the satire helps to turn types into, as the text's title has it, "probable" characters. Conversations between Democritus and the Abderites, Democritus and Hippocrates, and even the Abderites among themselves convey individualities without ever threatening the polarization.

Consider the representative of organized religion, the high priest Strobylus of the Latona temple with its sacred animals, the frogs. Latona is a second-rate Greek goddess, and frogs are somewhat lowly and ridiculous sacred animals. Democritus has withdrawn from the Abderites, and rumors spread about his cosmopolite scientific research. Democritus finds himself accused of experimenting with frogs, which would make him guilty of atheism, if not black magic. At the same time, a cousin with designs on Democritus' rich inheritance wants to have him declared insane (cf. 190). Threatened from both sides, Democritus evades the trial for contempt of frogs by sending a fried peacock to Strobylus who discovers that the bird is stuffed with one hundred gold "darics."

> There cannot be that much wrong with the man's reason, thought Strobylus. / The medicine worked immediately as it was supposed to work. The high priest greatly enjoyed the pheasant, drank Greek wine with it, pocketed the one hundred darics, and thanked Latona for the satisfaction, she had given her frogs. / "We all have our faults," said Strobylus the other day at a ball. "Although Democritus is a philosopher, I do not think, he means as ill as his enemies say of him . . . I hope his heart is better than his head! The latter is supposed to be somewhat wrong, and I believe it myself . . . I am sure he were the finest person in Abdera if philosophy had not spoiled his mind!" (215)[16]

Strobylus' final words are a bone to Democritus' cousin, a senator who wants Democritus certified (cf. 211–13, 218). As the narrator emphasizes (215), the elegant repast leads the high priest to show himself convinced of Democritus' inner worth without making him forget the dynamics of the power play in Abdera's senate. The narrator draws the line between folly and wisdom with his final comment that Strobylus "in all his . . . stupidity" was "a cunning fellow" (215). The word "cunning" (schlau) differentiates Strobylus from Democritus who is "wise" (weise, e.g. 143, 152, klug, e.g. 188).

Democritus is a lone individual in his attempts to convert the Abderites to his way of thinking. He finally comes to realize that he has failed in his efforts to reform the Abderite way of life, to replace corruption, derivation, and unreason with morality, originality, and reason. Their avid desire for using him as a source of amusement—that is, their constant need for distraction—is shown as adversely affecting Democritus' remaining task in life, that of the cosmopolite responsible to the world rather than one nation, or a city-state. Although willing to laugh at the Abderites' chatter, Democritus puts his scientific research first. In order to continue with his calling of a cosmopolite who contributes to the knowledge of humankind, he retreats first to a suburban country estate, and then to a kind of hermitage, a cabin in the forest that illustrates his isolation in old-order society (cf. 172–73, 188–89).

Ideologically, the satire opposes the dominance of the traditionally dominant culture, that of old-order society, and stakes a claim to power for the Enlightenment elite. Intellectual powers are to coincide with material powers. In this Enlightenment culture, wisdom is perceived to be a precious commodity, acquired by only a very few dedicated individuals, an intellectual elite (cf. 138).

Considering the rarity of cosmopolitism, this ideology is undemocratic, albeit based upon an evaluation of individual merit. The reader is to be convinced that an oligarchy with no legitimization of its power is to be replaced by a meritocracy that would define merit to accord with its particular view of humankind and the resultant obligations of each individual whose fulfillment would constitute merit. Thus, utopian Enlightenment culture puts its trust in humanity, and sets its ideology as absolute.

Johann Karl Wezel's *Belphegor* is skeptical about any absolute claims in the name of human norms or beliefs. The text achieves its critique by transposing both Voltaire's *Candide* and Wieland's *Abderiten,* which texts represent other Enlightenment cultures.

Voltaire's *Candide* (1759), like Samuel Johnson's *Rasselas* (1759), represents a self-contained Enlightenment culture in which the individual does not really have the "choice of life" Rasselas seeks. As Rasselas decides to return to Abyssynia, so Candide insists in the text's very last sentence that they "must cultivate [their] garden." Both heroes arrive at an inner balance after having experienced all walks of life and their inherently unsatisfactory nature. Their inner balance is based on a renunciation of the pursuit of happiness.

Wezel's "foreword," introducing the first "book" of *Belphegor,* attacks the utopian view of humanity explicitly, while its sketch of humanity also refutes the self-contained Enlightenment culture. The foreword claims that only a man who listened to nothing but "the goodness of his own heart and a small circle of sympathetic friends" would insist upon believing that "the human being [is] a creature of higher order, possessed with the most refined moral perfections, and the *world* [is] a sweet place of harmony, of contentment, of happiness." The foreword proposes to throw this same man into "the real world" instead. He would experience "the maelstrom of selfishness, envy, and oppression" that pervades the "history of humankind and its peoples," past and present. With experience beyond his narrow circle and ideal inner vision, he would be forced to abandon his illusions about humankind and the individual's potential, and come to perceive human beings as a kind of self-aware predators. "According to the author's theory, envy and ambition are driving human nature and are the cause of every good and evil on our planet at all times, in all places, in every estate of humankind and society, in all individual characters. He [the author] therefore put together a depiction of the world, in which envy and oppression are the main features, as the history of human beings and peoples presented them to him" (11).[17] The satire's backup is the evidence of experience and observation, and thus the assumption that there is objective evidence that each being can see for him or herself (11–12).

Whereas Wieland establishes the genre of satiric novel with great seriousness, Wezel maintains the irony he also shows in his text, an irony directed at both the self-contained and the utopian Enlightenment cultures. His foreword mocks the strategy pursued by the first attempts at satiric novels at the dawn of the Enlightenment, in which satirists assure the readers of their goodwill, and try to convince them that laughter is a virtue, since it shows that they are above the satire.

Wezel turns this topos into a conciliatory remark that promises a kind of anti-*Belphegor* to make amends for the savage portrayal of human beings in the satire. After having quoted Hobbes's famous words that "the condition of man . . . is the condition of a war of everyone against everyone" (*Leviathan*, 1651, pt. 1, ch. 4) as the motto of the satire's first book, Wezel ends his foreword by referring to the individual as the "wonderful composite that we call human being," "a true Janus with two faces, one ugly, the other beautiful" (12). Since the savagery of his critique is aimed at demolishing the utopian image of the human being, this about-face is hardly credible. Instead, it reinforces the focus upon the satiric object, just as Wieland did with his long spiel on how the Abderites were a product of nature.

Belphegor portrays four types of human beings in situations that incite envy and ambition. These types are the idealist Belphegor, the hedonist Medardus, the cynic Fromal, and the opportunist Akante. Despite their typical natures, they interact as individuals, their fates being interesting to the readers.

They experience typical situations, such as those known from the *Abderiten* and *Candide*, Swift's *Gulliver*, and the then-fashionable robinsonades. They survive religious and secular tyranny in Western, so-called civilized society, as Candide and his entourage do; they buy an estate on the North American frontier that compares to Candide's garden; and the idealist finds himself in settings other authors have used for utopian visions, such as the South Seas islands, colonies beyond the mountains, and hermitages to pursue "cosmopolite," humanity-saving work without interruption from the multitude or from material needs. In pursuit of utopia, Belphegor becomes the unwitting agent in the destruction of a mountain retreat, and while he goes into mental seclusion for developing a plan for universal peace, his then-wife—the opportunist Akante—turns his home into a whorehouse in order that they be able to pay the bills.

At the very beginning of the satire, Wezel refutes Voltaire's ironic picture of human innocence. The innocent kiss that leads to Candide's exile is transposed into a brutal kick that results in a broken hip for Belphegor. Wezel's hero is naive, green, overzealous, and impetuous, but not morally above the fray. This is shown when he succumbs to ambition, and sacrifices his friend, the cynic, thereby proving that good intentions are not tantamount to innocence, another dismissal of the Democritus-type individual.

Accordingly, the cynic Fromal is a transposition of Pangloss, Candide's teacher of faith in the best of all possible worlds, into a teacher of taking advantage of the worst of all bad worlds. Fromal tells Belphegor and the reader that envy and ambition have been around since time began, and thus, participation in the "war of everyone against everyone" (*bellum omnium contra omnes*) is justified. The text's structure makes Fromal seem the intellectual of the group, and as he never misses an opportunity for treachery, his formidable presence could lead the reader to believe that Wezel, unlike Voltaire, speaks with the voice of the teacher.

The hedonist Medardus stands for the fatalist of Voltaire's satire, but in *Belphegor*, this fatalism is the result of intellectual stupor as evidenced in Medardus' favorite stock phrases, "Destiny is everywhere" (*Die Vorsicht ist überall*) and "Who knows how this might do me some good?" (*Wer weiß, wozu mir's gut ist?*). They are his stereotyped reactions to any new misfortune.

Finally, the opportunist Akante transposes the aristocratic Cunégonde into what in the eighteenth century was known as a wanton woman. She is not referred to in the foreword, although she is the one who sets events into motion by literally kicking Belphegor out of her paradise after his fortune was gone. While Cunégonde is unavailable for social reasons, because of Candide's ineligibility, Akante becomes unavailable because, out of ambition, she feels that she should look for a better prospect. She turns to the highest bidder in an effort to make her way in the world.

It is important that neither the cynic Fromal or the opportunist Akante gain anything from their treacheries. Their lack of success seems tied in with the structure of society. Despite their attempts to pursue their fortunes, Murphy's Law applies to those who share fully in the corruption and immorality of the powers that be while having neither their luck (*Glück*) nor their superior force (*Obermacht*). The unlucky, powerless figures do not win, or cannot keep, money and love in ancien régime society, but it seems almost as if the illusion keeps the vicious circle going and the powerful in power. At the end, Akante is dead from one treachery to many, and Fromal vegetates on an estate like Candide's garden. The difference is that Fromal is a failure, whereas Candide has gained a precarious balance and some peace of mind.

Major and minor characters in the first book are portrayed as individuals who are locked in the war of everyone against everyone. Thus, after the first book demonstrates that individuals cannot live together without devouring one another, the second proves that, utopian or escapist visions notwithstanding, we have no choice in this matter. Its motto comes from John Gay's *Beggar's Opera* (1729, Act 3, scene 2), quoted by Wezel in English. "Of all Animals of Prey, Man is the only sociable one. Every one of us preys upon his Neighbour, and yet we herd together." Wezel's individuals are equal in their shared predicament, as even those with luck and superior force—though more equal in terms of power—are not protected against unforeseeable vicissitudes. Rather than achieving an equilibrium like Candide and Rasselas, Belphegor and his fellow seekers must live with chance as the only constant in human life. As Wezel's final paragraph emphasizes, this goes for those who retreat as well as those who commit themselves to a common goal.

Belphegor, by this time a citizen of the British colonies in North America, assumes "a different name" in the very last paragraph of the satire and—true to his nature but against the entreaties of the cynic—joins the fight for American independence. He goes on to become one of the most effective commanders and propagandists (329). Apparently, Wezel saw many Belphegors, so to speak, among the American leaders whose struggle had just begun when the book was published.

As the outcome of this venture is as uncertain as that of any historical or personal striving, the satire does not end with a firm affirmation of one attitude over the other. "[T]he outcome of the war will decide who of the participants is right, and whether Belphegor shall become commonly known as a patriot and philanthropist, or whether he shall die in the fight for freedom as an unsung hero" (329).[18] The open ending of the satire reflects the open ending of history, and the satiric critique of utopian concepts, especially the concept of individual self-realization and self-reliance. Despite everything that happens to him, all the

Candide-like injuries and maimings, Belphegor is still true to his nature in trying to break with the past. Wezel does not affirm Belphegor's course of action, and neither does he criticize it. He implies, however, that even a victory by the colonists would not vindicate Belphegor's decision, which is based on drives. It would merely make Belphegor one of the powerful who write history rather than being overwritten. The new society of a new world may or may not be a continuation of the old world's old order, and the satire has demonstrated before that Belphegor too is not immune to the lures of ambition and not above the pursuit of his luck.

Belphegor is not, as has sometimes been contended, nihilistic in the sense of seeing no meaning in human life. Meaning is a subjective term, and Belphegor certainly sees meaning in his commitment. While the satire is opposed to unrealistic expectations regarding individuals, it also opposes their exploitation or victimization. The text's refutation of utopias is not equivalent to a rejection of meaning as such, and it is an indication of how much Wieland's position is regarded as the "true" Enlightenment in Germany that Wezel's position could be misunderstood.

Rather than signifying an absolute, the sign /fool/ is absorbed in a critique of utopian Enlightenment culture while the critique of ancien régime culture works by appealing to a natural moral sense in the reader. /Folly/ signifies something like /self-delusion/ rather than lunacy. /Fools/ believe that they can resist the wake of their drives. Hence, Democritus is a /fool/, or rather Wieland is for having invented him, and so is Voltaire.

Culturally, the satire Belphegor emphasizes practical experience over hopeful theories. Its skeptical Enlightenment culture negates the utopian and the self-contained Enlightenment cultures. It also refutes the powers that be. Human beings of all walks of life and intelligence must contend with the whirlpool of chance around them and are equal in their vulnerability to it. Luck and power may offer brief respites; they are not solutions. Hence, neither ruling elites nor intellectuals can legitimize the claims to power that their cultures file for them. In fact, power is unwarranted and unwarrantable, a somewhat anarchic perspective that defies those who look for certainties in their lives, be it divine or reasonable guidance.

Early modern complex satire and the satiric novel are two transpositions of the genre of satire. Sebastian Brant's Ship of Fools is an early modern complex satire. While the text's Christian culture shows signs of almost being undermined by the contemporary mercantile culture,[19] it is still sufficiently related to late medieval cultures so as to allow a continuation of medieval premises regarding satires. Its form of expression and entertaining features serve to enhance the impact of its didactic purpose. Subtlety or stealth is unnecessary, as the satirist is backed by an awesome authority, that of a God and His text, the Bible.

With the displacement of Christian cultures in favor of human authorities, a change of satiric procedure was inevitable. The satiric novel introduces subtle techniques of manipulation. It (ab)uses the readers' sympathy for the hero to manipulate them into accepting the satire's premises. It additionally keeps the reader on its straight-and-narrow path by narrative comments as in Wieland's *Abderiten*, by absurd situations as in Wezel's *Belphegor*, or sometimes by paralogic as in Swift's *A Modest Proposal*. Its narrative structure individualizes satiric stereotypes, both characters and situations, and gives rise to new satiric strategies that in turn become a fountain of new opportunities to empower the word, and to deny the legitimacy of any power derived from premises unacceptable to a satire's contextual culture. Wieland and Wezel were among the first to make use of these new opportunities, transposing earlier literary texts, historical settings, or both, in order to challenge ascendant cultures inimical to their own.

Whereas the Middle Ages and the Renaissance strive to uphold certain collectively valid standards, Enlightenment cultures do not have a common guideline as to what constitutes the acceptable. Cultural fragmentation, one of the signs of our times, began 200 years ago when the individual rose above the creator. At the close of the fifteenth century, Sebastian Brant assembled his fools on a ship, calling his satire a "mirror for fools" (Prologue 31) in which each fool was to know him or herself. Since the eighteenth century, the fools have abandoned ship, their lifeboats carrying pieces of this mirror. Culturally, modern satire resembles a kaleidoscope rather than a Proteus. In its shifting patterns, the fool's image twists and contorts.

NOTES

1. By contrast, Randolph theorized that formal-verse satire by Roman and eighteenth-century French and English authors juxtaposed "specific Reason" and "specific Unreason" (375). Unlike later English and American theorists, Randolph unequivocally regards satire as normative. In order to present the opposing norms—Randolph does not use this term—"the Satirist utilizes miniature dramas, sententious proverbs and quotable maxims, compressed beast fables . . . anything and everything to push his argument forward to its philosophical and psychological conclusions" (373). "[P]urely rhetorical devices" are used to "give . . . the special effects necessary to good satire" (373). Satire relates to "formal dialectic, psychology and medicine; . . . didactic literature and the organized forces of religion and law; while the miscellaneous illustrative materials utilized connect it with the daily activities of man" (373). Thus, Randolph moves within the formally recognized genre of verse satire, while acknowledging its relationship to other genres in creating its surface, to rhetoric in its strategy of persuasion, and to didacticism in its deep structure. Randolph overlooks that medieval satires, for instance, are concerned with "reason" only as divine reason. Nonetheless, her approach points toward regarding satire as a genre informed by cultural rather than literary norms, although Randolph herself does not explicitly distinguish between literature and culture.

2. Cf. Highet 158; Elliott, *Society* passim; Rosenheim 25; Paulson 5; Tronskaja 7; Schönert, *Tucholsky* 56. Gaier's theory (331–46) is based on satire's aesthetically conceived relationship to reality.

3. I developed my approach in an argument with Schönert who argues along lines similar to Randolph (n. 1), though with a system derived from communication theory and applicable to the satire as a whole. His theory derives from research on the eighteenth-century satiric novel and twentieth-century short prose satires. Like all German scholars, Schönert regards satire as a mode of writing rather than a genre (*Tucholsky* 53). Schönert views satire as a communication between author, topic, recipient, and normative reference (54, cf. *Roman* 28–31). According to Schönert, the textual system consists of three structural levels. In the deep structure, satirical texts invariably contrast two normative principles with each other, norm and antinorm with the antinorm being of higher value. Some texts depict the antinorm; others leave it to the reader to decode it from the context. This decision takes place on the level of strategy, and does not affect the deep structure (*Tucholsky* 55). Schönert does not explain how norms and antinorms refer to cultures. Furthermore, medieval and early modern satires, which challenge prevalent antinorms as opposed to the divine norm they represent, are not really covered by this theory.

4. This description of satire is based upon cultural semiotics, as developed in present-day cultures. In reference to the aforementioned inevitable distortion of cultural observations, it is important to note that the terms *ideology* and *manipulation* are meaningless within the medieval humanist culture of first-generation German humanism that referred to a divine truth. Where the existence of a God is not in doubt, trying to lead readers back to Him cannot be perceived as manipulation.

5. In Germany, the "older" humanism of Brant represents a time of transition from late medieval to Renaissance cultures. For the problems of periodization cf. Skalweit 18–20; Mensching 10–11.

6. The term *Enlightenment* refers to cultures from the late seventeenth century to the early 1790s. Despite many differences, their primary point of reference is the individual.

7. Manger provides a survey of research on the *Ship of Fools*. Bohnert's "Narrenschiff" discusses its place in early modern culture.

8. Sebastian Brant, *The Ship of Fools*, trans. with introd. and comm. by Edwin H. Zeydel [1944] New York: Dover, 1962, 57. All English quotations are from this edition. The original with line numbers is given in the notes with verses separated by dash. Early modern German diacritical marks are rendered by modern equivalents.

   "All land syndt yetz voll heylger geschrifft—Vnd was der selen heyl antrifft /—Bibel / der heylgen vätter ler—Vnd ander der glich buocher mer /—In maß / das ich ser wunder hab / Das nyemant bessert sych dar ab /—Ja würt all gschrifft vnd ler veracht—Die gantz welt lebt in vinstrer nacht—Vnd tuot in sünden blint verharren / all strassen / gassen / sindt voll narren—Die nüt dann mit dorheit umbgan—wellen doch nit den namen han—Des hab ich gdacht zuo diser früst—Wie ich der narren schiff uff rüst" (1–14).

9. I thank Stefanie B. Pafenberg (Queen's University) for suggesting this relationship to me.

10. "Hie ist an narren kein gebrust—Ein yeder findt das in gelust—Vnd ouch war zuo er sy geboren—Vnd war vmb so vil sindt der doren /—Was ere vnd freud die wisheit hat / Wie sörglich sy der narren stat / Hie findt man der gantzen welt louff—Diß buochlin wurt guot zuo dem kouff—Zuo schympff vnd ernst vnd allem spil / Findt man hie narren wie man wil /" (47–56).

11. "Warlich hab jch on arbeit nicht—So vil narren zuosamen bracht—Ich habe ettwan gewacht zuo nacht—Do die schleyeffent der ich gedacht—Oder villicht by spyl und win—Sassent / Vnd wenig dochtent myn /" (88–93).

12. The two slanted lines characterize a sign. Signs consist of a signifier, or "word," a signified, or "matter," and an interpretant that is another sign. Thus, the interpretant of

/dog/ could be /man's best friend/, or in China, /delicacy/, or for those with phobias, /fear/. The interpretant relates the sign to an infinite semiotic network, as it in turn is a sign (cf. Eco 53).

13. Wieland explains his concept of "cosmopolite" in *Die Abderiten* (230–32, cf. Bohnert, "Weg" 551–53); Lessing implies his special meaning of "Freemason" in *Ernst and Falk: Conversations for Freemasons* (1778, cf. Bohnert, "Worlds" 5–8).

14. I quote from Christoph Martin Wieland, *Die Abderiten: Eine sehr wahrscheinliche Geschichte*, Books one and two [1774 in *Teutscher Merkur*], in *Werke*, vol. 2, Munich: Hanser, 1966, 121–241, 729–37. All page numbers in the text refer to this edition. Translations in the notes are my own.

"Der wahre Grund, meine Freunde, warum die Abderiten aus ihrem Mitbürger Democritus nicht viel machten, war dieser: weil sie ihn für—keinen weisen Mann hielten. / "Warum das nicht?" "Weil sie nicht konnten." "Und warum konnten sie nicht?" / Weil sie sich alsdann selbst für Dummköpfe hätten halten müssen. Und dies zu tun, waren sie gleichwohl nicht widersinnig genug."

15. "Ein Maler kann Ideale, Bildnisse, and Grotesken machen, je nachdem es ihm gefällt; aber Ideale und Grotesken sind keine Bildnisse; und wenn es sich zutrifft, daß sie jemanden ähnlich sehen, so hat vermutlich Natur oder Zufall die Schuld daran. Es ist schwer, sich in Gedanken zu einem Grade von Schönheit zu erheben, der das schönste in der Natur merklich übertreffe; aber vielleicht ganz unmöglich, eine Karrikatur zu erfinden, die keinem Geschöpfe Gottes ähnlich sehe."

16. "Es muß doch nicht so gar übel mit dem Verstande des Mannes stehen, dachte Strobylus. / Das Mittel wirkte unverzüglich, wie es wirken sollte. Der Oberpriester ließ sich den Pfauen herrlich schmecken, trank griechischen Wein dazu, strich die hundert Dariken in seinen Beutel, und dankte der Latona für die Genugtuung, die sie ihren Fröschen verschafft hatte. / "Wir haben alle unsre Fehler, sagte Strobylus des folgenden Tages in einer großen Gesellschaft. Democritus ist zwar ein Philosoph; aber ich finde doch, daß er es so übel nicht meint, als ihn seine Feinde beschuldigen. [. . .] Ich hoffe, sein Herz ist besser als sein Kopf. Es soll nicht gar zu richtig in dem letztern sein; und ich glaub es selbst. [. . .] Ich bin gewiß, daß er der feinste Mann in ganz Abdera wäre, wenn ihm die Philosophie den Verstand nicht verdorben hätte!"

17. Wezel's *Belphegor* has not yet been critically edited. I quote from Johann Karl Wezel, *Belphegor oder Die wahrscheinlichste Geschichte unter der Sonne* [1776], eds. Hubert Gersch and Insel Taschenbuch, Frankfurt a. M., 1984. Page numbers in the text refer to this edition, and translations are my own.

"Nach des Verfassers Theorie sind Neid und Vorzugssucht die zu allen Zeiten, an allen Orten, in allen Ständen der Menschheit und Gesellschaft, bey allen Charakteren allgemeinsten Triebfedern der menschlichen Natur und Urheberinnen alles Guten und Bösen auf unserm Erdballe. Er stellte also in dem Leben jener drey Personen ein Gemählde der Welt auf, in welchem Neid und Unterdrückung die Hauptzüge sind, wie sie ihm die Geschichte der Menschen und Völker darbot."

18. "[. . .] der Auszug des Krieges wird lehren, wer von beyden Theilen recht behalten und ob Belphegor als Patriot und Menschenfreund allgemein bekannt werden oder im Streite für die Freyheit ungerühmt umkommen soll."

19. In *Sinners—Fools—Paradise Lost: Satires and Cultures*, I show that both the Christian and the mercantile cultures form a somewhat unholy alliance in late-sixteenth-century Protestantism. This Christian mercantile culture is evident in the prose satire *Historia von D. Johann Fausten* (1587). Its biographic format also demonstrates the rise of the concept of the individual. It made it possible for Marlowe to turn the satire that depicted Faust as damned because of his individual defiance of God, into the tragedy of a misguided great man (1592).

WORKS CITED

Auerbach, Erich. "Figura" [1944]. Tr. Ralph Manheim. In *Scenes from the Drama of European Literature*. Minneapolis: U of Minnesota P, 1984. 11–76.

Bohnert, Christiane. "Der Weg vom Wort zur Tat: Ma_stab und Wirklichkeitsbezug der Satire 1774–1792." *German Quarterly* 60 (1987): 548–66.

——. "Sebastian Brants 'Narrenschiff': Satire und Wirklichkeit an der Schwelle zur Neuzeit." *Daphnis* 14.4 (1985 [i.e. 1986]): 615–45.

——. *Sinners—Fools—Paradise Lost: Satires and Cultures*. St. Louis, Mo: Unpubl. ms., 1993.

——. "Enlightenment and Despotism: Two Worlds in Lessing's 'Nathan the Wise'." In *Impure Reason: Dialectics in the Age of Enlightenment*. Detroit: Wayne State UP, 1993. 40 msp.

Corti, Maria. *Introduction to Literary Semiotics* [Italian, 1976]. Bloomington: Indiana UP, 1978.

Danielou, Jean. *From Shadows to Reality: Studies in the Biblical Typology of the Fathers*. Engl. Tr. of *Sacramentum Futuri: Etudes sur les Origines de la Typologie biblique*. Paris: Beauchesne, 1960. London: Burns & Oates, 1960.

Eco, Umberto. *Theory of Semiotics*. Bloomington: Indiana UP, 1976.

Elliott, Robert C. "Satire" (1973). In *Encyclopedia Britannica*, 23 (1989): 182–84. Flögel, Carl Friedrich. *Geschichte der Komischen Litteratur*. 4 vols in 2 [1784]. Repr. Hildesheim: Olms, 1976.

——. "The Definition of Satire: A Note on Method." In *Yearbook of Comparative and General Literature* 11 (1962): 19–23. Repr. in *SATVRA: Ein Kompendium moderner Studien zur Satire*. Ed. Bernhard Fabian. Hildesheim: Olms, 1975. 67–71.

——. "The Satirist and Society." *ELH: A Journal of English Literary History* 21 (1954): 237–48. Repr. in *Satire: Modern Essays in Criticism*. Ed. Ronald Paulson. Englewood Cliffs, N.J.: Prentice-Hall, 1971. 205–16.

Gaier, Ulrich. *Satire. Studien zu Neidhard, Brant, Wittenwiler und zur satirischen Schreibart*. Tübingen: Niemeyer, 1967.

Haug, Walter. *Literaturtheorie im deutschen Mittelalter: Von den Anfängen bis zum Ende des 13. Jahrhunderts. Eine Einführung*. Darmstadt: Wissenschaftliche Buchgesellschaft, 1985.

Highet, Gilbert. *The Anatomy of Satire*. Princeton: Princeton UP, 1962.

Jacobs, Jürgen. *Prosa der Aufklärung: Kommentar zu einer Epoche*. Munich: Winkler, 1976.

Kernan, Alvin B. "Robert C. Elliott, 1914–1981." In *English Satire and the Satiric Tradition*. Ed. Claude Rawson with Jenny Mezciems. Oxford: Blackwell, 1984. 1–5.

Kindermann, Udo. *Satyra: Die Theorie der Satire im Mittellateinischen. Vorstudien zu einer Gattungsgeschichte*. Nürnberg: Bang, 1978.

Kristeva, Julia. *Revolution in Poetic Language*. Tr. Margaret Waller. New York: Columbia UP, 1984.

Kuiper, Koenraad. "The Nature of Satire." *Poetics* 13 (1984) 459–73.

Lemmer, Manfred. "*Ich hab ettwan gewacht zu nacht*: Zum Narrenschiff-Prolog, Vers 90." In *Kritische Bewahrung: Festschrift Werner Schröder*. Berlin: Erich Schmidt, 1974. 357–70.

Lotman, Jurij M. "Problems in the Typology of Culture." [1967]. In *Soviet Semiotics: An Anthology*. Ed., tr. Daniel P. Lucid. Baltimore and London: Johns Hopkins UP, 1977. 215–21.

Manger, Klaus. *Das "Narrenschiff": Entstehung, Wirkung und Deutung*. Erträge der Forschung. 186. Darmstadt: Wissenschaftliche Buchgesellschaft, 1983.

Martini, Fritz. "Wieland: 'Geschichte der Abderiten' (1963 [rev. 1981])." In *Christoph Martin Wieland*. Ed. Hansjörg Schelle. Darmstadt: Wissenschaftliche Buchgesellschaft, 1981. 152–88.

Mensching, Günther. *Das Allgemeine und das Besondere: Der Ursprung des modernen Denkens im Mittelalter*. Stuttgart: Metzler, 1991.

Paulson, Ronald. *The Fictions of Satire*. Baltimore: Johns Hopkins UP, 1967.

Randolph, Mary Claire. "The Structural Design of the Formal Verse Satire." *Philological Quarterly* 21 (1942) 368–84.

Die Römische Satire. Ed. Joachim Adamietz. Darmstadt: Wissenschaftliche Buchgesellschaft, 1986.

Rosenheim, Edward W. *Swift and the Satirist's Art.* Chicago: U of Chicago P, 1963.

Rosmarin, Adena. *The Power of Genre.* Minneapolis: U of Minnesota P, 1985.

Schönert, Jörg. "'Wir Negativen' —Das Rollenbewußtsein des Satirikers Kurt Tucholsky in der ersten Phase der Weimarer Republik." In *Kurt Tucholsky: Sieben Beiträge zu Werk und Wirkung.* Ed. Irmgard Ackermann. Munich: Text + Kritik, 1981. 46–88.

———. *Roman und Satire im 18. Jahrhundert: Ein Beitrag zur Poetik.* Stuttgart: Metzler, 1969.

Skalweit, Stefan. *Der Beginn der Neuzeit: Epochengrenze und Epochenbegriff.* Erträge der Forschung. 178. Darmstadt: Wissenschaftliche Buchgesellschaft, 1982.

Snyder, John. *Prospects of Power: Tragedy, Satire, the Essay, and the Theory of Genre.* Lexington: U of Kentucky P, 1991.

Traugott, John. "The Yahoo in the Doll's House: *Gulliver's Travels* the Children's Classic." In *English Satire and the Satiric Tradition.* Ed. Claude Rawson with Jenny Mezciems. Oxford: Blackwell, 1984. 127–150.

Tronskaja, Maria. *Die deutsche Prosasatire der Aufklärung.* Berlin (GDR): Rütten & Loening, 1969.

Uspenskij, Boris et al. "Theses on the Semiotic Study of Cultures (As Applied to Slavic Texts)." In *Structure of Texts and Semiotics of Culture.* Eds. Jan van der Eng, Mojmir Grygar. The Hague, Paris: Mouton, 1973. 1–28.

Weinbrot, Howard D. *Eighteenth-Century Satire: Essays on Text and Context from Dryden to Peter Pindar.* Cambridge: Cambridge UP, 1986.

Wellbery, David E. "Zu den Vorträgen Kaes, Lützeler, Hohendahl [on issues of postmodernism and New Historicism. C.B.]." In *Geschichte als Literatur: Formen und Grenzen der Repräsentation von Vergangenheit.* Eds. Hartmut Eggert, Ulrich Profitlich, Klaus R. Scherpe. Stuttgart: Metzler, 1990. 381–84.

Williams, Brooke. "What has history to do with semiotic?" *Semiotica* 54:3/4 (1985): 267–333.

Winner, Irene Portis. "Ethnicity, Modernity, and Theory of Culture Texts." In *Semiotics of Culture.* Eds. Irene Portis Winner, Jean Umiker-Sebeok. Approaches to Semiotics. 53. The Hague, Paris, and New York: Mouton, 1979. 103–47.

Winner, Thomas G. "Structural and Semiotic Genre Theory." In *Theories of Literary Genre.* Ed. Joseph P. Strelka. Yearbook of Comparative Criticism. University Park and London: Pennsylvania State UP. 255–268.

Worcester, David. *The Art of Satire.* New York: Russell & Russell, 1960. First publ. Cambridge, MA: Harvard UP, 1940.

·9·

The Culture Market, The Marriage Market, and the Exchange of Language: Swift and the Progress of Desire

Erin Mackie

Satire is a form of cultural criticism and, as such, an eminently social production; it is as well often doggedly antisocial. Rational and benevolent reform is satire's social alibi, but is often maintained on only the shakiest ground. Posing as the upstanding custodian of social and cultural correction, satire often stumbles, revealing motivations and producing effects irrelevant to reform. By this I mean not so much those visceral, primitive impulse of misanthropy (though these are also at work), as the satirist's often obsessive commitment to a rigorous logic of exposure that is *not* identifiable with reform, and may indeed stymie any positive impact by drawing into the web of scandal the very conditions of satire's own possibility.

The most crucial condition for the satirist is that of his own authority, his license to speak. One convention of satiric discourse grants the satirist a privileged distance above or outside the object of his critique; this provides his immunity from the conditions he exposes and so validates his own authority. Yet, satire also involves a kind of excruciating self-consciousness that, as it does in the satire of Jonathan Swift, can foreclose the satirist's purchase on any privileged position of distanced immunity and authority. And of course, without this immunity, the satirist's critique risks invalidation. Satire, then, may comprise the conventions of its own invalidation. But, in a final turn of the paradoxical screw, the performance of self-cancellation, again as it does in Swift, may stand as a kind of suicidal confirmation of satiric control: the satirist's authority may be realizable, finally, only in his annihilation. Epitomizing those deconstructive qualities that Kirk Combe and Brian Connery speak of in the introduction, Swift leaves a kind of conceptual void where the terms offered up by the play of the satire (Fool/Knave, Houynhnhnm/Yahoo, and, as I will suggest here, Wife/Whore and Satirist/Satirized) are *all* canceled out.

In Swift's poetic satires these paradoxes of implication and distance, social reform and antisocial reaction, authority and annihilation, emerge with laser precision. As he formulates it, the networks of desire-driven exchange (linguistic, sociosexual, and economic) where relations and significance are *produced,* are as well the channels through which they are *corrupted,* even nullified. Ultimately, I argue, Swift's satire strikes at the heart of desire itself. Desire propels men and women into the narratives and economies that determine and undo them; in response, Swift puts the progress of desire under siege. Swift's satire cannot tolerate desire; it negates desire by representing its outcome as death in various guises: reified, exhausted language; people reduced to pure fetish; commodified texts torn and tattered into wastepaper; starved and alienated authors; diseased whores; excrement; and impossibility.

Swift's bleak satiric disaffection reflects both the specifically generic challenges of satiric authority and the historical conditions of early modern commercialization. Swift is an early, and reactionary, critic of modern commercial culture; the poems I discuss here are saturated with anxieties about contamination through exchange, reification, and cultural, as well as personal, entropy and dissolution. These anxieties respond to the deep and broad commercialization of early eighteenth-century England that brought with it the commodification of literature, culture, social relations, and even, some feared, of subjectivity itself. The text and the subjectivity embodied there realizes itself in networks of exchange where they are both recognized and perplexed, both granted significance and laid open to a system of appropriation where significance can never be commanded. Venturing into the marketplace of public opinion, the satirist risks losing control over his text and his self in the treacherous networks of the printing industry, with its piratical entrepreneurs, and the culture industry, with its increasingly commercial and popular standards.

Concerned with the constraints of his own medium, Swift often meditated darkly on language. And language is more than the medium of textual work, it assumes as well a central role in the formation of cultural institutions and so of the human subject. As such, language becomes a focal point of Swift's anxiety and satire. Intensely concerned with the construction and dissolution of the textual self, Swift's satire presents the subject's movement in language as a tragic spectacle.[1] The entrance into language is a fall into alienation and a subjection to forces that determine us while remaining "without our power" ("To Stella, Who Collected His Poems" 63). To put it dialectically, language cuts both ways: the medium of self-recognition and self-construction, of interaction and communication, it also, inevitably, alienates, jeopardizes, distorts, and limits. But, treating the positive potential of language as little better than a ruse that lures us into a false sense of security with its seductive promises of communication, expression, and identification, Swift tends to cancel out the dialectical interplay of the subject in language.

Recently, in an attempt to cast a finer net over Swift's perplexed subject, critics have taken up the methodological instruments of Lacanian psychoanalysis. According to Jacques Lacan, entrance into language subjects one to the signifier and to the (phallic) law that governs the symbolic. The symbolic order and the language through which the subject enters it have laws of their own that shape the existence of the subject in ways that *necessarily* involve self-alienation and unfulfillable desire. This subject loses her place in language as much as she finds it. As Lacan explains, identity formation takes place through the medium of the other that reflects the self back to its self. Premised on alienation, doubling, loss, and the other, identity is actually nothing of the kind.[2]

While there do seem to be certain formal similarities between Swift's and Lacan's delineations of a subject driven by desire into the symbolic networks that both constitute and estrange her, there are as well crucial differences. Swift's equation—I would call it a confusion—of instability and impossibility, lack and nullity, unfulfillability and futility, is *not* a necessary implication of the psychic economy described by Lacan.[3] Swift's satire does vividly enact the complex incommensurabilities of subjectivity and language, the self and other, desire and its object that Lacan foregrounds in his own psychic paradigms.[4] But where Lacan's description of lack, of the instability of signification, of the absence of origins, of the contradictions of identity, may be read as a mapping of the tensions that *create* desire, meaning, and subjectivity, Swift's account shows these conditions *annihilating* desire, meaning, even the subject. The self's "radical ex-centricity to itself," its dependency on the other for its own "signifying place," the prevention of "'total personality,'" of "being whole" by the subject's entrance into the metonymic chain of signification that is the movement of desire—these Lacanian principles can be read as the conditions of human existence; Swift tends to present them as the conditions of mortal doom.[5] The satiric personae are themselves prey to this systemic incoherence and contradiction that cancels their authority. And behind these personae the poet Swift becomes almost pathologically evasive in his flight from the conflicted boundaries of any subject-position and the estrangement of any desire.

While Lacanian paradigms may be useful in the articulation of some of the formal operations of Swift's satire, there are more explicitly historical aspects of Swift's distrust of language that links it to his distrust of concretely commercial and social (rather than sheerly symbolic) exchange. The inherent imperfection of sociocultural institutions like language was seen by Swift as dangerously aggravated by conditions of the market.[6] It was as a commodified author circulating on the marketplace of public opinion that Swift felt the greatest fear for his integrity. Publication mirrors and aggravates the functions of Lacan's symbolic order; both constitute and alienate the subject through language and circulation in networks of desire that are beyond the full comprehension or determination of that subject.[7] As a satirist who must mark his ideological territory with the stakes of language, his misgivings about language threaten to deprive Swift of the very tools of his trade.

Obsessed with the logics of sexual, social, and symbolic circulation, Swift prods the very foundations of our being in the world. With little confidence in the institutions through which people construct their cultures and themselves, Swift is a remarkably pessimistic and reactionary critic. Swift was threatened by nothing less than culture itself, specifically the economies through which it produces itself. For Swift, human institutions, like the clothes with which we hide our nakedness, are at best mystified supplements for human lack that expose, even as they seek to conceal, inadequacy and vulnerability. In this essay I identify the ideologies that Swift shows being reproduced in the self-canceling paradigms he constructs and take into some account the cultural logic of Swift's own severe skepticism. The impasses in Swift's work are symptoms of the conditions he satirizes, but ones to which his own ideology of human history and culture offers him few, if any, sustainable alternatives.

In his earliest published poem, "Ode to the Athenian Society," Swift laments the inevitable decay that time wreaks not only on our physical bodies, but also on those cultural institutions that we establish in order to counter personal mortality by providing, through them, an extrapersonal continuity through time:

> I grieve, this noble work so happily begun,
> So quickly, and so wonderfully carried on,
> Must fall at last to interest, folly, and abuse.
> . . . .

No conquest ever yet begun
And by one mighty hero carried to its height
E'er flourished under a successor or a son;
It lost some mighty pieces through all hands it passed
And vanished to an empty title in the last.
    For when the animating mind is fled,
        (Which nature never can retain,
            Nor e'er call back again)
The body, though gigantic, lies cold and dead. (275–91)

A human history of generation through time can only be, as Swift sees it, a
chronicle of loss. Inheritance is not accretion but diminution. In Swift's view,
the transmission from one generation to the next, far from guaranteeing the
continuity of knowledge and value instead corrupts and diminishes them. The
very act of passing on power and knowledge through political and cultural
institutions empties sociocultural entitlement of all meaning and import: "It
lost some mighty pieces through all hands it passed/ And vanished to an
empty title in the last." Human institutions provide no safety nets for fallen
man. Things wear out; institutions succumb to the same all-too-human
entropic forces that they are established to resist. This narrative of human history always staggering towards an implosion of value, matter, and meaning,
controlled Swift's vision of the limits and possibilities of those cultural institutions through which we seek the earthly redemption of reproduction, representation, and reform.

The narrative of progress-as-dissolution apparent in this early ode pervades
as well the set of powerful satires on desire that I have selected from Swift's
poetry to exemplify his anxieties about movement through the discursive channels of culture. In "Phyllis, or, The Progress of Love," "Strephon and Chloe," "The
Progress of Beauty," "The Progress of Poetry," and "On Poetry, A Rhapsody,"
movement in narrative time—the "progress" that Swift reverses—leads only to
debasement, dissolution, decay, disgust, and doggerel. Of course, the narrative
logic Swift discredits is a feature both of subjective structures of desire and also
of a larger historical paradigm, associated in its early religious form with narratives of spiritual development such as John Bunyan's *Pilgrim's Progress,* and later
with the more worldly, yet still highly providential, fictional narratives of Daniel
Defoe, Samuel Richardson, Tobias Smollett, and Henry Fielding, and finally with
the teleology of progressive (whiggish) historiography. Among other things, in
these poems Swift satirizes this whole progressivist ideology of human amelioration in historical time and through human institutions.

Swift sabotages the narratives of desire using tactics that are historically and
culturally specific. They involve the undermining of fetishization and narcissism,

two features especially visible in the eighteenth-century sentimental mythology of decarnalized woman.[8] Swift is as concerned to discredit this bourgeois erotic logic as he is to thwart the narrative logic through which the bourgeoisie consolidates its power in the sociocultural realm and inserts itself in history.[9] Swift's assault on desire is radical: it dismantles not merely the offending folly, vice, or idea, but the very ideological modes of their psychic and social production. Swift shows how desire itself is produced by dominant discourses in ways that undermine and exploit, rather than fulfill, the potentials of the subject so driven by them. The most necessary desire in commercial culture is the drive to enter into the market—either as subject or object, buyer or seller, consumer or commodity; and it is the degrading, sometimes lethal progress of this excursion into circulation that Swift's poems expose.

Focusing on circulation in the markets of sociosexual exchange, "Phyllis, or, the Progress of Love," tells the tale of a bourgeois woman's elopement with the stable boy. Phyllis runs off with the wrong groom; her "progress" is actually a regression through a debasement of signification into a total degradation—social, moral, and physical—of her life and her body. In a somewhat superficially positive reading of the poem, Phyllis cuts herself off from her position in the legitimate system of exchange as marriage and so finds herself in the illegitimate system of exchange as prostitution. From a bride with all the legal, social, and familial seals of legitimacy, Phyllis quickly devolves into a sluttish inn hostess resorting to prostitution to support her dissolute husband:

> How oft she broke her marriage vows
> In kindness to maintain her spouse
> . . . .
> For John is landlord, Phyllis hostess;
> They keep, at Staines, the Old Blue Boar,
> Are cat and dog, and rogue and whore. (89–100)

Yet the illegitimate desires that result in Phyllis's elopement, in her sexual transgression of class, are themselves fostered by the ostensibly legitimate bourgeois culture she only apparently scandalizes. Phyllis's errant desires are in no way peculiar to her, or even generated by her participation in any *unauthorized* discourses of desire. Her perversity is a product of, rather than a departure from, middle-class sexual norms. Her desires replicate the conventions of sentimental romances and play out the hypocrisies of bourgeois sexuality embedded in those conventions. This poem finally says that Phyllis *fulfills* rather than *violates* the values of her class and its culture. So Swift scrawls an ineradicable question mark over the ostensibly legitimate sphere of sociosexual exchange—marriage—that Phyllis "transgresses" in her elopement.

Swift's picture of the still virginal Phyllis highlights her manipulation of the conventions of sexual hypocrisy that mark the manners of "nice" girls:

> Desponding Phyllis was endued
> With every talent of a prude:
> . . . .
> She'd rather take you to her bed,
> Than let you see her dress her head
> . . . .
> In church, secure behind her fan
> She durst behold that monster, man:
> There practised how to place her head,
> And bit her lips to make them red;
> Or on the mat devoutly kneeling
> Would lift her eyes up to the ceiling,
> And heave her bosom, unaware,
> For neighbouring beaux to see it bare. (1–18)

Acting out seduction with the gestures of resistance in her pantomime of chaste ardor, Phyllis is well aware of the signifier's capacity for overdetermination: she exploits the signs of modesty as tokens of both sexual inexperience and sexual invitation. This is a prudish (i.e. hypocritical) form of coquetry and it works. Phyllis successfully hooks herself a husband—but only to betray him and her family by running off with the groom of the stables. Young women like Phyllis cannot be trusted because they are constrained by the imperatives of decency to lie: they can only express desire by denying it at the same time. The irony is that "decent" bourgeois culture itself supplies the arsenal of artifice and cliché that support Phyllis's transgression of its class structure. Bourgeois sexual ideology, Swift says in this poem, produces whores.

This ideology is anchored into cultural place by means of a stock of texts and social practices that, taken together, make up a highly accessible, commercialized, and fetishized discourse of desire. Phyllis's own sexual and textual practices operate within this discourse. Armed with a storyline and a rhetoric from the popular sentimental romances she has read, Phyllis pieces together an apology for her elopement with the groom:

> To my much honoured father,—these:
> ('Tis always done, romances tell us,
> When daughters run away with fellows)
> Filled with the choicest commonplaces,
> By others used in the like cases. (46–50)

She begins by justifying her love—"She'd do it if 'twere to do again"—yet soon changes her tune to placate her father—"She'll never do't another time." The letter's illogic of inconsistency and self-negation marks Phyllis's whole "progress," from her duplicitous coquetry and broken engagement on through the "romantic" quest that transforms her from a bourgeois bride to a public-house slut. Phyllis's tautological patchwork of fine phrases culminates in an attempt to remove herself from the standards and liabilities of public discourse: "She valued not what others thought her,/And was—his most obedient daughter" (71–72).

Phyllis, as author, reproduces public discourse, "the choicest common-places," in order to claim a place outside it. She imitates the letters used "By others . . . in the like cases" to show how hers is a unique case, outside conventional moral dictates. Phyllis's abuses of language and morals are in essence those of all Swift's bad writers. In his poem on a modern woman author, "Corinna," Swift represents exactly the sort of modish, commodified life and text that Phyllis emulates in her own. Turning briefly to this poem, I want to emphasize how Swift's satires against desire focus on specifically commercial networks of textual and sexual exchange that do not simply represent, but actually produce desire.

Corinna is the product of a denatured, defeminized birth. With Apollo acting as midwife she falls from nowhere into language and time, falls onto earth where she will fall again and again through the degradation of her body and of her language. The mock mythology of Corinna's birth and first days prefigure her fate and her doom: "This day (the year I dare not tell)/ Apollo played the midwife's part,/ Into the world Corinna fell./ And he endowed her with his art" (1–4).

Apollo endows Corinna with "art," but the form this art takes is determined by the charms Cupid and a satyr pronounce on the infant Corinna in the cradle: "Then Cupid thus: 'This little maid/ Of love shall always speak and write;'/ 'And I pronounce', the satyr said,/ 'The world shall feel her scratch and bite'" (9–12). So "art" is here, as often, an overdetermined term. It refers to poetic arts and to all the little erotic arts of coquetry. Corinna is in the fullest sense artful; she exploits erotic and satiric arts in her life as well as in her texts. Swift's entire representation of Corinna works through an overdetermination that conflates the sexual and textual. The scratching and biting the satyr pronounces resonates with aggressive erotic, as well as satiric, impulses. That Corinna's ardor will touch the whole world predicts her sexual promiscuity as much as her literary success and insinuates the equation between publication and prostitution that is graphically established by the end of the poem.

As an author, Corinna's physical body is identified with the body of her texts; the progress of her life becomes one with the progress of her works. For Swift linguistic representation is self-construction. That there is no guarantee of a self-identical subject, immune from the displacements of language and alienating appropriation, becomes for Swift not a license for endless free play but an imperative for prudent, highly self-conscious control. Corinna is less than scrupulous in her negotiations of her life; she breaches the moral limits of marriage and of discursive decorum. Finally her texts and her body are put outside her control, enthralled in an infinite prostitution to the public: "At twelve, a poet, and coquette;/ Marries for love, half whore, half wife;/ Cuckolds, elopes, and runs in debt;/ Turns authoress, and is Curll's for life" (25–28).

Corinna is what looks at first glance like a duplicitous subject—"a poet, and coquette," a woman who is "half whore, half wife"—just as she is a producer of two modes of discourse—the erotic and the satiric. These pairs of opposites, which remind us of the female contraries that offered such a fertile site of disdain and attraction in Pope's "Epistle to a Lady," lose their charm as well as their opposition in Swift. The apparent differences established by these pairs are collapsed: Corinna is a female poet *and so* a coquette, a promiscuous wife *and so* a whore; her satire is informed by her own satyr-ic nature, her own lechery. Her sexual promiscuity culminates in her lifelong prostitution to the printer Curll, who is in the same equation a pimp. Publishing is prostitution and a woman's publication in the town makes her a woman of the town: "A COPY of Verses kept in the Cabinet, and only shewn to a few Friends, is like a Virgin much sought after and admired; but when printed and published, is like a common Whore whom any may purchase for half a Crown" (Swift "Thoughts on Various Subjects" 249).

The public circulation of Corinna's erotic discourse threatens the public with infection of diseased language just as surely as the progress of the diseased prostitute threatens it with venereal infection. Corinna's venereal texts constructed out of her scandalous commonplace book ("all gallant is") and distributed by the printer/pimp Curll under the name of "romance" are analogues to the whore who, under the name of Cupid, inflames and accommodates lust and contaminates the town.

In "Corinna," Swift blasts the abuses of the modern female writer. The social effects of the scandalous romances that Corinna both lives and writes are apparent in the retrograde "progress" of Phyllis who uses such texts to choreograph the performance of her own desire. Phyllis, like Corinna, is a true modern. Her life falls outside conventions not to transcend them but to sink below them. Her "romance" is at the same time conventional and unconventional in the worst senses. Asserting herself outside and beyond the realm of public circulation of discourse, ironically as a prostitute she, like Corinna, enters into the most public and debased circulation of all.

Swift's critique in "Phyllis, or, The Progress of Love," shows how the ground for illegitimate sociosexual exchange may be found in the very niceties of convention and in the commonplaces of bourgeois popular culture. In other poems such as "Strephon and Chloe," "A Lady's Dressing Room," and "Cassinus and Peter," Swift likewise concentrates on the hypocrisies of legitimate, sentimental narratives of desire. "Strephon and Chloe," a tale of courtship and marriage, centers on the moment when all the artificial and quite literally inhuman supports of (masculine) desire are stripped away on the wedding night, leaving the couple in a condition of disgusting, if complaisant, familiarity. But Strephon and Chloe, unlike Phyllis and her groom John, remain solid middle-class citizens, fully confirmed and fully comfortable in their "beastly way of thinking" (209).

Typically, Swift performs the ideology he attacks by parodying its characteristic idiom; in "Strephon and Chloe" this idiom is sentimental pastoral. Swift uses a wooden, clumsy pastoral idiom to signal the inertia of this commercialized, overcirculated discourse and the ruinous effects it has on those who buy into the love stories it promotes. The desires and subjects that this discourse produces are heavily reified and fetishized; it is a perfect instrument for the production of commodities on the marriage market. Epitomizing the ideal, decarnalized, bourgeois woman—Chloe is just such a commodity:

> Of Chloe all the town has rung;
> By every size of poet sung:
> . . . .
> By nature formed with nicest care
> And, faultless to a single hair.
> Her graceful mien, her shape, and face,
> Confessed her of no mortal race
> And then so nice, and so genteel;
> . . . .
> You'd swear, that so divine a creature
> Felt no necessities of nature. (1–2; 5–9; 19–20)

The Chloe that circulates on the marriage market is the ethereal, waxen "goddess" idol that the poets construct from their commonplace books. The emphasis that Swift places on the stereotypicality of his Chloes, Celias, Strephons, and Phyllises, foregrounds the equivalency and so exchangeability of these reified characters produced by conventions that simultaneously govern both texts and social practices. Bad poetry, like the fashionable society it serves, empties its subjects of their individuality, autonomy, and self-determination, rendering them mere two-dimensional, cutout figures. So not only Chloe, but also the eligible beaux who court her are reduced by metonymy to the fashion fetishes and reified conventions through which they conduct sociosexual relations:

> What powdered wigs! What flames and darts!
> What hampers full of bleeding hearts!
> What sword-knots! What poetic strains!
> What billet-doux, and clouded canes. (35–38)

More mannequin than man, Strephon moves through a progress of desire that eventually strips him of his canes and clothes, his poetic strains and bleeding heart, and every last shred of his decency. As the wedding night approaches, Swift lingers at length on Strephon's sexual anxieties. "The hardest part" of the whole marriage ordeal, achievement of its "*crowning joys*" presents to Strephon an almost insurmountable difficulty (70–71). At first his fear is represented as the fear of giving offense to his love goddess, Chloe: "Can such a deity endure/ A mortal human touch impure?" (89–90). But in the next stanza gender roles are reversed and the real ground of Strephon's fear is exposed.

Calling to mind, with no great accuracy, classical precedents for goddesses condescending to sleep with mere mortals, Strephon first heartens himself:

> And goddesses have now and then
> Come down to visit mortal men:
> To visit and to court them too:
> A certain goddess, God knows who,
> (As in a book he heard it read)
> Took Colonel Peleus to her bed. (97–102)

But Strephon's rumination over the tatters of classics culled in his school days next calls up a less inviting image of woman's sexuality:

> But, what if he should lose his life
> By venturing *on* his heavenly wife?
> For, Strephon could remember well,
> That, once he heard a schoolboy tell,
> How Semele of mortal race,
> By thunder died in Jove's embrace;
> And what if daring Strephon dies
> By lightning shot from Chloe's eyes? (103–110)

While still sustained by the surface logic of sentimental discourse, Strephon's sexual anxiety casts him as the agent of sexual violence that offends the delicate Chloe; but as his meditations sink deeper, this is revealed as a displacement that veils the fear of the castrating female that is the actual source of

Strephon's sexual reluctance. Gender is skewed in this allusive memory that casts Strephon not as a mortal man consumed by the erotic fire of a goddess, but as a mortal woman (Semele) slain by the sexual potency of a god (Jove). Strephon's fear of sex is a fear of feminization, of emasculation. Swift shows how, by masking it as adoration, the sentimental discourse of goddesses, flames, darts, and the rest of it, accommodates and so perpetuates a fear of women and their bodies that is inseparable, finally, from loathing.[10]

At the eleventh hour, Strephon is spared sexual confrontation with the phallic woman, the potent goddess of his dark erotic fantasies. Interrupting Strephon's stalwart, if diffident, advances, Chloe steps off her pedestal down to the chamberpot and pisses. This smelly, undeniable proof of her female and mortal body divests Chloe of all Strephon's fantasies: "He found her, while the scent increased, / As *mortal* as himself at least" (185–86). The couple commences, then, a relationship played out through excrement rather than sex. Love is banished and replaced by a kind of mutually agreeable domestic swinishness: "How great a change! how quickly made! / They learn to call a spade, a spade. / They soon from all constraint are freed. . . . / And, by the beastly way of thinking, / Find great society in stinking" (203–10).

Strephon's and Chloe's "progress" from courtship to marriage descends from one degraded and deathly form to another. Their circulation as empty tokens on the marriage market has its outcome on the chamberpot where humanity is reduced to this lowest common denominator of the mortal, deathly body. So the waste of human potential and the reductive equivalency implicit in the images of the lovers as mere shells of dead language and dead commodity is explicitly re-presented in the excremental outcome of their matrimonial transaction. This romance plot ends in death, appropriately figured here as the death of sexual desire in a fetishization of excrement. As the filthy outcome of the circuit of human desire, excrement is in Swift a frequent emblem of death. So Swift riddles on a privy in "The Gulf of All Human Possessions": "This cave within its womb confines / The last result of all designs:/ Here lie deposited the spoils / Of busy mortals' endless toils" (11–14).[11] The proximity between the womb and the tomb in a psychic economy centered on fears of castration before the Medusa's head of female sexuality is compounded in Swift's imagination with other self-canceling pairs of (re)production and death: work ends only in waste, design ends in chaos. The accretion of cultural capital in such an economy can only be the hoarding of filth; the investment of libidinal energy can only give returns in deathly fetishes.

"Violence," performance theorist Joseph Roach says, "is the performance of waste." And if in "Strephon and Chloe" Swift exposes the waste that results from the veiled violence (against the female body, against human dignity) of bourgeois desire, in the "Progress of Beauty," he exposes the violence of desire's assault on the prostitutes who function as culture's human refuse. As the commodified woman's body on the illicit market, the prostitute occupies a less-than-human position of illegitimate sexual circulation in contradistinction to which the legitimate exchange of marriage is produced. As in "Strephon and Chloe," in "The Progress of Beauty" Swift draws on pastoral conventions; but here they are used to narrate the decay of a professional whore rather than the devolution of a bourgeois marriage. Showing that both these narratives can be produced by the same discourse, Swift rejects the distinctions between them and so dismantles the categories through which bourgeois ideology of class and gender claims its legitimacy.

That the objects of their desire are mortal and unstable, that they change through age and decay, that these objects are even corporeal are notions not tolerable to the ideals of feminine beauty produced by this ideology. As we have seen in "Strephon and Chloe," Swift's satire discredits these ideals. In poems such as "The Progress of Beauty," "Strephon and Chloe," "A Lady's Dressing Room," "A Beautiful Young Nymph Going to Bed," and "Cassinus and Peter," Swift exposes the way patriarchal exchange creates its objects by requiring that women construct themselves according to models of masculine desire and so become admissible signifiers in the systems of exchange—marriage or prostitution. While Swift's poems graphically depict socioeconomic structures of woman's place, they simultaneously reveal the psychosexual complement of these structures: the phallic construal of woman as the fantastic other, the support for man's own fantasies of wholeness. In Luce Irigaray's terms, Swift's reading of phallic inscription on women's absence becomes a way to disconstrue male myths of presence—sexual and linguistic.[12] Patriarchal privilege, especially in its newly developing bourgeois and domestic inflections, is undermined in Swift's satires on women in ways that revise societal norms and satiric conventions.

"The Progress of Beauty" narrates the gruesomely physical decomposition of a woman whose body, life, desires, and future are consumed by the disease, disorder, and exploitation of the prostitution market. Celia is not the agent, nor even the dupe, but the victim of an exchange that, along with slavery, epitomizes human commodification and exploitation in its most lethal forms. The "progress" of Celia's "beauty" recites the hideous process of her decay into a body-in-pieces.

Before her disintegration is complete, Celia is able to mask the signs of age, disease, and poverty by artful application of cosmetics: "But Celia can with ease reduce, / By help of pencil, paint and brush, / Each colour to its place and use, / And teach her cheeks again to blush" (45–48). This literal self-inscription as a recognizable signifier in the sexual economy is highly self-alienating. Once

Celia has composed herself according to the pattern of fashion and of male desire, "She knows her early self no more" (49). What her freshly painted surface conceals are the signs that time and labor have written on her body. These marks attest both to Celia's mortality and to her exploitation. If a paper of verses published is like a whore, this whore trying to patch herself back together is like a tattered paper of verses.

By focusing on the work and the material that go into women's self-production, Swift exposes the lack of identity between the body of woman and the commodity/signifier (of masculine desire) she becomes. This exposure represents the female body as a product of female labor that works, often explicitly against women's own interests, for corrupting sociocultural institutions. Again and again Swift's narratives of desire pass through a central specular scene: the woman working for hours before the mirror, transforming herself into a ghostly commodity because her life depends on it. Swift exposes the processes of specularization and standardization through which this alienated labor is performed and this lack of identity magnified. In "The Progress of Beauty," Celia stands before the mirror, constructing a double that supports the illusion of an integral self. This painted, dyed, dressed, coiffed, spectacular body-on-the-market reflects back the fetish image of masculine desire, the picture of herself as the desire of the other.

Celia's self-inscription eventually runs aground. Like the modern writer of *A Tale of a Tub,* at last condemned by the deficiency of his own invention to write upon nothing, so the modern nymph of Drury Lane, reduced by the depredations of venereal disease, tries to write upon the absent site of her own face: "Two balls of glass may serve for eyes, / White lead can plaster up a cleft, / But these alas, are poor supplies / If neither cheeks nor lips be left" (113–16). Here Swift dramatizes the Lacanian notion of woman's access to the phallus through a masquerade in which she denies her self in order to become the signifier of an other's desire: "It is for what she is not that she expects to be desired as well as loved" ("The Meaning of the Phallus" 84). This masquerade in dress and manner echoes the poet's own masquerade in the discursive conventions through which he forfeits himself in order to gain access to an audience, a lover, a market where he may be reflected back to himself in the fullness of an other's fantasy of plenitude. And as I discuss later, Swift the poet and lover backs away from this masquerade and will deny his own desire before admitting his own lack.

Both whore and poet are left with the futile task of writing, of composing the fantastic commodity fetish woman. In "To Stella, Who Collected His Poems," Swift maligns the poet who rhymes on female faces subject to decay:

> So Maevius, when he drained his skull
> To celebrate some suburb trull;

His similes in order set,
And every crambo he could get;
Had gone through all the commonplaces
Worn out by wits who rhyme on faces;
Before he could his poem close,
The lovely nymph had lost her nose. (71–78)

The commonplaces with which the Grub Street poet writes are as corroded as the nose of his trull. The possibility of composing an integral image of the subject is always precluded in advance by a tattered and tired medium. Like the cosmetic arts whose application, in Swift's vision, attests only to the decay beneath and becomes identified with that decay, so the poetic arts—indeed mediation itself—are corrosive.

Of course there are important distinctions to make between the hack poet Maevius and the nymph/prostitute Celia. Maevius is the subject of exploitation and Celia the object. She is "the lovely nymph" who "had lost her nose" before the poet could immortalize it and her in verse. Yet, by looking at Swift's vision of the poet's position in the culture market, we can see how these distinctions between exploiter and exploited, victimizer and victim, knave and fool, often collapse under the pressures of a bad economy where any victory is Pyrrhic: "If, on Parnassus' top you sit, / You rarely bite, are always bit: / Each poet of inferior size / On you shall rail and criticize;/ And strive to tear you limb to limb" ("On Poetry: A Rhapsody" 345–49). It is not only the paper of verses and the prostitute, but also the poet himself whose body is torn, racked, and ruined. A victim of competitive malice rather than frustrated Maenads, the modern-day Orpheus falls to the exigencies of an aggressive marketplace.

Driven by capital, spurred by deregulation when the Licensing Act expired in 1695, suffused by a growing force of professional authors, the publishing market swelled, producing waves of literary fashions that, according to some including Swift, threatened to erode the bulwarks of culture. The rise of the printing industry went hand-in-glove with the decline of the aristocratic patronage system. More and more often working for wages, the writer's alienation from his labor and easy exploitation was guaranteed in the absence of copyright laws. One of the earliest modes of mass production, printing produced textual objects whose physical and graphic uniformity emphasize those qualities of equivalency and exchangeability that mark the commodity per se. It was in this hypercommercialized mode that Western culture would dress itself and so, according to the dark prognostications suggested in Swift's satire, put on the shirt of Nessus fated to poison and consume the body beneath.

In "The Progress of Poetry" and "On Poetry, A Rhapsody," Swift explores the narratives his culture scripts for the poet. Processes of creative production are shown enthralled to economies that distort value, erode meaning, engender hypocrisy, and starve poets as surely as they do prostitutes. Poverty becomes in these poems not merely an attendant, but a necessary condition for poetic production. Uninspired and unproductive, the well-fed poet "fresh in pay" wallows in comfort; but his money spent, lying starving in a garret, his imagination soars: "And up he rises like a vapour, / Supported high on wings of paper; / He singing flies, and flying sings, / While from below all Grub Street rings" ("The Progress of Poetry" 43–46). A professional writer who sells his work piecemeal to the printer, the Grub Street hack's creative powers are subject to the laws of the market-economy in which his texts circulate. Surplus shuts down and scarcity drives on the mills of poetic production.

The conditions of his text's production and consumption are outside of the poet's determination and usually operate at his expense. Embodied in his verse, the poet is subjected to the exploitation and violence of publishing-as-prostitution; his role as cultural producer necessarily concludes in his circulation as commodity consumed by a voracious and devouring public. And this consumption is death:

> Poor starveling bard, how small thy gains!
> How unproportioned to thy pains!
> And here a simile comes pat in:
> Though chickens take a month to fatten,
> The guests in less than half an hour
> Will more than half a score devour.
> So, after toiling twenty days,
> To earn a stock of pence and praise,
> Thy labours, grown the critic's prey,
> Are swallowed o'er a dish of tea;
> Gone, to be never heard of more,
> Gone, where the chickens went before.
>   ("On Poetry" 59–70)

As a textually constituted subject, Swift's poet, in good Orphic tradition, is torn to pieces. But here the poet isn't merely dismembered and scattered, but also eaten alive—just another product that feeds the rituals of modish consumption. And here in a figure that calls up, even as its parodic inflection mocks, the horror of evil's banality, these rituals are rendered as cannibalism. The poet's desire to "earn a stock of pence and praise" by entering into the commerce of discourse ends in his death.

Pain, humiliation, even death, through textual abuse was a fate Swift envisioned not only for Grub Street hacks, but also for himself and for poets, like Pope, he admired. In "Verses on the Death of Dr. Swift," the poet projects a paranoid fantasy of Curll's posthumous production of an unauthorized biography and pirated edition of his works (201–04). The life, will, and letters of the writer are resurrected from the trash heap—"Now Curll his shop from rubbish drains; / Three genuine tomes of Swift's remains"—only to be enthralled to Curll in a kind of undeath of illicit publication.

Just as the textual body of the poet meets an ignominious end in the dustbins of culture, so does it emerge from an equally inglorious origin in the kennels of polluted fancy, discarded language, and base interest. In "On Poetry, A Rhapsody" the poet's congenital illegitimacy—*a condition of his very status as poet*—is figured with images of base birth: "the spawn of Bridewell," "infants dropped," "the spurious pledges / Of gypsies," the "bastard of a pedlar Scot," "beggar's brat, on bulk begot" (33–38). Motivated by these anxieties about the generation and decay of the textual self, Swift resists subject positions he sees as especially vulnerable. Trying to outdistance time and the limits of subjectivity, in "Verses on the Death of Dr. Swift" he refuses the first person "I" and so tries to speak from a perspective beyond the death of the author. Musing on the uncertain outcome of fame in the hands of a "careless and ignorant posterity," Swift associates this danger with the displacement and misappropriation inherent in the naming systems of language itself: "And though the title seems to show / The name and man, by whom the book was writ, / Yet how shall they be brought to know / Whether that very name was he, or you, or I?" ("Ode to the Athenian Society" 165–68).

Perhaps most generally, Swift fought against subjection to those forces that put the determination of our selves outside our control. "To Stella, Who Collected His Poems" enacts this contest through the issues of desire and its representation as determination. Concerned with evading the snares of conventional erotic and poetic paradigms, the poet displaces the language of love with a desireless and so invulnerable discourse "Without one word of Cupid's darts, / Of killing eyes, or bleeding hearts" (11–12). The poet's relationship to Stella is removed from the progress of love and stands still and impassive. Both the emotion and the course of desire that love entails are inoperative: "I ne'er admitted love a guest;" ". . . his pursuits are at an end, / Whom Stella chooses for a friend" (14; 23–24).

Just as "friendship" with Stella seems to offer a positive alternative to the disastrous discourse of sexual desire, so there seems to be a class of "true poets" whose language is transacted in economies of truth that create solid values invulnerable to the meretricious trade on Grub Street:

> True poets can depress and raise;
> Are lords of infamy and praise:
> . . . .

Unjustly poets we asperse;
Truth shines the brighter, clad in verse;
And all the fictions they pursue,
Do but insinuate what is true. (53–54; 57–60)

In these lines, mediation seems fully under the thumb of truth. But this security is immediately undermined by the very terms that represent it:

Now, should my praises owe their truth
To beauty, dress, or paint or youth,
What Stoics call without our power,
They could not be insured an hour. (61–64)

Here "dress" and "paint" are associated with forces of mediation that threaten the poet with their independence from his control and this threat echoes back to the sartorial figure used immediately before to illustrate, not the liabilities but the advantages of poetic mediation—"Truth shines the brighter, clad in verse" (58; my emphasis). What, we must ask, guarantees that the "dress" of poetic language is any less superficial and ephemeral than the "dress" or "paint" that cover the decayed bodies of the nymph/prostitutes celebrated by those Grub Street "wits who rhyme on faces"? (76).

This question remains unanswered; the conflict between the desire for a stable ground that insures meaning, value, and autonomy, and the awareness that no such ground exists remains unresolved. Indeed, as we have seen, Swift pits this awareness (of lack) against desire (for satisfaction) and its narratives, which Swift tracks to their dead ends. In a sense, Swift's final engagement is with this site of frustrated possibility itself, this dead end of desire's trajectory.

Discussing this condition of impossibility, this self-canceling lack of resolution in Swift, one critic cites it as the condition of his work's "truth" (Rawson 167). But simply because the irresolvable tensions generated from a deconstruction of one and another ideological paradigms often form the final epistemological horizon of Swift's satire does not mean that they need remain the final critical horizon of our readings of that satire. Swift has much to tell about the conditions—often exploitative, dehumanizing, and contradictory—that sustained bourgeois culture during the watershed period of financial, commercial, and imperial growth in England around the first quarter of the eighteenth century. But his irresolution, his inability to sustain a vision of possibility within and for cultural institutions should not, I think, be confirmed as the "truths" of his texts.

Impossibility is the trump card in Swift's satiric hand. But there is no reason to keep the game closed. The "irresolvable ambiguity," the impasse in this satire by no means partakes all the inevitability of a "truth." Rather Swift's pervasive performance of entrapment by impossibility offers information about some of the ideological structures that dominated his culture and one set of refusals of them. But this refusal, along with the snares it would avoid, is just as much a *product*, as a negation of (or escape from) the sociocultural conditions he assails. Swift's well-nigh apocalyptic skepticism may itself be a component truth of the context it denies rather than a judgment-as-truth on that context.

NOTES

1. See Wyrick, ch. 6 "Investments: Swift and the Tragedy of Language."
2. See "Agency of the Letter in the Unconscious" (171–72).
3. See, for example, Lacan's "The Function of Language in Psychoanalysis," "The Agency of the Letter in the Unconscious," "Function and Field of Speech and Language," and "The Meaning of the Phallus."
4. In "Swift and the Subject of Satire," Elizabeth Maddock takes on these analogies and describes in both Swiftian and Lacanian terms the limitations faced by the linguistically constituted subject (110).
5. Lacan, "The Agency of the Letter" 71–72; "The Meaning of the Phallus" 79-82. See Fredric Jameson who acknowledges both the conservative overtones in Lacan's thought and "the dialectical possibilities inherent in it" (373). Pollak notes how "to Swift, no self was ever fully 'proper' to itself. . . . all identity as he conceived it was perforce, in part, extrinsically derived" (178).
6. For a history of what has come to be called the "commercial revolution," see McKendrick, Brewer, and Plumb. P.G.M. Dickson provides a detailed history of the "financial revolution" that went hand-in-glove with England's entrance into modernity at the turn of the eighteenth century. For the contest over, and the gradual legitimation of materialism and consumption, see Joyce Appleby.
7. I think it is best to think through the psychic paradigms of Lacan, and for that matter, Freud, in relation to historical pressures that produce the structures of consciousness these paradigms articulate. On the relation between Lacanian psychoanalysis and marxian materialist historiography, see Jameson who outlines the similarities between these two thought systems (385–86).
8. See Pollak's discussion in ch. 2, "The Eighteenth-Century Myth of Passive Womanhood." See also Ian Watt on "the decarnalization of the public feminine role" (163–64).
9. See Pollak, especially ch. 6, "The Difference in Swift." As Carole Fabricant points out, Swift's texts are usually antagonistic to the normative categories of their age (17).
10. Pollak discusses how Swift "is intent on exposing not only the male anxiety engendered by the fact of sexual difference, but also the process by which the fetishized female 'normally' displaces the masculine fear" (160). On Swift's discreditation of the phallic order in *Gulliver's Travels*, see Ruth Salvaggio (421–23).
11. On Swift's use of excremental figures to comment on circulation and as an allegory of writing itself, see Wyrick (95; 114–27).
12. For another analysis of woman's sociocultural role in exchange see Gayle Rubin's "The Traffic in Women." Both Rubin and Irigaray work in the context established by anthropology (Levi-Strauss), psychoanalysis (Freud and Lacan), and marxian conceptions of the commodity. I discuss Swift's treatment of women on the market at more length in "'The anguish, toil, and pain,/ Of gathering up herself again'": The Fabrication of Swift's Women."

Works Cited

Atkins, G. Douglas. "Going Against the Grain: Deconstruction and the Scriblerians." *The Scriblerians and the Kit-Cats* 17 (1985): 113–17.

Appleby, Joyce Oldham. *Economic Thought and Ideology in Seventeenth-Century England.* Princeton: Princeton UP, 1978.

Brown, Marshall. "Deconstruction and Enlightenment." *The Eighteenth Century: Theory and Interpretation* 28 (1987): 259–263.

Fabricant, Carole. *Swift's Landscape.* Baltimore: Johns Hopkins UP, 1982.

Irigaray, Luce. "Women on the Market." *This Sex Which Is Not One.* (1977). Tr. Catherine Porter. Ithaca: Cornell UP, 1985. 170–91.

Jameson, Fredric. "Imaginary and Symbolic in Lacan: Marxism, Psychoanalytic Criticism, and the Problem of the Subject." *Literature and Psychoanalysis: The Question of Reading: Otherwise.* Ed. Shoshana Felman. Baltimore: Johns Hopkins UP, 1982. 338–95.

Lacan, Jacques. "The Meaning of the Phallus." *Feminine Sexuality: Jacques Lacan and the Ecole Freudienne.* Eds. Juliet Mitchell and Jacqueline Rose. Tr. Jacqueline Rose. New York: W. W. Norton & Co./Pantheon Books, 1985. 74–85.

———. "Agency of the Letter in the Unconscious." *Ecrits: A Selection.* Tr. Alan Sheridan. New York: W. W. Norton & Co., 1977. 146–78.

———. "The Function and Field of Speech and Language in Psychoanalysis." *Ecrits: A Selection.* Tr. Alan Sheridan. New York: W.W. Norton & Co., 1977. 30–113.

McKendrick, Neil, John Brewer, and J. H. Plumb. *The Birth of a Consumer Society: The Commercialization of Eighteenth-Century England.* Bloomington: Indiana UP, 1982.

Mackie, Erin. "'The anguish, toil, and pain,/ Of gathering up herself again': The Fabrication of Swift's Women." *Critical Matrix* 6.1 (1991): 1–19.

Maddock, Elizabeth. "Swift and the Subject of Satire." *Qui Parle* 4.2 (1991): 91–118.

Pollak, Ellen. *The Poetics of Sexual Myth: Gender and Ideology in the Verse of Swift and Pope.* Women in Culture and Society Series. Ed. Catharine R. Stimpson. Chicago: U of Chicago P, 1985.

Rawson, Claude. "The Nightmares of Strephon: Nymphs of the City in the Poems of Swift, Baudelaire, Eliot." *Order from Confusion Sprung: Studies in Eighteenth-Century Literature from Swift to Cowper.* London: George Allen & Unwin, 1985. 154–92.

Roach, Joseph. "'Windsor-Forest': Culture and Performance in the Circum-Atlantic World." Plenary address delivered at "Eighteenth-Century Views Reviewed: New and Old Historicisms," 1993 Western Society for Eighteenth-Century Studies Conference. U of California, Santa Barbara, February 13, 1993.

Rubin, Gayle. "The Traffic in Women: Notes on the 'Political Economy' of Sex." *Toward an Anthropology of Women.* Ed. Rayna Reiter. New York: Monthly Review Press, 1975. 157–210.

Salvaggio, Ruth. "Swift and Psychoanalysis, Language, and Woman." *Women's Studies* 15 (1988): 417–34.

Swift, Jonathan. *The Complete Poems.* Ed. Pat Rogers. Penguin English Poets. Gen. ed. Christopher Ricks. New York: Penguin, 1983.

———. *A Tale of a Tub. The Writings of Jonathan Swift.* Eds. Robert A. Greenberg and William B. Piper. New York: W. W. Norton & Co., 1973. 263–372.

———. *Thoughts on Various Subjects.* Vol. 4 of *Prose Works of Jonathan Swift.* Eds. Herbert Davis and Louis Landa. Oxford: Basil Blackwell, 1957. 241–54.

Watt, Ian. *The Rise of the Novel: Studies in Defoe, Richardson, and Fielding.* Berkeley: U of California P, 1957.

Wyrick, Deborah Baker. *Jonathan Swift and the Vested Word.* Chapel Hill: The U of North Carolina P, 1988.

·10·

Economic Discourse in the Savoy Operas of W. S. Gilbert

Linda V. Troost

Playwright, poet, and lawyer William Schwenck Gilbert is perhaps best known for the satirical operas written in the last quarter of the nineteenth century with Arthur Sullivan, the works known collectively as the Savoy Operas, "a 'divine emollient' for the well-educated and well-to-do" (Rowell *Theatre* 6).[1] Most critical work on Gilbert has focused on biography or theater history (both scholarly and anecdotal), but a few scholars have looked at his operas in more theoretical ways.[2] Those examining his work as a satirist have countless observations on Gilbert's mockery of popular theatrical genres (nautical drama, sentimental drama, melodrama), revered institutions (law, politics, the peerage), human frailties (pride, greed, hypocrisy), and social trends (aestheticism, women's education, colonial expansion). This chapter, in contrast, looks at his broader methods of satire and works toward a clearer definition of the eponym, "Gilbertian."

Of all modes of literary discourse, satire depends most on underscoring difference, of isolating the "other," usually for attack. For Gilbert, the other consists of the exotic, the mysterious, romantic, the theoretical, all pitted against the commonplaces and realities of Victorian capitalism. Instead of idealizing the other, Gilbert the satirist denigrates it by exposing its dependence upon the standard against which it supposedly revolts. In each of the satiric operas, the idealized other collapses into the mundane, often expressed as commercialism.

Toward the end of his career with Sullivan, Gilbert implicates capitalism itself, now pitted as an ideal against its hard-nosed self, and destroys the hierarchy exploited by the earlier operas.

I first wish, however, to distinguish among the various forms of that evasive term *burlesque,* the category under which one must put the intentional mismatch of subject and style of presentation that lies at the heart of his method. First, there is *theatrical burlesque,* a "grotesque" parody of the subjects and styles of a theatrical genre like melodrama or opera (Booth, *Prefaces* 174–75). Although not so blatant as Gilbert's theatrical burlesque on Donizetti's *The Elixir of Love—Dulcamara; or The Little Duck and the Big Quack* (1866)—the comic opera *Ruddigore* (1887) comes closest to the theatrical burlesque with its parody of the conventions of Victorian melodrama and nautical opera: bad baronets, good old men, Gothic settings, wholesome sailors, fantastic scenic transformations, and patriotic sentiment.

Literary burlesque can take two basic forms and appear in any genre. *High burlesque* describes a low or ordinary subject with an inappropriately high style. The most common version, the "mock-heroic," creates comic incongruity by describing the commonplace in language normally applying to the magnificent and noble. The most noted exemplars, John Dryden and Alexander Pope, use this strategy largely to attack personal hypocrisy by highlighting the discrepancy between the low subject and the high style the subject tries to exploit. *Low burlesque* inverts the principles of the high burlesque: a high or serious subject or character gets a seemingly inappropriate and degrading description. The exemplars of this style—François Rabelais, Paul Scarron, and Samuel Butler—primarily use it to attack the hypocrisy behind revered institutions—religion, politics, literature—by showing the fundamental lowness of the exalted topic.

The Savoy operas use all three types of burlesque, but they are best remembered for the distinctive texture and tone we call "Gilbertian." Gilbert's genres, technique, and the object of his focus vary throughout his professional career, but the basic pattern of burlesque remains: he unites two opposite forces, generally "the ordinary and the extraordinary" (Rowell "Introduction" 1). Sometimes he inverts the two in logical topsy-turveydom, exemplified by the Bab Ballads—the comic poems written for *Fun* in the 1860s—and his extravaganza, *Topsy-turvydom* (1874).[3] Just as often, however, he fuses the high and the low, uniting both literally and metaphorically what seem antithetical. I wish to look at one strain in the operas that illustrates this method: the fusing of the discourses of the economic and the romantic.

Gilbertian burlesque, as I shall name it, mismatches subject and style but holds each in suspension. In particular, Gilbert marries a grandiose concept, such as poetry, to something ordinary, like shopkeeping. Literary burlesque describes one thing in terms of an extreme other, but in the Gilbertian world, the incongruities do not seem to exist because the subject and its mode of presentation become one thing: poetic rapture and business profits live happily together.[4]

In addition, Gilbertian burlesque generates a tension between what the audience expects and what the author gives, and therefore, it serves as a suitable vehicle for the satiric exposure of a seeming ideal. To distance the audience, however, Gilbert treats the serious farcically, and also, to borrow his comment on *H.M.S. Pinafore*, addresses "a thoroughly farcical subject in a thoroughly serious manner" (in Smith 48). The audience wants to indulge in escapism at the theater, but the author forces it, through the earnestness of the characters' dialogue and the realistic technical details, to see the deception of the real world embedded in the theatrical fiction.

For Gilbert, the process of creating the tension of incongruity first required fabricating a realistic visual world. Carrying on the tradition for scenic verisimilitude that Madame Vestris started in the 1830s and that Tom Robertson developed later in the century,[5] author-director Gilbert paid great attention to accurate scenery and costumes. For example, the Peers' costumes in *Iolanthe* were made by the court robemakers to her Majesty,[6] and the Bucks and Blades in *Ruddigore* wore historically accurate uniforms belonging to twenty different regiments, each listed in the first-night program. The scenery was as carefully planned: when designing the deck for the *H.M.S. Pinafore*, Gilbert spent a day in Portsmouth sketching rigging (Pearson 97). And, as the reviewer for the *Standard* noted with glee, Gilbert disciplined his singers, even those in minor roles: "Here we find that marvel of marvels, a chorus that acts, and adds to the reality of the illusion" (in Allen 76).

Why should Gilbert lavish such artistic detail upon fantastical comic operas? David Eden argues that this obsession derives from Gilbert's "sublimations of an original anal erotism" (70), but Jane Stedman's explanation is more essential: Gilbert wanted a strong visual link between this fantasyland and our own world to deepen his satire (200–01).

With a material world in the audience's view, Gilbert now can invent absurd characters with skewed values to populate it. Upon closer examination, however, we see Gilbert has attacked some genuine delusion or correctable human frailty: an obsession with family pride, for example, or a besotted passion for the latest fashion in art or literature. The seemingly realistic world onstage, after a few twists, finally proves to be genuinely realistic after all, with its characters reflecting, with painful accuracy, the nonsensical attitudes of some humans. Also, the commodified comic-opera stage visually supports Gilbertian burlesque by fusing the illusory ideal with the commonplace to expose the materialism behind the romantic.

The Sorcerer (1877) provides a simple example of Gilbertian burlesque invoked through what will become one of Gilbert's favorite modes: the discourse of ordinary business and trade. The title of the opera suggests to the audience magic, spells, and spirits; when the sorcerer makes his appearance, he turns out to be John Wellington Wells, of "J. W. Wells & Co., the old-established Family Sorcerers in St. Mary Axe" (35). Instead of an elusive spirit, like Mephostophilis in Marlowe's *Doctor Faustus,* Gilbert gives his audience a full-fledged businessman, "a dealer in magic and spells" (37) with a permanent address, business cards, and advertisements in all the papers. Gilbert derived this technique of combining the sublime and the domestic from the fairy extravaganza, a whimsical entertainment descended from the pantomime and related to the burlesque (Booth *Prefaces* 169), but he does more with the device than James Robinson Planché did in the previous generation. The domesticated magician's first speech, most aptly, is a sales pitch:

> Yes, sir, we practise Necromancy in all its branches. We've a choice assortment of wishing-caps, divining rods, amulets, charms, and counter-charms. We can cast you a nativity at a low figure, and we have a horoscope at three-and-six that we can guarantee. Our Abudah chests, each containing a patent Hag who comes out and prophesies disasters, with spring complete, are strongly recommended . . . Our penny Curse–one of the cheapest things in the trade–is considered infallible . . . We can't turn 'em out fast enough (36).

Gilbert reduces Wells from a Merlinesque sorcerer to a common tradesman who sells magic the way others sell soap. No matter how exotic the talisman or spell, Wells sees it as merely a stock item: if anyone burns for knowledge, he or she can purchase "*an extremely small prophet, a prophet / Who brings us* [the firm] *unbounded returns*" (37). The pun on prophet/profit collapses the magical into the commercial, allowing neither to gain the upper hand.[7]

Admittedly, Wells can conjure up frightening images in his Incantation, but in every respect, he represents a model tradesman with excellent marketing strategies. He is "not in the habit of puffing [his] goods" (39) because he has his reputation to keep up as "an old-established house with a large family connection" (39). As a shrewd salesman, he offers 10 percent discounts for "prompt cash" (39) and 25 percent discounts to members of the Army and Navy Stores. Not everyone sees the magician's prosaic side. The heroine, Aline Sangazure, fears Wells will turn her into a guinea pig: she holds the conventional romantic view of magicians, the one the audience holds, too.

Her fiancé, Alexis, wins her over by reassuring her that Wells fits into the ordinary world of the comic opera: "He *could* turn you into a guinea-pig, no doubt, but it is most unlikely that he would take such a liberty. It's a most respectable firm, and I am sure he would never be guilty of so untradesman-like an act" (36). Alexis sees no discrepancy between the commercially mundane and the magically fantastic side of Wells. Such blindness to absurdity always warns us of satire in Gilbert's comic worlds: the contrast lies in Alexis's deadpan acceptance and the audience's awareness of the absurdity. We laugh because Alexis does not. We want escape in our entertainment, but Gilbert forces us to see that behind the mysterious, lurks the profitable.

Gilbertian burlesque appears in other operas as well, but with greater sophistication and satirical force. In *The Pirates of Penzance* (1880), for instance, the pirates (all noblemen in disguise) view their exotic and escapist calling as a vocation. They even have apprentices, as carpenters and plumbers have. Unlike Wells, the Pirate King does not "think much of [his] profession" (110), but, like the professional sorcerer, he thinks his pirate band conducts itself in a businesslike fashion: they aim to make a profit. Unfortunately, they are not successful capitalists: "We don't seem to make piracy pay" (108).

Why not? The band allows noblesse oblige to interfere with their piracy instead of practicing laissez faire: they "make a point of never attacking a weaker party" and therefore, "invariably get thrashed" (108). Nor do these noble pirates molest orphans because they, too, are orphans. They operate according to the gentleman's code of honor and the Victorian's sense of duty, collapsing the values of the day into the trade of piracy and commenting thereby on the lack of these values in business.

Even Major-General Stanley, who buys his way into the social hierarchy, acquires an aristocratic ideology with his ancestors: "Frederic, in this chapel are ancestors: you cannot deny that. With the estate, I bought the chapel and its contents. I don't know whose ancestors they *were,* but I know whose ancestors they *are,* and I shudder to think that their descendant by purchase (if I may so describe myself) should have brought disgrace upon what, I have no doubt, was an unstained escutcheon" (128). With his new acquisition, the Major General puts on its matching values. Having fibbed his way out of pirate clutches in Act 1 by pretending to be an orphan, he has the noble decency to feel guilty in Act 2.

The nobly born Pirate King sees the corruption of the society from which he has fled:

> Oh, better far to live and die
> Under the brave black flag I fly,
> Than play a sanctimonious part,
> With a pirate head and a pirate heart.
> Away to the cheating world go you,
> Where pirates all are well-to-do;

But I'll be true to the song I sing,
And live and die a Pirate King! (110)

The King astutely remarks in the dialogue before his famous song that, "contrasted to respectability, [piracy] is comparatively honest" (110). Gilbert openly condemns the hypocrite who pleads utter respectability while conducting business far shadier than selling penny curses for profit. If piracy and necromancy are honest trades, then what has happened to society's standards of conduct? *The Sorcerer* asks this question in a distant way by using magicians as the subject; *The Pirates of Penzance* tackles the issue more directly.

The French philosopher Henri Bergson notes the pervasiveness of Gilbert's method of satirizing his subject. In his treatise on laughter, published in 1900, Bergson notes that: "To express in reputable language some disreputable idea, to take some scandalous situation, some low-class calling or disgraceful behaviour, and describe them in terms of the utmost '*respectability,*' is generally comic. The English word is here purposely employed, as the practice itself is characteristically English" (142). Gilbert manipulates this English form of comic transposition by doubling it upon itself: as piracy becomes a "respectable" trade, respectable businessmen become pirates. The pirates of Penzance are noble earls, dukes, and barons underneath their pirate outfits, which prevents them from hunting profit efficiently: their noble values incapacitate them.[8] The successful businessman, however respectable on the surface, is only a robber baron underneath and therefore can pursue his self-interest without the aristocratic impediment of honor. In the conservative, comic world of *Pirates,* nobility makes a difference, even if, as the Major General shows, obtained by purchase. It is altruistic nobility of character, not showy romanticism or desire for profit, that Gilbert asks us to admire.

The combining of the romantic and the economic appears yet again in the next collaboration between Gilbert and Sullivan: *Patience* (1881). The two aesthetic poets, Reginald Bunthorne and Archibald Grosvenor, are presented as tradesmen "in the high aesthetic line" (164). Bunthorne affects the conventional picture of Inspired Poet to impress the Rapturous Maidens that follow him everywhere, but he does not see his occupation as deriving from divine inspiration. He is a machine generating poetry in shifts. For example, after appearing to suffer "*all the agonies of composition,*" he reassures his audience, "It was nothing worth mentioning, it occurs three times a day" (160). Bunthorne's muse seems to ship inspiration regularly. The repetitive element, incongruous for a profession that relies on the spontaneous, reveals the lowness of what he is *really* doing: fabricating an illusion.

Grosvenor, however, does not fabricate anything—he merely supplies the goods. As the idyllic poet who steals the affections of almost all the Rapturous

Maidens from Bunthorne, Grosvenor explicitly sees himself as an ordinary shopkeeper and makes no show of divine poetic inspiration: "Ladies, I am sorry to appear ungallant, but this is Saturday, and you have been following me about ever since Monday. I should like the usual half-holiday. I shall take it as a personal favour if you will kindly allow me to close early to-day" (182). Like the Family Sorcerer, Grosvenor runs his shop and controls the hours of poetic rapture as easily as a shopkeeper can regulate his hours. And Grosvenor reduces his mystic power to a commodity.

The world, to quote the rapturous maiden Angela, is a "whirlpool of grasping greed" (167). As Bunthorne confides to Patience the dairy maid, "What's the use of yearning for Elysian Fields when you know you can't get 'em, and would only let 'em out on building leases if you had 'em?" (166). Bunthorne is all too human in trying to impose upon others, but he does recognize his hypocrisy, unlike the self-deceptive Grosvenor and the Rapturous Maidens. Next to the frank commercialization of the rival Grosvenor, however, Bunthorne must fail, but not because of his hypocrisy. Capitalist economics ensures the survival of the blandest, and Grosvenor's product outsells Bunthorne's.

Bunthorne understands that noble aspiration is doomed to failure in a materialistic, changing world. Nevertheless, he maintains the pose of the pure aesthetic poet instead of blending art with the shop, as Grosvenor so successfully does. Unfortunately, when Grosvenor abandons aestheticism to become an "*arithmetical/Every-day young man*" (197), the Rapturous Maidens follow his fashion, and Bunthorne finds himself alone. It seems a harsh punishment for the one character who sees through false, fashionable poetry, but his market timing is not as good as Grosvenor's.

Gilbert's operas of the late 1880s and early 1890s deal less with trade and shopkeeping and more with mechanization and finance. *Patience* introduces factory-generated poetical raptures, but the full development of the human assembly line appears later. For example, *Ruddigore* (1887) boasts "professional bridesmaids who are bound to be on duty every day from ten to four" (376), and who mechanically burst into the same song at the slightest hint of a wedding. The opera's accursed baronet performs evil deeds on a regular schedule (with bank holidays off, of course), and the ancestral ghosts view being a bad baronet as a vocation: "It is our duty," says Sir Roderic, "to see that our successors commit their daily crimes in a conscientious and workmanlike fashion" (417). Even evil and the supernatural operate according to a set of mundane regulations.

The dehumanization caused by an increasingly industrial Victorian society becomes more extreme in *The Gondoliers* (1889) and *Utopia, Ltd.* (1893). In these works, humans become not machines, but corporations.[9] Economic

priorities engulf the human element. In *The Gondoliers*, the formerly penniless
Duke and Duchess of Plaza Toro, now "registered under the Limited Liability
Act" (551), make a nice living for themselves in questionable operations. The
Duke, for example, helps start bogus corporations:

> I sit, by selection,
> Upon the direction
>   Of several Companies bubble . . .
> As soon as they're floated
> I'm freely bank-noted—
>   I'm pretty well paid for my trouble. (552)

The Duchess hires herself out for equally dubious assignments: whitewashing
the reputations of shady ladies, providing testimonials for bad dressmakers,
endorsing patent medicines and facial soaps she does not use. The advertising aristocrats conclude their song with a verse clarifying the moral dangers
of such dehumanization:

> In short, if you'd kindle
> The spark of a swindle,
>   Lure simpletons into your clutches . . .
> Or hoodwink a debtor
> You cannot do better
>   Than trot out a Duke or a Duchess. (553)

We laugh at them in the context of the opera because of their double levels,
but their reduction into a company encourages them to profit from personal
dishonesty: "Honesty, patriotism, courage, a high sense of honor are being
replaced by the morality and ethics of the counting house" (Lawrence 167).

Utopia, Ltd. carries Gilbertian principles to an extreme. King Paramount's
daughter, Princess Zara, returns from Girton College, Cambridge, with guests
for her languorous homeland, which wants to imitate England, a "powerful,
happy, and blameless country" (595) "where every virtue flourishes" (587).
Among her seven guests (the "Flowers of Progress"), she includes Mr.
Goldbury, a Company Promoter. The Utopians immediately launch national
reform: "But perhaps the most beneficent change of all has been effected by
Mr. Goldbury, who, discarding the exploded theory that some strange magic
lies hidden in the number Seven, has applied the Limited Liability principle
to individuals, and every man, woman, and child is now a Company Limited
with liability restricted to the amount of his declared Capital! There is not a
christened baby in Utopia who has not already issued his little Prospectus!"
(606). Freed from the need to ally with six other people before metamor-

phosing into a corporation, the Utopian can do so alone. Once they become businesses, however, they exempt themselves from everything that controls the moral individual. They can declare bankruptcy and avoid paying their debts, thereby driving others into financial ruin. For example, Scaphio and Phantis find themselves in financial trouble when none of their debtors will pay up. Nor can they fulfill their job of controlling despotic King Paramount: "we are helpless! He's no longer a human being—he's a Corporation, and so long as he confines himself to his Articles of Association we can't touch him! What are we to do?" (615). Their solution is political revolution.

Gilbert's satire, however, is, like that of many other satirists: essentially conservative. Like Juvenal or Pope before him, Gilbert sees a threat in the contemporary political, social, or literary system, and he longs for the values that existed in the good old days predating the interlopers. Gilbert may attack the same bourgeois, greedy attitudes Karl Marx, William Morris, and Bernard Shaw attack, but his solution differs from theirs. He exposes the flaws of the system to warn a credulous public, but when it comes to major economic and social overhaul, he prefers to obliterate the reformers and their ideologies instead of establishing a new order.

Like Swift, Gilbert sees a life run by theory as absurd and sometimes dangerous to humanity, but unlike the author of *Gulliver's Travels*, Gilbert frees his creations from their traps instead of misanthropically following them to their doom. For instance, Alexis Pointdextre and the Palmieri brothers espouse extreme socialist positions when it comes to reform, but Gilbert gives each a comeuppance instead of an outright condemnation. He shows that self-interest invariably undermines ideology. In *The Sorcerer*, Alexis sees, to his horror, his aristocratic father about to marry the humble pew-opener and promptly abandons his revolutionary theories about the positive value of interclass marriage. In *The Gondoliers*, Marco and Giuseppe Palmieri learn that absolute equality for all, even with everyone's being elevated to high station, does not work in practice. People long for distinctions:

> When you have nothing else to wear
> But cloth of gold and satins rare,
> For cloth of gold you cease to care—
> Up goes the price of shoddy. (543)

Socialist ideology goes contrary to human nature, and even with new economic and social ideologies in place to suppress rank, the old love of making discriminations will eventually surface.

Gilbertian burlesque, which flattens two levels (high and low) into one, serves as a concrete example of social leveling and its consequences. Socialism is as absurd, Gilbert suggests, as a comic opera. Of course, proper levels reassert themselves in all the operas, but happiness lies in restoring the past, not in establishing a utopian future. In *The Gondoliers,* for instance, the real ruler of Barataria, once discovered, re-establishes the traditional class system at the end of the opera, and all characters end happily, with each Baratarian and Venetian united to the correct beloved and returned to his or her correct place in the hierarchy. Gilbert may attack the evils of capitalism, but he regards social radicalism as the greater evil. He prefers the devil he knows to the one he doesn't.

Even the incorporated royal subjects in *Utopia Ltd.* reject the reforms advocated by Princess Zara although the reforms have eliminated war, disease, and lawsuits. They adopt instead a real English system instead of the idealized one: "Government by Party! Introduce that great and glorious element—at once the bulwark and foundation of England's greatness—and all will be well! No political measures will endure, because one Party will assuredly undo all that the other party has done; and while grouse is to be shot, and foxes worried to death, the legislative action of the county will be at a standstill. Then there will be sickness in plenty, endless lawsuits, crowded jails, interminable confusion in the Army and Navy, and, in short, general and unexampled prosperity!" (626). Princess Zara's economic paradise brought bad times to lawyers and doctors when the country reformed its legal and sanitation systems. Now, however, humanity's ills will restore profits to the middle classes. A reviewer for the *Daily Graphic* called the opening night's longer version of Zara's speech "about the bitterest speech Gilbert has ever penned" (in Allen 380), prompting Gilbert to tone it down (Allen 413). Gilbert shows the social price the Victorians have paid for their prosperous economic system, but he also warns that changing the system will lead to other problems. As the opera shows, capitalism as an ideal ultimately undermines itself.

In the final operas, Gilbert sees plot complications resulting, not from one person's obsession or some arbitrary law, but from a larger "predicament"— the fault lies in the entire political-economic system (Sutton 92–93). Gilbert's shift to a larger scope for his satire explains the shift in discourse from that of trade in the early works to that of corporations in *The Gondoliers* and *Utopia, Ltd.* To mitigate the increasingly severe satire, he transplants his works from contemporary British settings to distant ones.[10] The first seven operas (excluding the anomalous *Thespis*) are set in Victorian Britain; the last six have either foreign or historical settings (and sometimes both).

As literary burlesque goes after both public and personal targets, so does Gilbert in his quest to purge his audience through laughter. Radical political reformers and rampant capitalists may come under fire, but so does the rigid Victorian moralist obsessed with a Kantian sense of duty.[11] Jay Newman argues

that this aspect of Teutonic philosophy opposes the "classical liberalism" and util-
itarianism Gilbert's comic operas generally bring forward as a preferred system
of morality (276–80). The skeptical Gilbert would bristle at being associated with
any kind of ism, but he definitely does pillory "the power of a concept—if not
a mere word—to affect behavior" (Sutton 100), especially because he sees devo-
tion to a seemingly noble ideology as a cover for material gain.

For example, *Ruddigore's* Rose Maybud, a slave to her book of etiquette, feels
compelled to switch fiancés rather than act in a manner contrary to her book's
teachings. Interestingly enough, she has just realized that Robin the farmer is
wealthier than the sailor, Richard: "I knew not that thou didst seek me in wed-
lock, or in very truth I should not have hearkened unto this man, for behold,
he is but a lowly mariner, and very poor withal, whereas thou art a tiller of the
land, and thou hast fat oxen, and many sheep and swine, a considerable
dairy farm and much corn and oil!" (392). The biblical discourse does not conceal the pragmatism of her statement although she thinks it does. *The Mikado's*
Pooh-Bah, uses the same ruse. In a desperate attempt to "mortify [his] pride
continually" (320), he does penance by filling multiple "degrading" governmental posts (and accepting all their salaries). Again, pious words do not conceal his abuse of a moral code for personal profit. As Sutton notes, "Duty . . .
means obeying one's impulses" (101).

Gilbert attacks entrapment by a theory by making names and concepts independent entities and allowing assorted characters obsessed by them to run the
comic-opera worlds. People become things or ideas to be shuffled. Bergson
sees this comic pattern of thinking as a reflection of industrialized life: these
characters are "looking upon life as a repeating mechanism, with reversible
action and interchangeable parts" (126). All one need do is start the machinery and let the plot run. Captains, kings, babies, spouses, dukes—all are
interchangeable parts in the comic-opera machine. Hayter argues that Gilbert
attacks the fundamental "meaninglessness of the class system" (95), but more
specifically, Gilbert mocks narrow thinking about class. All people become, to
social snobs, mere names and titles, and Gilbert's satire exposes their false code
by parodying the mental and social rigidity caused by confounding the signifier and the signified.

The confounding takes ludicrous form in early works such as *H.M.S. Pinafore*
(1878). When Little Buttercup reveals that she inadvertently switched two babies
many years ago, the system of the opera demands that the two adults—one a cap-
tain and one an able-bodied seaman—now exchange places so they match their
new labels. Their identities, their accomplishments in life and the Navy become
hollow because of the sudden switch. Sir Joseph Porter, ruler of the Queen's Navy,
who rose to his exalted position by polishing door handles and by voting only

at his party's call, also illustrates the meaninglessness of the label "First Lord of the Admiralty." The maidens in *The Gondoliers* and *The Grand Duke* switch allegiance to whoever, at the moment, happens to be the King of Barataria or the Grand Duke because they see themselves as betrothed to a title and its income, not a person.[12] To the snob, the name itself is the substance, and Gilbert satirizes snobbery's dehumanizing nature by treating its premise literally and logically. For Gilbert, social snobbery's valuing name and rank over accomplishment illustrates theory's smothering of humanity. The snobs hope to create difference through titles and rank; instead, they cause a collapse of that difference because anyone can wear the label of "King of Barataria" or "Grand Duke of Pfennig Halbpfennig." A title no longer marks a person as an exalted and valuable "other"; that person's humanity collapses into the title—the signified person becomes the signifier, or worse, part of a signifier. In *The Gondoliers,* "King of Barataria" and "fiancée of the King" consist at one point in the second act of five people instead of two, but that poses no problem to a clever accountant: "Three wives—two husbands . . . That's two-thirds of a husband to each wife" (545). Treat a label as more important than the person, and the pie divides neatly, if absurdly.

The Savoy operas attack capitalists, socialists, social climbers, snobs who denounce social climbers, slaves to duty, and those who evade their duties. What, then, is Gilbert really attacking through his burlesque? Narrow-mindedness and hypocrisy, be it of the audience, of conservatives, or of radicals. The double level of Gilbertian burlesque evokes the laughter of ridicule, the audience's cure. The comic fusing of the two levels—the noble and the materialistic, the theoretical and the practical—provides the audience with a flexible perspective to see the arbitrariness of both fictional and actual social constructs. Gilbert reprimands us for misreading the poetical, the theoretical, or the socially acceptable—too many of these are disguises for self-interest. By giving them a commercial or financial slant, Gilbert exposes the illusion to us and trains us to be skeptical of both present and future social, political, and economic deception.

Gilbert shields us, however, from the harsh satiric corrective and gives us distance through absurdity. His play *Engaged* (1877), staged a month before *The Sorcerer,* had a disappointing run because it lacked sufficient comic distance.[13] It savagely portrays, through its hypocritical characters, a "sacrifice of identity . . . to money" (Cardullo 465). The same material reworked for *Ruddigore* and other operas, however, went over well with the audience. These works allow us to laugh to scorn the absurd representatives of the world's materialistic dangers and mankind's narrow-mindedness, all safely distanced by song and dance. In the first Savoy opera, *The Sorcerer,* the satire is so mild that we see no warning at all; by *The Mikado,* eight years later, we cannot miss it; in *Utopia, Ltd.,* it becomes blatantly Swiftian.

Reginald Allen postulates that the generalized satire "is an important factor in the permanence of their appeal" (378). The operas occasionally lampoon individuals—Gilbert clearly is going after W. H. Smith, bookseller turned politician, in the character of Sir Joseph Porter—but Smith's type exists in every decade and every country.[14] The Savoy operas survive because they entertain on many levels (visual, aural, farcical) while flattering our intelligence, although *H.M.S. Pinafore, The Pirates of Penzance,* and *The Mikado,* which focus on the conventional satirical targets of pride and greed, are more popular than the works of the 1890s, which attack depersonalized political and economic systems, and demand more worldliness and detachment from their audiences.

Few amateur G & S troupes (bastions of the upper-middle class) touch *Utopia, Ltd.,* a work explicitly attacking capitalism and two-party politics although its satire has stood the test of time. It even offers warnings for an age that has made it both possible and financially advantageous for an individual to incorporate, something Gilbert proposed as a joke. Despite the opera's fantasy setting, Gilbert's comments hit too close to home for many of us who live off this competitive and predatory system. A satirist can successfully attack individual traits and manners without alienating his audience, but when he goes after an inescapable way of life, he will breed only resentment. In reaching for the satire of a system in *Utopia, Ltd.,* Gilbert paradoxically makes it too personal.

As G. K. Chesterton notes of the Victorians, "most respectable people still believed in liberty, because they still believed that no liberty could ever in *practice* invade respectability" (184). Gilbert wants to warn his listeners of the dangers of complacency. There are genuine threats to the liberty of Britain's citizens, not only from populist upheaval but from the dehumanizing effects of conformity (Sutton 123) and respectability. Even "the corporate idea" denies "the uncertainties of human life," protecting "the incompetent and the irresponsible man from the consequences of his own failure" (Borowitz 1279). The present systems, Gilbert argues, may be fraught with problems, but changes will be worse. The "other" may call seductively from this mundane world; Gilbert warns us that it is not an improvement.[15]

NOTES

1. The name derives from the Savoy Theatre, built in 1881 to house the works, previously performed at the Royalty and the Opera Comique.
2. Frye (46, 109) and Sutton (94–98) see elements of Frazerian mythic ritual in *The Mikado.* Borowitz, Sutton, Hayter, Fischler, and Cannadine contextualize the comic operas in Victorian history and culture. Munich studies Gilbert's contraltos from a feminist approach. Eden uses Gilbert's operas, plays, and poems more to psychoanalyze the

author than to illuminate the writings, but he nonetheless raises some insightful points amid the Freudian theory.

3. Gilbert uses the phrase for the first time in 1870 as the title for the Bab Ballad, "My Dream." James Ellis (360) notes that Gilbert may have gotten the inspiration for this inversion from William Sawyer's 1868 poem "Turvey Top."

4. Munich notes the similarity between romantic "rapture" and economic "rapacity" in the operas, which "delimits the transformations of conquest, allowing for the transposition between public and private significance" (30).

5. For a history of verisimilitude in stage scenery, see Appleton 126–27, 135–36 and Rowell, *Victorian* 18–19.

6. Messrs. Ede and Sons, as noted by the first-night reviewer for *The Era* (quoted in Allen 174).

7. Relentless punning comes into the Savoy operas via the fairy extravaganza and theatrical burlesque. See Rowell, *Victorian* 68–71.

8. Lawrence observes that Gilbert often regards the aristocracy in his operas as "irresponsible ciphers, and certainly not the men of common sense that Great Britain needs" (182).

9. Gilbert used the idea of literal human machines in *The Mountebanks* (1892), a comic opera with a score by Alfred Cellier. Two characters drink a magic potion and find themselves transformed into clockwork Hamlet and Ophelia dolls. For an analysis of Gilbert's satire on the Companies Act of 1862, see Borowitz 1276–79.

10. Hayter argues that this shift in setting accompanies "a decrease in social satire" and an increase in "music, comic characterization, and spectacle" (44–45). On the contrary: the farther the setting moves from late-Victorian England, the more caustic the satire becomes.

11. For a discussion of Kant's influence on Victorian morality, see Eden 127. For a summary of the Evangelical influence, see Hayter 101–103.

12. Oscar Wilde develops this Gilbertian idea in *The Importance of Being Earnest* (1895) by having both Cecily and Gwendolyn regard themselves as engaged to someone named Ernest.

13. Fisher notes that "Gilbert used the license of farce . . . to distance his audience" (281), but as the mixed reviews of *Engaged* indicate, liberal doses of farce did not compensate for attacking Victorian ideals (Booth, *Theatre* 187 and Sutton 79).

14. Gilbert learned his lesson from *The Happy Land* (1873). By portraying onstage Prime Minister Gladstone and his Liberal cabinet (thereby incurring the wrath of the Lord Chamberlain), the burlesque was too specific to outlast its target and closed before Gladstone's government fell. See Lawrence for a discussion of this burlesque.

15. A shorter version of this essay was first presented at the W. S. Gilbert Sesquicentennial Conference sponsored by the Massachusetts Institute of Technology in November 1987.

WORKS CITED

Allen, Reginald, ed. *The First-Night Gilbert and Sullivan.* Revised centennial ed. London: Chappell, 1975.

Appleton, William W. *Madame Vestris and the London Stage.* New York: Columbia UP, 1974.

Bergson, Henri. *Laughter.* Tr. Fred Rothwell. In *Comedy.* Ed. Wylie Sypher. New York: Doubleday, 1956. 61–190.

Booth, Michael R. *Theatre in the Victorian Age.* Cambridge: Cambridge UP, 1991.

———. *Prefaces to English Nineteenth-Century Theater.* Manchester: Manchester UP, 1980.

Borowitz, Albert I. "Gilbert and Sullivan on Corporate Law." *American Bar Association Journal* 59 (1973): 1276–81.

Cannadine, David. "Gilbert and Sullivan: The Making and Unmaking of a British Tradition." In *Myths of the English.* Ed. Roy Porter. Cambridge: Polity P, 1992. 12–32.

Cardullo, Bert. "The Art and Business of W. S. Gilbert's *Engaged,*" *Modern Drama* 28 (1985): 462–73.

Chesterton, G. K. "Gilbert and Sullivan" in *Cornhill Magazine* 69 (1930). Rpt. in *W. S. Gilbert: A Century of Scholarship.* Ed. John Bush Jones. New York: New York UP, 1970. 183–205.

Eden, David. *Gilbert and Sullivan: The Creative Conflict.* Rutherford: Fairleigh Dickinson UP, 1986.

Ellis, James, ed. *The Bab Ballads.* By W. S. Gilbert. Cambridge: Belknap P-Harvard UP, 1970.

Fisher, Judith. "W. S. Gilbert: The Comedic Alternative." In *When They Weren't Doing Shakespeare.* Eds. Judith L. Fisher and Stephen Watt. Athens: U of Georgia P, 1989. 280–98.

Fischler, Alan. *Modified Rapture: Comedy in W. S. Gilbert's Savoy Operas.* Victorian Literature and Culture Series. Charlottesville: U of Virginia P, 1991.

Frye, Northrop. *The Anatomy of Criticism: Four Essays.* Princeton: Princeton UP, 1957.

Gilbert, W. S. *The Savoy Operas.* London: Macmillan, 1926; rpt. 1975. All quotations from the Gilbert and Sullivan operas come from this edition, with song lyrics in italics.

Hayter, Charles. *Gilbert and Sullivan.* Modern Dramatists. New York: St. Martin's P, 1987.

Lawrence, Elwood. "*The Happy Land:* W. S. Gilbert as Political Satirist." *Victorian Studies* 15 (1971): 161–83.

Munich, Adrienne Auslander. "'Capture the Heart of a Queen': Gilbert and Sullivan's Rites of Conquest." *The Centennial Review* 28 (1984): 23–44.

Newman, Jay. "The Gilbertianism of *Patience.*" *The Dalhousie Review* 65 (1985): 263–82.

Pearson, Hesketh. *Gilbert: His Life and Strife.* New York: Harper, 1957.

Rowell, George. "Introduction" in *Plays by W. S. Gilbert.* British and American Playwrights: 1750–1920. Cambridge: Cambridge UP, 1982. 1–21.

———. *Theatre in the Age of Irving.* Drama and Theatre Studies. Totowa: Rowman and Littlefield, 1981.

———. *The Victorian Theatre: A Survey.* London: Oxford UP, 1956.

Smith, Geoffrey. *The Savoy Operas: A New Guide to Gilbert and Sullivan.* New York: Universe, 1983.

Stedman, Jane W. "Gilbert's Stagecraft: Little Blocks of Wood" in *Gilbert and Sullivan: Papers Presented at the International Conference Held at the University of Kansas.* Ed. James Helyar. Lawrence: U of Kansas Libraries, 1971.

Sutton, Max Keith. *W. S. Gilbert.* Boston: Twayne, 1975.

.Index.